"The Heart and Stomach of a King

"The Heart and Stomach of a King"

ELIZABETH I AND THE POLITICS OF SEX AND POWER

Carole Levin

University of Pennsylvania Press

Philadelphia

University of Pennsylvania Press
NEW CULTURAL STUDIES

Joan DeJean, Carroll Smith-Rosenberg,
and Peter Stallybrass, Editors

A complete listing of the books
in the series appears at the
back of this volume

Copyright © 1994 by the University of Pennsylvania Press
All rights reserved
Printed in the United States of America

Library of Congress Cataloging-in-Publication Data

Levin, Carole.
    The heart and stomach of a king : Elizabeth I and the politics of sex and power /
Carole Levin.
        p.   cm. — (New cultural studies)
    Includes bibliographical references and index.
    ISBN 0-8122-3252-6
    1. Elizabeth I, Queen of England, 1533–1603.   2. Sex role—Political aspects—
Great Britain—History—16th century.   3. Great Britain—History—Elizabeth,
1558–1603.   4. Queens—Great Britain—Biography.   5. Power (Social sciences)
I. Title.   II. Series.
DA355.L458   1994
942.05′5′092—dc20
                                                                        94-7315
                                                                        CIP

to
my niece Rohana
my nephews Tristan and Leon,
and to
Joe, Desirée, Heather, and Adam & Christina
who are also my family

Contents

Illustrations

Acknowledgments

My interest and fascination with Elizabeth is long-standing and I have worked on this study for a long time. The research for the first major portion of it was accomplished in the summer of 1980 at the University of Kansas as part of a Ford Foundation fellowship on changing public roles for women. In the more than a decade since I have had financial support and reduced instructional responsibilities from institutions where I have taught, particularly SUNY College at New Paltz. I am greatly appreciative of the generosity of this institution. The support and encouragement I have received from SUNY/New Paltz and the New Paltz Foundation were critical in allowing me to finish this project. I was also able to do a substantial portion of the research for this project while a Monticello College Foundation Fellow at the Newberry Library in 1987. The major portion of this book was completed while at the Folger Shakespeare Library on a National Endowment for the Humanities Fellowship in 1991–92. The staff and other scholars at the Folger were especially helpful as I moved into the final stage of this project. I am deeply grateful to these institutions for their generosity and help as well as to the librarians at Harvard University, the University of Chicago, and Princeton University where some of the research was accomplished. I also thank the British Library for allowing me to quote from the Lansdowne Manuscripts, which I used in microfilm while at the Folger Shakespeare Library.

Many scholars have been most generous in their help and support, particularly Carol Brobeck, Sara Eaton, Ronald Fritze, Joan Kessler, Elaine Kruse, Amos Lee Laine, Elizabeth Mazzola, Cary Nederman, Carol Neely, James Schiffer, Martha Skeeters, Howard Solomon, Gerald Sorin, Maarten Ultee, Retha Warnicke, and Jenny Wormald. Jo Eldridge Carney, Patricia Crawford, Dennis Moore, Malcolm Smuts, and Lena Cowen Orlin each read portions of the manuscript. Ilona Bell, Ruth Elwell, John King, Karen Lindsey, Terry Murphy, Geoffrey Parker, Winfried Schleiner, and A. J. Slavin each read the manuscript in its entirety. I am deeply grateful to all of them. Their comments and suggestions were immeasurably helpful and I hope made this a better book. What errors remain are of course my own.

I am also most appreciative of Rona Ackerman, Arlen Feldwick, Katy Currey, Rick and Casey Gershon, Nancy Kassop, Pamela Laird, Mary Ann Lee, Jo Mano, Banisa St. Damian, Lynn Spangler, Pat Sullivan, and Jeanie Watson, friends and colleagues who listened and gave me support and encouragment when I needed it. Joe Silvestri, Desirée Moyer, Bill Shields, and Adam Schenkman provided research support and Ruth Elwell was responsible for the index.

The staff, particularly Jerry Singerman, at the University of Pennsylvania Press were wonderful people with whom to work. I am especially grateful to my series editor, Peter Stallybrass.

Portions of this book were published in very different form in the journals *Albion* and *The Shakespeare Yearbook*, and in the collections, Jean R. Brink, Allison P. Coudert, and Maryanne C. Horowitz, eds., *The Politics of Gender* (Sixteenth Century Essays and Studies, Volume XII, 1989) and Janet Sharistanian, ed., *Gender, Ideology, and Action: Historical Perspectives on Women's Public Lives* (Westport, CT.: Greenwood Publishing Group, 1986). I appreciate permission to use this material in this book.

1. Introduction

"I may have the body of a weak and feeble woman, but I have the heart and stomach of a king," Elizabeth I is said to have proclaimed in a moment of national crisis in 1588, as she faced the possibility of a Spanish invasion.[1] Whether or not this is an accurate transcription of what she said at Tilbury, it is hardly surprising that it has passed into tradition as one of the most famous of her speeches, since it so neatly encapsulates the struggles and contradictions for a woman in a position of power. Elizabeth had from her earliest memories known the difficulties and dangers for women when their lives were caught in the intersection of sexuality and politics, of gender and power. Not only must she have early learned her mother's fate, she also saw the progression of stepmothers at her father's court. At fifteen she had to listen to rumors that she had become pregnant by Thomas Seymour, widower of her last stepmother Katherine Parr, as he awaited his execution in the Tower. Only her quick wits and self-possession saved her own reputation and allowed her to protect her servants Katherine Ashley and Thomas Parry. During her sister Mary's reign she herself was in the Tower, afraid she would follow her cousin Jane Grey to the block. Few would have believed in November 1558 that her reign would last for forty-five years. To rule successfully Elizabeth may well have believed she must have "the heart and stomach of a king."

Traditionally, western society has viewed women as weak and incapable of a public role; to be successful a woman must move away from the expectations of her gender and "act like a man." But to do so makes her unwomanly, possibly even monstrous. Moreover, the way a society views a woman in a position of power not only impinges on her use of that power, but may reflect wider societal expectations about women's roles.[2] Elizabeth I was very skillful in how she represented herself and her authority as monarch. She was able to capitalize on the expectations of her behavior as a woman and use them to her advantage; she also at times placed herself beyond traditional gender expectations by calling herself king. Elizabeth was able to overcome the powerful resistance to her rule, and she did so by making her evident weaknesses as an unmarried woman ruler into sources of strength. Elizabeth's own motto was "Semper Eadem"—"Always the same." But her success came from how fluid and multi-faceted her representations of self were. As we shall see, Elizabeth was also fortunate and her success as monarch combined competence with good luck. Examining Elizabeth I's actions, means of self-representation, and contemporary responses to the queen, can yield some answers to some important questions about the connections between gender, politics, and culture.

Tudor England witnessed the rule of Mary I and Elizabeth I for fifty years. Their Scottish cousin Mary Stuart ruled until her forced abdication in 1568. From Mary Stuart's arrival in England until her execution in 1587 she plotted to usurp Elizabeth's throne. Discounting Matilda's disputed reign in the twelfth century, this was the first time in England since the Conquest that women ruled in their own right; and such rule brought about a number of social, political, and psychological repercussions. Attitudes toward women and their status changed dramatically. This pattern was mirrored in much of the rest of Europe as well. There was not only Mary Stuart, whose attempts to rule Scotland in the 1560s were so spectacularly unsuccessful,[3] but her mother, Mary of Guise, who until her death ruled as regent for her daughter while the latter was in France. Mary Stuart, who had been sent to France as a child of five, did not return to Scotland until 1561 after the death of her young first husband, Francis II, the year before. Francis's death changed the lives of his widow and his mother. The next king of France, Charles IX, was a child, and for close to thirty years Catherine de Medici dominated French politics as the Queen Mother. Protestants hated Catherine as the architect of the St. Bartholomew's Day massacre of 1572, and at the time of her death in 1589 France was being torn apart by religious wars that would soon claim the life of her last son, Henry III, through an assassin's knife.

Queenship provoked questions about the legitimacy of female rule, in an age already troubled about legitimacy because of religious division. It is hardly surprising that the misogynist Scottish reformer John Knox referred to this political phenomenon as a "monstrous regiment of women." The very existence of a woman ruler challenged traditionally-held beliefs that the monarch as God's representative ought, by definition, to be male.

This study focuses on the special difficulties of self-representation of the unmarried, childless Elizabeth and explores the way her Court, foreign ambassadors and the countries they represented, and the mass of English people responded to her. A central concern is how gender construction, role expectations, and beliefs about sexuality influenced both Elizabeth's self-presentation and other's perception of her. A crucial question this study examines is how such issues affected the methods of power used by a woman ruler as opposed to the traditional king. The way people regarded a queen and her use of power will also be valuable in answering more general questions about attitudes toward women during the English Renaissance.

In the sixteenth century the monarch was God's representative on earth, an even more potent force with all the confusions and dislocation brought on by Henry VIII's break with the Church of Rome and subsequent attempts to reform the church. Henry VIII became Supreme Head of the Church, and his daughter Elizabeth, in language that already showed the difference in attitudes toward queenship, was Supreme Governor. Elizabeth went far beyond this official role in the religious functions she practiced as monarch. Throughout her reign Elizabeth practiced a number of rituals of medieval kings that demonstrated the continuing power of the aspect of sacred monarchy but, as female monarch, her approach to these rituals was rather different and she also followed a tradition of female saintliness.

Many of the English reacted with ambivalence to the idea of a woman ruler. The ambivalence centered directly on the conflict between her rule and her femininity. If a queen were confidently to demonstrate the attributes of power, she would not be acting in a womanly manner; yet womanly behavior would ill-fit a queen for the rigors of rule. When Elizabeth became queen in 1558 she was an unmarried woman of twenty-five. Everyone expected she would marry and solve the problem of being a woman ruler by turning the governance over to her husband. Yet the question of who could be a satisfactory consort to her was never answered. Instead, Elizabeth embraced the ideal of chastity and presented herself as a Virgin Queen who was also the mother of her people. Yet she also engaged in extended marriage negotiations with many of the courts of Europe, such as France and the Holy Roman Empire, and in highly ritualized courtship games with many of the men at her own court. These centered particularly on Robert Dudley and Christopher Hatton earlier in her reign and the Earl of Essex at the end, suggesting that her dedication to virginity was more ambiguous and multifaceted than many scholars argue. Elizabeth's image as Virgin Queen was powerful but it was countered with the rumors and gossip throughout her reign about her supposed sexual relationships with her favorites and the illegitimate children she bore—and sometimes supposedly destroyed.

For many people in the sixteenth century, the desire for a king was powerful. Elizabeth refused to marry and have a child, thus providing England with the male leadership and stability so many craved. Instead, Elizabeth dealt with this concern in part by fashioning herself as king as well as queen in the ways she represented herself. This expansion of gender roles was reflected in some of Shakespeare's plays in terms of cross-dressing heroines and women characters using what might be perceived as "male" language.

In studying Elizabeth we can ask, how did she transcend her gender and her unmarried, childless state, and in what ways was she trapped by it? What strategies did she use that were successful and which ones failed? What were the different ways in which her people responded to her? How did the image of the queen change in the reign of her successor, James I? This book attempts to answer some of these questions.

This volume is not a biography of Elizabeth, though it certainly uses biographical information about her.[4] The study is chronological in only the broadest sense in that in its early chapters consider the problem of the succession and responses to Elizabeth at the beginning of her reign. And the last chapters consider Elizabeth at the end of her reign, the connections between images/representations of her and of some of Shakespeare's female characters, and the impact of the Essex rebellion. The chapters in between deal thematically with such issues as Elizabeth as a religious figure, her courtships, rumors about her sexual behavior, and rumors about the survival of her brother Edward VI and other attempts to suggest that she was not the legitimate monarch.

Many different sources were used to do this study: tracts and pamphlets, religious works, Parliamentary statutes and speeches, sermons and homilies, ceremonies and progresses, plays and ballads, diaries, gossip, rumor, calendar and holy days, liturgy, sixteenth-century books, records of the Privy Council, Elizabeth's own speeches and letters, and recorded dreams about Elizabeth. Much of the evidence we have for popular reaction to the queen comes from first-hand descriptions of her public ceremonies and progresses, letters, ambassadors' reports, and, especially, court cases involving people arrested for slandering the queen. While these sources, which abound in rumor and gossip, do not always provide accurate factual information about Elizabeth's life, they tell us a great deal about the social-psychological response to queenship, to a woman in power, particularly in terms of attitudes toward sexuality and power. Jan Vansina suggests that "Rumor is the process by which a collective historical consciousness is built. . . . Hence a tradition based on rumor tells more about the mentality of the time of the happening than about the events themselves."[5]

Some of the richest sources are the letters of foreign ambassadors, who frequently wrote long letters home about what was going on at Elizabeth's court. As D. M. Loades has noted, "Everything, from weighty affairs of state to the most trivial court gossip, tended to go into such dispatches, partly because court gossip could hold important clues, and partly because the ambassador was always anxious to demonstrate his zeal, and, if possible, his closeness to the centre of power."[6] The dispatches from Guzman de Silva, the Spanish Ambassador from 1564 to 1568, are especially valuable, as de Silva seems to have been able to develop a close relationship with Elizabeth and reported many conversations they had. James Melville, the Ambassador from Scotland, also has provocative insights about Elizabeth, though they have to be taken with more caution as they are from his *Memoirs* and written down long after the fact. Melville also repeated gossip as well as first-hand experience. The letters home from Elizabeth's ambassadors at other courts and from members of her Privy Council are also very useful. All these sources have to be used with extreme care, and cannot necessarily be taken at face value. They may reflect more about the person giving the evidence than about the queen herself or may tell us more about what Elizabeth wanted someone to believe than what her actual feelings were. But, pieced together, all these sources can help illuminate the issues of gender and rule in sixteenth century England.

*   *   *

When Elizabeth was born on September 7, 1533, no one had any idea that she would become the queen of England only twenty-five years later. Her birth was a deep disappointment to her father, Henry VIII, who had turned his world upside down, divorced his wife Catherine of Aragon, and broken with the Catholic Church so that he might marry again. But it was not simply passion for Anne Boleyn that caused this, though winning Anne became an obsession with Henry; the real passion was for a son who would secure the Tudor line and save England from a disputed succession that might cause the repeat of the chaotic War of the Roses of the previous century. In the 1520s Henry became convinced that God was punishing him for making an incestuous marriage with the widow of his dead brother Arthur, to whom Catherine had been briefly married, by giving the couple no sons to survive infancy.[7] Henry's concerns, however fanatical we may suppose he was about them, are understandable and make sense in sixteenth-century terms, when many saw a king as a necessity to stability. Though Henry and Catherine had a daughter, the future Mary I, the idea of a queen regnant was not acceptable to Henry. He had to have a son to inherit and to keep the Tudor line secure. When Pope Clement VII, after years of procrastinating, refused to give Henry his annulment, the king eventually had Parliament declare, "This realm of England is an empire"; no pope, no emperor, could tell its king or its people what to do. Thomas Cranmer, Archbishop of Canterbury, as the highest churchman in the realm, declared the marriage of Henry and Catherine null and void in January 1533 and Henry married the by now pregnant Anne Boleyn. Despite the assurances of all the soothsayers the king consulted that this child would be a boy, the infant was a daughter, Elizabeth. Anne Boleyn's next pregnancy, which would have been a son, ended in miscarriage, perhaps with a deformed fetus.[8] In 1536 she was arrested, accused of adultery with five men, one of them her own brother, and beheaded. Henry celebrated Anne's death by announcing his betrothal to Jane Seymour, who in 1537 gave Henry the son, Edward, he craved, though the disease contracted with childbirth cost her her life. Henry married three more times, but none of these later marriages yielded any children. The accusation that her mother had lovers, and at least the hint she might be a witch, must surely have had an influence on Elizabeth. Some of Elizabeth's enemies at times suggested she was not even Henry's daughter, and her strong public identification with him once she was queen may have been an answer to such an unspoken question.

As a child Elizabeth experienced at first hand the dangerous politics of royal marriages. Her own mother was executed, her first stepmother died of complications caused by childbirth, and her next step-mother, Anne of Cleves, was cast off by Henry because she did not sufficiently attract him. Katherine Howard, Henry's fifth wife, was also a kinswoman of Elizabeth. Her execution in 1542 when Elizabeth was eight for the same crime as Anne Boleyn's must have been particularly shocking. Elizabeth had an especially warm and close relationship with her last stepmother, Katherine Parr, who encouraged her education and tried to create more of a family for all Henry's children. But Katherine as well did not have an easy tenure as queen. She narrowly escaped arrest for heresy. Katherine's passionate marriage to Thomas Seymour only months after Henry's death,

Elizabeth's own involvement with Seymour as a young teenager living in her stepmother's house until Katherine asked her to leave, and Katherine's death in childbirth a year later must have also had an impact on Elizabeth. Since Thomas Seymour was husband to Elizabeth's stepmother, any relationship would have been almost incestuous, putting Elizabeth in an even more ambivalent position.[9] Seymour's pursuit of Elizabeth, along with his many other plots and misdeeds, led to his arrest and those of Elizabeth's governess, Katherine Ashley, and her steward, Thomas Parry. Elizabeth herself was closely examined by Sir Robert Tyrwhit. Elizabeth learned quickly the danger of slander and rumors and the need to protect her damaged reputation. In a letter to Edward Seymour, the Lord Protector, Elizabeth noted that "there goeth rumour abroad, which be greatly both against my honour and honesty (which above all other things I esteem) . . . that I am in the Tower; and with child by my Lord Admiral. My Lord, these are shameful slanders." Elizabeth asked that she "might come to the Court . . . that I may show myself there as I am." When the Lord Protector refused this request, Elizabeth was ready with another. She asked that the Council "send forth a proclamation into the counties, that they refrain their tongues, declaring how the tales be but lies."[10] We do not know the lessons Elizabeth learned from her father's marriages and the Seymour episode but it is revealing that Robert Dudley claimed years later that Elizabeth had told him at the age of eight that she would never marry.[11]

Despite all Henry's marital adventures, in 1547, the year of his death, he had only the one son, Edward.[12] On June 8, 1536 Parliament passed a new act of succession, which declared both Mary and Elizabeth illegitimate and entailed the crown on the children of the marriage of Henry and Jane Seymour. A provision was added that, if there were none, Henry might dispose of the Crown by will. Some people thought this provision was instituted so that Henry could place his illegitimate son, Henry Fitzroy, whom he had created Duke of Richmond, in the succession ahead of Mary. But Richmond died on July 23, 1536, and an Act of Parliament in 1543 officially restored Mary and Elizabeth to the succession, though it did not restore their legitimacy. The will Henry finally wrote before his death in 1547 declared that

> a full and plain gift disposition assignement declaration limitation and appoinctement wt' what conditions our doughters Mary and Elizabeth shall severally have hold and enjoye the sayd imperial Crowne and other the premiss's after our deceasse and for default of issue and heyres of the severall bodyes of us and of our sonne prince Edward lawfully begotten and his heyres.[13]

Yet it is doubtful that Henry really considered that a woman would be the ruler, though both his daughters received a fine humanist education in foreign languages and classical texts. In 1553, however, with the death of Edward VI, this possibility of female rule became reality. All potential heirs were female. Despite the Duke of Northumberland's plot to divert the succession to the Tudor cousin, Lady Jane Grey, who had been forced to marry his youngest son, Mary was popularly acclaimed queen. In the mid-sixteenth century the English people not only had to deal with the new phenomenon of a woman ruler,[14] but had to deal with it at a time of great religious unrest. England, within about thirty years, was under Henry VIII to be Catholic, also under Henry to maintain Catholic dogma but without allegiance to the pope; become far more Protestant in ritual under Edward VI; return its allegiance to the pope under Mary; and with Elizabeth's accession experience the development of an Anglican church hierarchy. There was really not one Reformation in England but a series of ebbing and flowing of different beliefs and practices among different groups of people.[15] At the same time as this religious confusion came queenship. Women were to rule in England for the entire second half of the sixteenth century.

Elizabeth was often in peril in her sister's reign. The Protestant alternative to a Catholic queen, she was the focus of a number of plots and conspiracies. The most dangerous one was led by Thomas Wyatt against the planned royal match of Mary with her cousin Philip of Spain. It caused Elizabeth to be placed in the Tower in 1554, and made her fear she might be executed as her cousin Lady Jane Grey recently had been. Elizabeth was convinced she survived Mary's reign through the Providence of God. When she became queen she was also determined not to make the same mistakes her sister had in forcing an unpopular religious settlement or marrying a hated foreigner. Marriage to anyone would have robbed Elizabeth of power and have been potentially divisive. Despite the long courtships, Elizabeth may well have always been aware of the risks; her success as monarch was inextricably woven into her refusal to wed.

Elizabeth was far more successful than Mary and the other women rulers of her time. She presided over a broadly based religious settlement, for many years kept England out of expensive and dangerous foreign entanglements, and was the symbol of national unity, especially at the time of the Spanish Armada. During her reign England was not engulfed in civil war as happened to neighboring Scotland or France. Elizabeth, though reluctantly, was one of the leading Protestant monarchs of sixteenth-century Europe. Her reign was a time of great cultural achievement. But there were also serious problems. Elizabeth—and as a result England—was fortunate. We can understand the terror her refusal to name an heir caused, and the pressure Parliament tried to exert. Had Elizabeth died in the first decade of her reign there might well have been a disputed succession and bloody civil war. The last decade of her reign was also particularly difficult. Inflation and poor harvests caused misery for many of the English, and there was deep fear that the Spanish might attempt another invasion. Elizabeth was a well-beloved sovereign, and one reason for her success was her love for her people and the way she manifested that love. Shortly after her death, her godson, Sir John Harington, wrote "We did all love hir, for she said she loved us, and muche wysdome she shewed in thys matter. She did well temper herself towards all at home, and put at variance those abroad; by whch means she had more quiet than hir neighbours." [16] Yet, despite that love, in those last years the grumblings about woman's rule were louder. Elizabeth's failure to provide for the royal succession was the price she had to pay for the successes of her forty-five-year reign as an unmarried woman. But it is also important to realize that some of the problems of Elizabeth's reign would have been problems for any ruler, male or female. All early modern English sovereigns had problems controlling their nobility and dealing with the demands of Parliament. The way these problems manifested themselves in Elizabeth's reign had to do with her sex, but the problems themselves were more universal. So were the troubling issues with religion. Elizabeth as an unmarried woman ruler was unique in sixteenth-century England; she was also one of the five Tudor monarchs who had to deal with maintaining power in a time of religious and social unrest. A study of Elizabeth I helps us to understand the intersection of politics with gender, of sexuality with power.

2. Elizabeth as Sacred Monarch

In 1558 the Scots reformer John Knox published his *First Blast of the Trumpet Against the Monstrous Regiment of Women*. Knox vehemently described female rule as blasphemous against God, given the essential quality of woman's nature. "I am assured that God hath reveled to some in this our age, that it is more then a monstre in nature that a Woman shall reigne and have empire above a Man. . . . howe abominable, odious, and detestable is all such usurped authoritie." Knox argued that God not only ordained that women were barred from authority, but given their weaknesses they would be incapable of wielding authority if they illegitimately usurped it. Yet women, who were avaricious, deceitful, cruel, oppressive, and proud, sought domination over men, and some men foolishly allowed it. "To promote a Woman to beare rule, superioritie, dominion, or empire above any Realme, nation, or Citie, is repugnant to Nature . . . it is the subversion of good order, of all equitie and justice." Men must "acknowledge that the Regiment of a Woman is a thing most odious in the presence of God . . . she is a traitoresse and rebell against God . . . they must studie to represse her inordinate pride and tyrannie to the uttermost of their power." Knox claimed divine authority for his views. "By the Holy Ghost is manifestly expressed in these words, I suffer not a woman to usurp authority above the man. So both by God's law and the interpretation of the Holy Ghost, women are utterly forbidden to occupy the place of God in the offices 'foresaid, which he has assigned to man, whom he hath appointed to be his lieutenant on earth. The apostle taketh power from all women to speak in the assembly." Aimed at Mary I, Mary Stuart, and her regent mother, Mary of Guise, Knox had the bad timing of having his work appear only a few months prior to the beginning of Elizabeth's reign. Though in no way arguing for the overthrow of Elizabeth, Knox was committed to the proposition that for a woman to be the head of government was "monstrous." In the "apology" he sent Elizabeth he stated, "I can not deny the wreiting of a booke aganis the usurped Authoritie, and injust Regement of Women; neither [yit] am I myndit to retract or call back any principall point, or proposition of the same, till treuth and verritie do farder appeir." Knox was not primarily a political theorist, and he was mostly concerned with matters of religion. But in the sixteenth century monarchy, politics and religion were completely intertwined.[1]

Knox was answered the following year by John Aylmer in his *Harborrowe for faithfull and trewe subjectes*. Tutor for Lady Jane Grey and friend of Roger Ascham, Aylmer was one of those who had fled abroad during Mary's reign. Though defending Elizabeth's right to rule, Aylmer in the end was almost as limiting to the power of a woman to rule as Knox, suggesting that Knox's wrong thinking came "not of malice but of zele." Aylmer conceded that God did not want women to be priests, but this is separate from "cyvill pollycie." Aylmer supports Elizabeth's right to rule, since God sent her "by birth" to the English people. But he adds, better in England, "then any where [since] the regiment of England is not a mere Monarchie," but rather a combination of "monarchy, oligarchy, and democratie." Parliament limited the power of the ruler, who "can ordein nothing without them. . . . if to be short she wer a mere monark, and not a mixte ruler, you might peradventure make me to feare the matter the more, and the les to defend the cause. . . . [but] it is not in England so daunger[ous] a matter, to have a woman ruler."[2] Aylmer accepted the view that women are less competent, but that hardly means they are incompetent. "The male is moore mete to rule then the female" does not mean the woman is unfit, but only less so. "Chalke is whyter than cheese, ergo cheese is black" is ridiculous, he argued. When the Bible is opposed to women and children ruling, Aylmer argued, this is a metaphor for poor rule. "Not boyes in age, but in manner . . . not women in sexe, but in feblenes of wit . . . such as women be of the wurst sort, fond, folish, wanton, flibbergibbes, tatlers, trifles, wavering witles, without counsell, feable, careles, rashe, proude . . . talebearers, evesdrippers, rumor raisers, evell tonged . . . and in everyre wise, dotefied with the dregges of the Devils dounge hill. . . . No Deborah, No Judiths, no Hesters, no Elyzabethes."

When Aylmer spoke specifically of Elizabeth he praised her greatly, but perhaps hardly in ways she would appreciate. He discussed how she behaved "so humbly without pride, so moderately without prodigalitie, so maydenly without pompe. . . . I am sure that her maidenly apparel, which she used in kyng edwardes tyme, made the noble mens daughters and wyves, to be ashamed, to be drest and paynted lyke pecockes, being more moved with hir most vertuous example: then with all that ever Paule or Peter wrote, touchyng that matter." Here Aylmer echoed Knox, who asserted that "gorgious apparell is abominable and odiouse in a woman."[3] Aylmer assured his readers that there would be no problem in the queen marrying. "Say you, God hath apoynted her to be subject to her husband . . . therfore she may not be the heade. I graunte that, so farre as perteining to the bands of mariage, and the offices of a wife, she must be a subjecte: but as a Magistrate she maye be her husbandes heade. . . . Whie may not the woman be the husbandes inferiour in matters of wedlock, and his head in the guiding of the commonwelth." Aylmer's vision of an ideal woman ruler was someone modest, who wore simple dress, listened to advice, and married. All of these were not what Elizabeth wished to be. William Haugaard may well be right that *Harborrowe* did Aylmer's career no good.[4]

Medieval monarchs had not made the claims of being God's lieutenant that began to emerge under Henry VIII. The position of the monarch and the nature of kingship emerges in the sixteenth century as an office so awe inspiring and powerful it could even encompass a female ruler, thus making it possible for her to perform religious acts—priestly acts—inconceivable for a woman in previous centuries. The idea of queenship was difficult for a people used to a monarch by definition male, but the change in the conception of monarchy, and the practices that went with this change, aided the English in accepting a woman monarch.[5]

Early in her reign Elizabeth may have yielded that modesty, simplicity, and obedience were acceptable behaviorial traits for other women, but she refused to accept them for a queen. *The Second Book of the Homilies*, produced by her bishops under the leadership of John Jewel in 1563, included a homily against excess of apparel and one on marriage that encouraged all women to dress simply and to marry and obey their husbands.[6] According to the homily against excess of apparel,

> the proud and hauty stomachs of the daughters of England, are so maintained with divers disguised sorts of costly apparell that. . . . here is left no difference in apparel between an honest matron and a common strumpet.

Even worse, the very wearing of such clothes by the "honest matron" might well, suggested the homily, lead her to "wanton, lewd, and unchaste behavior," since "such as delight in gorgeous apparel are commonly puffed up with pride and filled with divers vanities."[7] Yet Elizabeth's delight in gorgeous apparel, however she had behaved during her brother's reign, was notorious during her own and vital to her self-representation as monarch.

The homily on marriage also demonstrated the distance between Elizabeth's own code of behavior and the stance she allowed her government to take toward other women. The purpose of marriage, proclaimed the homily, was "that man and woman should live lawfully in a perpetual friendly fellowship." There are duties in marriage for both the sexes, but the duties of husbands and wives are different according to their natures. The husband:

> ought to be the leader and author of love in cherishing and encreasing . . . for the woman is a weak creature, not endued with like strength and constancy of mind: Therefore they be the sooner disquieted, and they be the more prone to all weak affections and dispositions of mind more than men be: and lighter they be and more vain in their fantasies and opinions.

If the husband has certain duties—to be kindly and guide his wife, she has certain ideals of behavior that she should follow as well.

> But as for their husbands, them must they obey, and cease from commanding, and perform subjection. For this surely doth nourish concord very much, when the wife is ready at hand at her husband's commandment, when she will apply herself to his will, when she endeavoureth herself to seek his contentation and do him pleasure, when she will eschew all things might offend him.

The homily stated that for a woman to obey her husband is her way of showing that she honors God, for women must understand that it is God's commandment that they acknowledge the authority of their husbands. The homily did recognize the difficulties of the married woman's lot. Women "must specially feel the griefs and pains of their matrimony, in that they relinquish the liberty of their own rule," yet it still urged all women to marry, and to honor and obey their husbands as their religious duty. Yet Elizabeth's assent to the publication of the homilies was ambiguous. "She allowed the book to be printed with only a vague suggestion of her authorization and with a specific proviso that would allow a clergyman to select those homilies he would read," Haugaard points out, though he suggests Elizabeth's problems with the homilies were over doctrine, not behavior models for women.[8] As a queen Elizabeth refused to follow dictates for behavior that would have effectively made her a puppet of the reformers. If she were furious with Knox, she may not have been that much better pleased with Aylmer.

Aylmer and Knox engaged in a public discussion of just what was the queen's role as monarch; this dispute was of great importance at the beginning of the reign, and one place it played itself out was in her title in regards to the Church of England. The Parliament of 1559 not only passed the Uniformity Act, setting forth the official doctrine of the Church of England, it also passed the Supremacy Act which gave Elizabeth the title of Supreme Governor over the Church of England. This title sounded less powerful than the one held by Henry VIII and Edward, "Supreme Head." Though some members of the House of Commons believed it was against the word of God for Elizabeth to refuse to be "Head," many reformers, as well as papists, had objected to the title, and there was pressure on Elizabeth not to use it. The returned Marian exile, Thomas Lever "wisely put such a scruple in the Queen's head that she would not take the title of supreme head," Edmund Sandys wrote with approval to Matthew Parker (April 30, 1559).[9] Perhaps on some level an element of that objection came not only from the idea of the monarch as head but from the perception of blasphemy that a woman could take this role. That people from a variety of perspectives opposed the idea of a female head of the Church must have been an important factor in Elizabeth's decision to seek instead the title of governor, Norman Jones suggests. When Supremacy was being debated in the House of Lords, Archbishop of York Nicholas Heath, arguing from a Catholic perspective, uncannily echoed Knox. He claimed that "Her highness, beyinge a woman by birthe and nature, is not qualyfied by God's worde to feed the flock of Chryst, it appeareth most playnlye. . . . To preach or mynister the holy sacraments, a woman may not. . . . A woman, in the degrees of Chyrst's churche, is not called to be an apostle, or evangelst, nor to be a shepherd, neyther a doctor or preacher. Therefor she cannot be supreme head of Christ's militant churche, nor yet of any part therof."[10]

Despite what pressure there was, it seems that it was Elizabeth's own decision and inclination not to the use the title of Head, or so Bishop John Jewel certainly believed. Jewel wrote to Henry Bullinger in May 1559 that Elizabeth "seriously maintains that this honor is due to Christ alone, and cannot belong to any human being soever."[11] But though Elizabeth would not take the title, she also was unwilling to relinquish the power over the church she believed was hers by right. Jones argues that, "in terms of her prerogative, the change from headship to governorship was meaningless."[12] Elizabeth took being Governor of the Church very seriously, and, argues Haugaard, "fought passionately to establish her vision of the

Figure 1. Elizabeth holding the Bible, from Bishop Burnet, *The History of the Reformation* (private collection)

national church."[13] Yet as Supreme Governor Elizabeth frequently was content to remain in the background in terms of dealing with church hierarchy, and often forced her archbishops to carry out the public fight for the shape of the national church without giving them the official support they desired.[14] For Elizabeth, the religious functions as monarch went far beyond this official role as Supreme Governor. As one popular book of the sixteenth century stated, "To worship the kinge is to worshippe

Religion and God." [15] Throughout her reign Elizabeth continued a number of rituals of medieval kings that demonstrated the continuing power of the aspect of sacred monarchy. We can see, however, the gendered nature of the way she approached these ceremonies.

Throughout her reign Elizabeth used the royal touch to cure people of the disease, scrofula, known as the king's evil. Being able to cure through touch suggests the power Elizabeth had as a religious figure, a sacred monarch, and the value of her self-presentation as Virgin Queen. It is even more remarkable when we note that only a hundred years earlier in 1462, in defense of the House of Lancaster, Sir John Fortescue wrote that Edward IV could not cure the king's evil by touching the afflicted since to do so one must not only be a king but also a legitimate one. To touch one needed not only to be anointed with holy oil but the person must also be the legitimate heir. Lancastrians claimed that Edward IV could not touch since he was not the rightful king. Wrote Fortescue, he "wrongly claims to enjoy this wonderful privilege. Wrongly . . . [since] this unction is powerless because Edward had no right to receive it." Sir John went on to argue by analogy, and scornfully asked: "Would a woman who received ordination thereby become a priest?" [16] Clearly not. Continuing this line of argument, Fortescue added that a usurper would not be the only one unable to cure by touch.

> Many duties likewise are incumbent on the kings of England in virtue of the kingly office, which are inconsistent with a woman's nature, and kings of England are endowed with certain powers by special grace from heaven, wherewith queens in the same country are not endowed. The kings of England by touch of their annointed hands they cleanse and cure those inflected with a certain disease, that is commonly called the King's Evil, though they be pronounced otherwise incurable. This gift is not bestowed on Queens. [17]

Yet less than a century later, both Mary and Elizabeth were touching for the king's evil, and following other practices including blessing metal for cramp rings (also used for healing) [18] and conducting other religious services attached to Easter, such as washing the feet of the poor on Maundy Thursday. It is worth considering how practices described as inappropriate and unworkable in one century could be accomplished the next, and the implications for understanding the nature of Elizabeth's role as queen and the function of monarchy and its religious aspects in the sixteenth century. It is useful to look as well at Mary's reign to see the similarities and differences in religious practices of a queen regnant, one Catholic who marries; the other a Protestant Virgin Queen.

We should not assume that Elizabeth appropriated these functions for purely political reasons as a means of encouraging loyalty, though that was a strong element. As Max Weber has noted, the use of religious conventions are helpful in establishing the legitimacy of rule. Further, some sociologists, of the Durkheim school, argue in a positive theory of ritual that "religious beliefs and practices not only create and sustain the fundamental social structure of a society, but maintain the members' sense of reality."[19] But religious feelings probably also infused Elizabeth's gestures. Historians have traditionally described Elizabeth as a politique who was very knowledgeable about Christianity but had little religious conviction. But the work of such scholars as William Haugaard and Margaret Aston suggests far otherwise. Scarisbrick is correct that Elizabeth was no zealot, which was a difficult issue for the Protestant zealots of her time to come to terms.[20] But because Elizabeth did not agree with their version of Christianity does not mean that she was not devout. It was serious enough for Elizabeth to organize worship in her chapel as she wanted it. The little silver cross she had in her private chapel infuriated reformers, but was important enough to her that she refused to remove it. John Jewel's letters to Peter Martyr are filled with the despair this caused him. Jewel wrote him November 16, 1559, "The doctrine is every where most pure; but as to the ceremonies and maskings, there is a little too much foolery. That little silver cross, of ill-omened origin, still maintains its place in the queen's chapel. Wretched me! This thing will soon be drawn into a precedent. There was at one time some hope of it being removed. . . . But as far as I can perceive, it is now a hopeless case. Such is the obstinacy of some minds."[21] Elizabeth had originally wanted the cross and candlesticks set up throughout her kingdom, but had finally agreed with church leaders to ban them, and in the central place of the proscribed crucifixion, the royal arms were displayed, thus conflating even more monarchy and worship. Elizabeth refused, however, to take the cross and candlesticks out of her own chapel.[22] Iconoclasts were so distressed that in both 1562 and 1567 they made attempts to destroy them. In 1562 an unknown reformer managed to do so. Bishop John Parkhurst wrote gleefully to Bullinger (August 20, 1562), "The crucifix and candlesticks in the queen's chapel are broken into pieces, and, as some has brought word, reduced to ashes. A good riddance of such a cross as that!" Elizabeth, however, replaced them and they were a target again five years later, as de Silva explained in a letter to Philip II (1 November, 1567). "On the 25th whilst they were performing what they call the service in the Queen's chapel an Englishman went up to the altar and cast down the cross and candlesticks upon which he stamped, and at the same time shouted heretical and shameful words." Elizabeth was inclined at first to treat this leniently. She told de Silva "that the man was mad and did not know what he was doing, recounting to me some of his follies, amongst others that he thought our Lady and St. John, who were on either side of the cross, were Jews who wanted to crucify Christ again." De Silva was far from convinced, calling the man "an evil-minded rogue." In December the man tried to destroy the sacred objects in the chapel again, and this time "he was at once arrested and taken to a private prison whence he was transferred to the Tower."[23]

Given the conflicts over Elizabeth's private worship, we might wonder what Elizabeth's true religious feelings were. De Feria reported to Philip in 1559 that she had told him "she differed very little from us as she believed God was in the sacrament of the Eucharist and only dissented from three or four things in the Mass." She went on to say that "she did not wish to argue about religious matters," something she tried to avoid whenever she could. Five years later she told de Silva, referring to the beginning of her reign, that "she had had to conceal her real feelings to prevail with her subjects in matter of religion, but that God knew her heart, which was true to His service."[24] Of course, we do not know how sincere Elizabeth was in her discussions with either of the Spanish ambassadors, or if she was concealing her real feelings here as well. Bacon said of Elizabeth that she did not want to make windows into men's souls, and neither did she want a window made into her soul.[25] She was content to believe that God knew what was in her heart, about her faith as in so many other matters, and to let it be. Yet her behavior in both the Maundy ceremony and the touch ceremony certainly give us hints as to her religious attitudes.

In performing these ceremonies Elizabeth not only continued kingly practices but also the practices of medieval women saints; though Catholics did not allow women to be priests, they had not excluded women from the miraculous, particularly miraculous cures, and this power seemed closely connected with the saints' purity and virginity. The many revered female saints, as Scarisbrick points out, "tempered male authority and . . . asserted the dignity of womanhood."[26] But these saints had been swept away, and many reformers had no use for virgins. Yet Elizabeth presented herself as a Virgin Queen, echoing the cult not only of the Virgin Mary, but also perhaps those of such saints as Frideswide and Uncumber, both of whose shrines had been destroyed in 1538, both of whom were said to be daughters of kings, and both of whose power came from their determined virginity. Uncumber, daughter of a pagan father, prayed to God for aid when her father attempted to force her to marry. She immediately grew a dense, curly beard, which was sufficiently off-putting for her suitor to leave her at the altar. Her father, in his fury, had her crucified. In England, especially from the fourteenth century onward, Uncumber was the saint to whom unhappy wives prayed for succor, to be "disencumbered" of their husbands as Thomas More scornfully put it.[27] There were images of Uncumber in Norwich, Bristol, and Somerset as well as Westminster itself. But Lord Mayor of London Sir Richard Gresham had the Westminster statue taken down in August 1538.

If Uncumber's beard might suggest a parallel with the male, kingly aspect of Elizabeth's self-representation, St. Frideswide, patron saint of Oxford, is a more direct comparison as a healer.[28] Frideswide supposedly lived in the late seventh and early eighth centuries.[29] The daughter of Didanus, an under-king, she was piously educated and early had a calling for a religious life. Despite her vows King Algar wished to make her his wife because of her beauty and wealth. He threatened to burn down Oxford if Frideswide was not delivered up to him. Frideswide managed to escape. When Algar caught her she prayed to St. Catherine and St. Cecilia, and he was immediately struck blind. It was Frideswide's own prayerful intervention, once he repented, that restored his sight. Frideswide founded a monastery and was known for her healing, possibly learned from her abbess/ aunt. Her shrine was decorated with delicately carved plants, all of which were known for their healing properties, to demonstrate Frideswide's great gift as a healer. Her most remarkable healing was when a leper conjured her in the name of Christ to kiss him. Despite what was described as his "loathsome condition" and her "fear of infection," Frideswide made the sign of the cross and gave the leper a kiss. "Immediately the scales fell from him, and his flesh came again like that of a child." She was able to cure a fisherman who was subject to violent fits, perhaps by casting the devils out of him. In some versions she also healed a blind girl, perhaps echoing the blindness and recovery of sight of Algar. The relics of St. Frideswide were preserved in a beautiful shrine at Oxford in a chapel dedicated to her. During Lent and again on Ascension Day, the Chancellor of Oxford, and principal members of the University, along with the scholars, came to the shrine in solemn procession proffering gifts. Especially during the twelfth century there were numerous instances of the faithful being miraculously cured after a pilgrimage to her shrine. Of those who came to be cured, women outnumbered men two to one, and many of these diseases had to do with specifically female maladies, including madness or severe pain caused by intercourse. Prayers at St. Frideswide's shrine also cured one knight's daughter of scofula, which makes the identitification of Frideswide with Elizabeth even more powerful. In the later Middle Ages St. Frideswide's shrine was Oxford's richest church, and St. Frideswide's fair, sanctioned by a charter from Henry I, was the most important one in Oxford. The fair received particular attention in 1382 and 1384 because of a dispute between the University and St. Frideswide's Priory over jurisdiction. St. Frideswide must have been a well-known saint in the medieval England. In "The Miller's Tale" Chaucer has the carpenter call out "Help us, seinte Frydeswyde!" We find references to the shrine in the early sixteenth century as well. In 1518 Catherine of Aragon made a pilgrimage there. Pope Clement VII allowed Cardinal Wolsey to dissolve the priory of St. Frideswide in 1525 and Cardinal College was established on its site. In 1546 Henry VIII re-established the college as Christ Church, and St. Frideswide's church became the college chapel as well as the cathedral of the new diocese of Oxford. The shrine was destroyed with many others in 1538, though the faithful rescued some of the saint's relics.[30]

The history of Frideswide's relics becomes more ambiguous in the mid sixteenth century, and more suggestive of the confusion over women's power and nature. During the reign of Edward VI, Peter Martyr, the foreign reformer, was appointed to the chair of Regius Professor of Theology at Oxford. He lived in college with his wife Catherine, a former nun. Catherine was one of the first two women to reside at college, and Peter and Catherine's windows were often broken by Papists indignant at a woman's presence.[31] Early in 1553 Catherine died and was buried in the church near where the shrine had been. In 1556 Cardinal Pole wrote to the dean of Christ's Church, Oxford, Dr. Marshall, to ask him to restore the devotion to St. Frideswide and punish reformers at Oxford, both living and dead. As part of this restoration, investigation, and punishment, Marshall had the bones of Catherine Martyr exhumed and reburied in the dunghill next to his stable, since she was a nun who had violated her vows to marry. The bones of Frideswide, if indeed they were hers, were disinterred, put into two silk bags and placed back in the church.[32] The relics of St. Frideswide were again exalted, though it does not appear that there was any attempt to rebuild her shrine. In 1561, as part of the Ecclesiastical Commission, Parker and Grindal inquired into the matter and issued instructions to the authorities of Christ Church to remedy the scandal done to Catherine's

body. The sub-dean, James Calfhill, had his servants again dig up Catherine Martyr's bones, which were by this time quite disjointed. The bones
were brought into the church, and on January 11 1561/2 there was a solemn
ceremony. An oration was preached praising Catherine for her modesty
and good works and referring to those who worshiped Frideswide as
"crazy old men." But Calfhill did not want to show disrespect to the bones
he found in the bags. "Since I hold that nothing less becomes a good man
than to copy hateful Popish sacrilege and barbarous cruelty, I was determined on no account to let anything unseemly or insulting be done with
them. So I hit upon a scheme by which the bones could be dealt with
decently, while at the same time all foolish superstition could be suppressed." The relics of Frideswide and the bones of Catherine were then
comingled, "that in case any cardinal will be so made hereafter to remove
this woman's bones again, it shall be hard for them to discern the bones
of her, from the other," John Foxe declared. Strype's version is more re-
spectful to Frideswide. "For the preventing of any future superstitions
with those relics, (and yet that no indecency might be used towards the
said saint and foundress's bones,) and withall, for the better securing of
this late buried holy woman's bones from being disturbed any more, by
the advice of Mr. Calfhill, the bones of both were mixed and put together." Calfhill informed Grindal that now no one could distinguish the
bones of one from the other, and so they were placed in the same coffin.[33]
One wonders, despite the supposed honor due to Catherine Martyr, if
there might have been an underlying element of contempt—in the attitude toward all women—in mixing up her bones with that of a discredited
saint. Or, despite some reformers' gibes at saints, it may be a reluctance
totally to let go of such a comforting and healing presence that her bones
too must be protected by being a placed with the Protestant good woman.
The ceremony also demonstrates the fragility of the Protestant settlement
in the minds of its leading exponents in the early Elizabethan period. Foxe
himself foresees there may be another time coming where cardinals again
rule England to the cost of the true believers.

We have no direct evidence that Elizabeth saw herself as a continuation of such saints as Uncumber and Frideswide. Nor that those who
thronged for her touch were consciously making such a connection. But
surely the tradition of the virgin saint as healer would resonate as well for
a Virgin Queen who healed by touch. Throughout medieval and early
modern England there was a strong belief in magical healers, and the king
was the most magical of all.[34] Kings had touched to cure the afflicted in

England since the time of the saintly Edward the Confessor. After the Norman Conquest it seems that English kings saw the effect of the French people spontaneously going to their king to be cured and copied the measure as an effective means to gain religious-political support.[35] Yet the practice seems to have waxed and waned in England in the Middle Ages. Despite Fortescue's concerns, there appears to have been relatively little touching for the king's evil by English kings in the fifteenth century, and we have no records of either Edward IV or Richard III touching, though Edward did have cramp rings made to distribute, another form of magical healing.[36]

Henry VII, after a century or more of comparative neglect, restored the ceremony of the touch to all its dignity and established a full ceremonial, with a set office of service.[37] Henry, whose claim to the throne by the right of primogeniture was weak, used a number of techniques to assure his prestige, including claiming his descent from the mythological King Arthur and producing a round table repainted in the Tudor colors of white and green which he claimed was the original round table.[38] In the same way he named his eldest son Arthur. Touching for the king's evil, which could only be accomplished by the Lord's anointed, and which suggested the work of Christ himself, would be another means to assure his position. The touching became highly ritualized, and Henry VII gave each of the afflicted a gold angel as well as the king's healing touch.[39]

Just as touching increased the monarch's prestige, so too did maintaining the practice of washing the feet of the poor on Maundy Thursday, the day before Good Friday and a time of year heavy with religious portent.[40] By the Tudor period the monarch had become clearly associated with the Maundy ceremony. The ceremony of washing the feet of the poor, done in imitation of Christ washing the feet of his disciples at the end of the Last Supper, was a part of the Easter vigil and had been included in the church service for many centuries. In the Bible Christ told his disciples, "If I then, your Lord and Master, have washed your feet, ye also ought to wash one another's feet / For I have given you an example, that ye should do as I have done unto you."[41]

The Mandatum, or rite of the Washing of the Feet, was thus originally a simple act of charity very common in the Church. It became a liturgical rite sometime between the fifth and the seventh century. By the eleventh century the practice was being carried out in Rome. The Pope washed the feet of twelve subdeacons at the end of the evening Mass on Holy Thursday. When the other Holy Thursday rites were moved to the morning hours during the fourteenth century, the Mandatum remained a separate service to be held in the afternoon. The ceremony of the Maundy was known in Britain by at least 600. In the eighth century St. Alcuin set forth the correct way to celebrate it in his Book of Offices.[42]

Medieval monarchs also began to be involved in the Maundy. King John gave thirteen pence to each of thirteen poor men at the Maundy ceremony held in Rochester in 1213. Apparently the thirteen represented the twelve apostles and either Christ or an angel who had visited the table of Pope Gregory the Great. But Edward II was the first English monarch actually to hold a Maundy himself. In the nineteenth year of his reign, Edward washed the feet of fifty poor men. Edward II may have extended the monarch's participation in the ceremony because he felt that he needed all the prestige he could acquire, given his political problems. Edward had already attempted to have the pope sanction a second coronation for him on the grounds that he had discovered some special holy oil given to St. Thomas à Becket by the Virgin Mary that should be used to anoint him. The pope, however, suggested if Edward wanted to use it to anoint himself privately he could go ahead; a second coronation was certainly not necessary. Edward may have felt an act in imitation of Christ himself to be a possible substitute.[43]

The Maundy ceremony developed gradually. It became customary for the sovereign to provide a meal and to also give gifts of clothing, food, and money to the poor people involved. For example, in 1363, when Edward III was fifty years of age, he provided for fifty of his subjects. By the age of the Tudors it had become so associated with the monarch that it came to be called the Royal Maundy.[44] The idea of having the number of participants equal the age of the sovereign became institutionalized by the beginning of Henry VIII's reign. Each year Henry washed the feet of the number of men who equaled his age and gave each of the poor men whose feet he washed a red purse with a number of pence in it that also equaled his age.[45]

Roy Strong suggests that in the Middle Ages the religious festivals were used as a way to augment royal power. He mentions the Royal Maundy and the king's touch as examples of the greatest spectacles of medieval royalty. While the Tudors inherited such occasions, they were "extended and overlaid by what might be described as a liturgy of state," as the sixteenth century monarchy developed even more its symbolic significance.[46]

The sixteenth and seventeenth centuries seem to have become the height of both ceremonies—touching and also blessing through the washing of the feet.[47] Henry VII may well have believed this would increase his prestige as he further ritualized these practices, and his son Henry VIII continued them. Yet Henry VIII seems to have been less interested in some of these rituals. As Raymond Crawfurd points out, apparently "the ceremonial of healing possessed no special sanctity and no exceptional importance in the mind of the 'Supreme Head of the Church.'" Some ceremonies, such as the washing of the feet on Maundy Thursday and blessing cramp rings, continued in the reign of his son, others apparently did not. We have no record of Edward VI touching for the king's evil. One might perhaps wonder if this were due to his youth, but we have records of French kings touching as early as age nine. When Mary became queen in 1553, she continued these ceremonies, investing them with great dignity as well as obvious personal feelings of piety. Elizabeth continued them as well. One reason that these ceremonies became so ritualized is that these functions were part of a larger theatricalization of royalty intended to achieve and demonstrate power. By the sixteenth century, the monarch had become even more important symbolically; the image of the monarch, idealized as God's representative on earth, was a means to secure the people's allegiance. The Tudors, who ruled without a standing army or an extensive police force, had their power "constituted in theatrical celebrations of royal glory," in Stephen Greenblatt's words. For queens ruling instead of kings, this aspect of power through ritual and spectacle could be particularly important, though Elizabeth took much more advantage of it than Mary.[48]

When Mary became queen in 1553 it is hardly surprising that she eagerly embraced the rituals of healing and touch. In part as a way to quiet the reservations of many of her subjects on her accession, Mary also gave more in royal alms in 1553 than any year in the previous reign. Yet Mary did not pursue these practices primarily for propaganda reasons. A genuinely pious woman, she exacted less than the full public effect from these rituals. After Mary's accession the newly restored Catholic Church made an effort to bring about a revival of many disused customs. Mary wrote to the Bishop of London in March 1554 "that the laudable and honest ceremonies which were wont to be used, frequented and observed in the church, be also hereafter frequented, used, and observed." Cardinal Reginald Pole, the Archbishop of Canterbury, issued similar injunctions: "That all parishioners shall obediently use all the godly ceremonies of the church as (amongst therein enumerated) creeping to the cross."[49]

For Mary, as a Catholic, the Easter season was an especially holy time. Mary continued the practice of washing the feet of the poor on Maundy Thursday. Mary's 1556 Maundy was commemorated with a painting on a table top by Nicholas Lizarde, which unfortunately has not survived. There is also a reference to one of Mary's Maundies in Robert Fleetwood's *Iterium ad Windsor.* The day following Maundy Thursday, Good Friday, Mary blessed cramp rings. In the final Marian version of this ritual the curative value of the cramp rings was explicitly stated to have come from being rubbed in the royal hands, and the rings were valuable due to the supernatural qualities of the monarch, supporting the view in the sixteenth century of the monarch's own almost magical power. Mary also touched for the king's evil on Good Friday, traditionally a particularly holy day for this ritual.[50]

The Venetian Ambassador, Marco Antonio Faitta, described Mary's 1556 Maundy and touching ceremony on Good Friday. Accompanying Mary to the Maundy ceremony were Archbishop Pole, some other bishops, and her Council. The choristers of her chapel provided music. Helping her in the ceremony were the Under Almoner, the Grand Almoner (the bishop of Chilchester), and her ladies in waiting and gentlewomen of the court. Faitta, who was at all the ceremonies, described them in great detail, paying especial attention to the role of the queen herself. "Her Majesty knelt down on both her knees before the first of the poor women, and taking in the left hand the woman's right foot, she washed it, . . . drying it very thoroughly with the towel which hung at her neck, and having signed it with the cross she kissed the foot so fervently that it seemed as if she were embracing something very precious." Mary did the like for each of the forty-one poor women, they being the same number as her age. "I vow to you that in all her movements and gestures, and by her manner, she seemed to act thus not merely out of ceremony, but from great feeling and devotion," Faitta wrote.[51] After providing the women with food, alms, wine, cloth, shoes and stockings, a purse with forty-one pence, and the aprons and towels carried by her gentlewomen, Mary then left the hall to take off her gown, which was a very rich one of purple lined with fur. After a half hour she returned, and again examined all the women very carefully. Mary then gave the gown to the woman who looked the poorest and most aged, as was the custom with the Maundy robe. On Holy Thursday as well alms were distributed to three thousand people who thronged the court.

The next day, Good Friday, Mary crept to the cross on her knees, blessed the cramp rings, and then withdrew from the service to bless those afflicted with scrofula,

> but she chose to perform this act privately in a gallery where there were not above twenty persons. She caused one of the infirm women to be brought to her, when she knelt and pressed with her hands on the spot where the sore was. This she did to a man and three women.
>
> She then made the sick people come up to her again, and taking a gold coin—viz. an angel—she touched the place where the evil showed itself, signed it with the Cross and passed a ribbon through the hole which had been pierced in it, placing one of them round the neck of each of the patients, and making them promise never to part with that coin, save in case of extreme need.

Faitta concluded his letter that "Having been present myself . . . at all these ceremonies, her Majesty struck me as affording a great and rare example of goodness, performing all those acts with such humility and love of religion, offering up her prayers to God with so great devotion and affection, and enduring for so long a while and so patiently so much fatigue; and seeing thus, that the more Her Majesty advances in the rule of this kingdom, so does she daily afford fresh and greater opportunities for commending her extreme piety."[52] All the ceremonies associated with the Easter Season, including touching for the king's evil, were clear demonstrations of Mary's piety if not her political pragmatism.

Elizabeth was far more aware of how to use spectacle to enhance the prestige of the monarchy, which she did from the very beginning of her reign in her coronation ceremony and procession through London the day before her coronation.[53] Thus we know even more about Elizabeth's practices, and have a number of accounts of both her Maundy ceremonies and her touching for the king's evil. For Mary as a woman to continue these practices was already an unusual situation, but as a Catholic Mary wanted to re-establish practices that were not only royal but Roman. For Elizabeth, the situation was more difficult and complex. She was a woman ruler, a "female-king" who had also to balance the variety of demands on her for religious reform. Looking at what ceremonial she retained and what she let go gives us an insight not only into Elizabeth's religious sensibilities, but also a glimpse into the cultural attitudes of the English Renaissance toward religion and queenship. The use of these religious ceremonies fit well with Elizabeth's self-presentation as the Virgin Queen, an image she presented to her people as a means to replace the Virgin Mary and help heal the rupture created by the break with the Catholic

Figure 2. Elizabeth in her coronation robes, c. 1600 (by courtesy of the National Portrait Gallery, London)

Church. Elizabeth and her Councillors deliberately appropriated the symbolism and prestige of the suppressed Marian cult in order to foster the cult of the Virgin Queen. This proved a powerful resource for Elizabeth in dealing with the political problems of her regime.[54]

The identification of Elizabeth with the Virgin Mary, which developed in the mid-1570s, was very effective in encouraging loyalty to the queen. The worship of the Virgin Mary had been especially popular in

England in the late Middle Ages, and well into the early sixteenth century.[55] Simply denying her power and prestige, as Protestant reformers did, did not lessen the tremendous appeal the Virgin had for the popular imagination; it simply left a void. The image of Elizabeth as a Virgin Queen helped to fill this void and at the same time was politically valuable since many English Protestants came to love and revere Elizabeth as they had previously loved and revered the virgin. People began to suggest that one ought to say, "Long live Eliza!" instead of "Hail Mary!" John Buxton describes the famous picture of Elizabeth being carried to Blackfriars as "like the Virgin Mary in a religious procession: a comparison her subjects did not hesitate to draw."[56] We can see this identification in many other contexts. A number of the symbols used to represent Elizabeth as Virgin Queen—the Rose, the Star, the Moon, the Phoenix, the Ermine, and the Pearl—were also symbols that had been used previously to represent the Virgin Mary. Roy Strong suggests that, although Protestant England banned religious images as idolatrous, images of the monarch were accorded the kind of ceremonial deference reserved for religious icons.[57]

In time, many of her subjects did accept Elizabeth as an acceptable substitute for the Virgin Mary, and their adulation assumed a religious coloring. For example, many of the members of Elizabeth's court believed that having the queen visit on progress was tantamount to having their house blessed. Lord Burghley wrote about Elizabeth's visit to Theobalds as "consecrating" it; Burghley treated her so splendidly there that she visited a number of times, which was a great if costly honor.[58] Elizabeth's progresses were critical in systematically promoting the cult of the Virgin Queen for people of all classes all over the country.[59] Sir Robert Burton suggested the very sight of the monarch could "refresh the soul of man." Magnificent, idealized portraits of Elizabeth also functioned to legitimate her power and gain loyalty.[60]

The celebration of Elizabeth's accession day, November 17, took on religious significance and the trappings of a religious festival, in part, suggests David Cressy, "to compensate for the reduction in holy days" in the calendar. In fact, this day was sometimes known as "the queen's holy day." The festivities included public thanksgiving for her safety, sermons, and the ringing of bells, in addition to the more expected and secular contests such as tournaments and signs of rejoicing and triumph. After the abortive rebellion in the north in 1569 and the bull of excommunication of 1570, public celebrations marking Elizabeth's accession began spontaneously. The first was in Oxford in 1570. They soon spread through the kingdom and were established officially. Elizabeth's government felt a need for a public display of celebration that demonstrated that all the threatening dangers had been overcome. The day "attracted much of the festive and liturgical energy that had formerly been reserved for saints' days."[61] Her accession was formally introduced as a church holiday in 1576, with a specific service and liturgy. Part of the service included the entire congregation.

> Minister: O Lord, save the Queen.
> People: Who putteth her trust in thee.
>
> * * *
>
> Minister: Let the enemies have none advantage on her.
> People: Let not the wicked approach to hurt her.[62]

From then onward November 17 was kept as a day of patriotic rejoicing, "in the forme of a Holy Day," as Thomas Holland said in a sermon in 1599 to answer those that "uncharitably traduced the honour of the realm." In at least some years, two days after the accession day festivities, on November 19, there were further sports to celebrate St. Elizabeth's day, the queen's namesake. "Then the nineteenth day, being St. Elizabeth's day, the Earl of Cumberland, the Earl of Essex, and my Lord Burgh, did challenge all comers six courses apiece; which was very honourably performed."[63]

Another day of organized public celebration was September 7, Elizabeth's birthday. There were prayers in church, ringing of bells, bonfires, and parties. One prayer asked God to bless Elizabeth and curse her enemies,

> to fight against those that fight against her. . . . Bless them that blesse her. Curse them that curse her. . . . Lett her rise. Lett them fall. Lett her flourish. Lett them perish.[64]

In a letter to William Cecil, the Recorder of London, William Fleetwood, described how London celebrated this day in the 1580's:

> This Weddensday morning all the bells of London do ring for joye, that upon the seven of this monethe, being on this daie . . . her Grace was borne. There will be on this daie but specially great feastings at supper. I have been bidden out this night to supper in six or seven places.[65]

The celebration of Elizabeth's birthday was particularly offensive to English Catholics because September 7 was, coincidentally, the eve of the feast of the nativity of the Blessed Virgin Mary. Catholics such as Edward Rishton complained that the English Protestants were ignoring this holy day, "and to show the greater contempt for our Blessed lady, they keep the birthday of queen Elizabeth in the most solemn way on the 7th day of September, which is the eve of the feast of the Mother of God, whose nativity they mark in their calendar in small and black letters, while that of Elizabeth is marked in letters both large and red. And what is hardly credible, in the church of St Paul, the chief church of London . . . the praises of Elizabeth are said to be sung at the end of the public prayers, as the Antiphon of our lady was sung former days."[66]

But many of her loyal subjects regarded the fact that Elizabeth should share the nativity of the Virgin Mary as more than simply coincidence; they considered it a divine omen. It proved to them that Elizabeth and the Anglican Church were sustained and sanctified by divine providence. This belief was further intensified by the date of Elizabeth's death, March 24, which was the eve of the Annunciation of the Virgin Mary.[67] Soon after the queen died one anonymous Latin elegy asked, "do you wish to know why it was on the Eve of the Lady that the holy Eliza ascended into heaven?" The answer emphasizes the direct parallels commonly perceived between Elizabeth and the Virgin Mary:

> Being on the point of death she chose that day for herself because in their lives these two were as one. Mary was a Virgin, she, Elizabeth, was also; Mary was blessed; Beta was blessed among the race of women. . . . Mary bore God in her womb, but Elizabeth bore God in her heart. Although in all other respects they are like twins, it is in this latter respect alone that there are not of equal rank.[68]

An engraving of the queen produced right after her death had as a caption, "She was, She is (What can there more be said?), In earth the first, in heaven the second Maid."[69] In 1607 Christopher Lever helped perpetuate this identification with a long poem about the sufferings Elizabeth endured under her sister Mary's reign. Lever placed Elizabeth among the saints and angels of Heaven, "as one far exceeding all others, the Virgin Mary only except."[70]

The continuation of the Maundy ceremony and touching for the king's evil were manifestations of the sacred aspect of monarchy Elizabeth represented to a people suffering from the dislocations of so many changes in church and state. Elizabeth deliberately performed these ceremonies with as much drama as possible, a holy or sacred theatre, what Richard McCoy calls the "increasingly threatrical and secular nature of Tudor power and its rites," or the "self-theatricalization that would characterize her entire reign" as John King describes it.[71] Blessing and curing with the queen's touch was yet another aspect of religious functions subsumed by the monarch. Some Catholics, however, would find this identification of Elizabeth as blasphemous, while for many Protestants these rituals and identification were examples of how Elizabeth had failed truly to purify the Church. Some Protestants explained Elizabeth's touching as merely prayerful intervention to God, not a miraculous cure. Reginald Scot put it thus: "God will not be offended thereas for hir maiestie onelie useth godlie and divine praier, with some almes, and referreth the cure to God and to the physician."[72]

The blessing of cramp rings did not extend into the reign of Elizabeth, and creeping to the cross was abandoned within a few years of her accession. Abandoning these practices may have been a concession to Protestants who perceived them as popish remnants. Elizabeth did, however, wash the feet of the poor on Maundy Thursday throughout her reign with elaborate ceremony that included, as had Mary's, drawing a cross on each foot as she finished. And touching for the king's evil became even more popular in her reign. Both her chaplain, William Tooker (1597), and her surgeon, William Clowes (1602), wrote books about scrofula and Elizabeth's remarkable talent for healing it through touch. It seems clear that Elizabeth chose to keep the ceremonies that were most public and had greatest value as spectacle and allow the less public ones to fall into disuse.

Elizabeth expressed herself eager to cure by touching throughout her reign. During her reign, instead of a fixed season for touching as had been done previously, occasions were arranged according to Elizabeth's inclinations, particularly when she felt a divine directive or when she was strongly importuned by the applicants or their patrons. Sufferers would give their names to the royal Surgeons, who would examine each patient carefully to be sure the disease was really the Evil and there were no impostures. They would then submit a list to the queen who would appoint a day, usually a Friday, Sunday, or feast day. The ceremony often took place at St. Stephen's Chapel in the ancient palace of Westminster, though Elizabeth also touched to heal while on progress, thus not only presenting the ceremony through the mediating filter of her Court, but also demonstrating this prestige through the theatricalization of ritual in other parts of her kingdom.

Her chaplain William Tooker described how intensely she prayed to be able to transmit the healing touch. "How often have I seen her most serene Majesty, prostrate on her knees, body and soul rapt in prayer . . . how often have I seen her with her exquisite hands, whiter than whitest snow, boldly and without disgust, pressing their sores and ulcers, and handling them to health . . . how often have I seen her worn with fatigue, as when in one single day, she healed eight and thirty persons of the struma." Tooker claimed that "most" of those touched eventually regained health. William Clowes also described in great detail specific cures Elizabeth had effected by touching when all other medical remedies had been tried and failed.[73]

We know some specific instances when Elizabeth touched. While on progress at Kenilworth in 1575 she not only knighted five gentlemen but also "by her hignes accustumed mercy & charitee, nyne cured of the penyfull and daugnerous diseaz, called the king's evill," wrote an eyewitness, Robert Laneham, who further explained in a private letter, "for that Kings and Queenz of this Realm, withoout oother medsin (save by handling and prayerz) only doo cure it."[74] Witnesses describe as well that Elizabeth actually touched the tumors and afflicted areas. We know that at least later in her reign the ceremony was fixed and elaborate, and presented in English rather than Latin. On August 18, 1596, a Venetian visitor observed the ceremony.

> This year at the touching the Queen touched ten, and then washed her hands, being served by the Lord treasurer, the Lord Chancellor, and my Lord of Essex, all three on their knees; the treasurer in the middle, opposite the Queen holding a basin, the Chancellor on his right with a ewer of water, and on the left the Earl of Essex with a napkin which the Queen used to wipe her hands.[75]

Though clearly aware of the value of the theatricalization of holy ritual, we may assume that Elizabeth did not touch simply for the propaganda value it afforded her. She apparently took the ceremony very seriously, and at times did not feel that at that specific moment she had the inspiration to cure by touching. At Gloucester, when throngs of the afflicted came to her for her aid, she had to deny them, telling them, "Would, would that I could give you help and succour. God, God is the best and greatest physician of all—you must pray to him." It is possible that Elizabeth may have refused to touch because she was menstruating, which would have made her touch polluting. This may also be why Elizabeth did not touch in a fixed season, since this sometimes might have coincided with her periods, which were irregular. Popular culture in medieval and early modern England believed the touch of a menstruating woman could have disastrous effects on men, cows, gardens, bees, milk, wine, and much more, even if medical authorities of the time denied it.[76]

The effectiveness of the queen's touch was a potent political force for her, and a weapon against the ire of the pope. Indeed, the Protestant English feared the pope, whom Sir Walter Mildmay, for one, described as England's "most mortal and capital enemy." They believed that each Maundy Thursday he pronounced a solemn anathema against all heretics and enemies. There was particular concern after the pope issued a bull of excommunication against Elizabeth in 1570. English Protestants publicly discounted the papal bull on the grounds that Elizabeth still had the God-given ability of a true monarch to cure by touch, and even English Catholics as well as Protestants continued to go to Elizabeth to be healed by her touch.[77]

As with touching, Elizabeth began celebrating the Maundy from the very beginning of her reign, and there are specific descriptions of a number of her Maundies, including 1560, 1565, 1572–1573, and 1595. The hall where the Maundy took place was prepared with long tables on each side, set with all the paraphernalia needed for the ceremony. There were carpets and cushions on which the queen could kneel and basins of holy water, alms, and other gifts for the recipients. The chaplain entered first, as did all the poor women who were to participate in the ceremony. There were the same number of women as years in the queen's age; thus the ceremony got longer as the queen grew older. These women would take their places, half on each side of the room. The Yeomen of the Laundry, with towels and a silver basin filled with warm water and flowers, washed each women's feet and then wiped them. The women's feet were then washed by the Sub-Almoner and again by the Almoner.

After all this had taken place the queen then entered the hall and prayers and songs were sung in her honor. For these occasions Elizabeth dressed very formally, sometimes in blue, the color of the Virgin Mary. Then the same number of ladies and gentlewomen as poor women addressed themselves with aprons and towels to wait upon the queen. Elizabeth, kneeling on the cushions, washed each woman's feet, and then kissed one, and then the other, after which she made on each foot the sign of the cross. After Elizabeth finished the foot washing itself, she gave each woman cloth for a dress, shoes, food, and wine. Then the aprons of the gentlewomen was given to the poor women. Each woman was also given a small white purse containing the same number of pense as the queen's age.

In Maundy ceremonies of earlier reigns the monarch had usually given his robes to one of the recipients at the close of the ceremony, as Mary did with the 1556 Maundy. Elizabeth instead, so that she might keep her gown, ransomed it from the women by giving each recipient twenty shillings in addition to what they had already received. She did this to avoid choosing one person at the expense of the others. She may also have not wanted to part with the dress, given how Elizabeth felt about her clothes. Once the lengthy ceremony was completed Elizabeth took "her ease upon the cushion of state," still the center of attention, and there was more music. Finally, the ceremony being lengthy and by this time it being evening, the queen withdrew and the company departed.[78]

The emphasis on having the number of poor correspond to the monarch's age, as opposed to having twelve recipients as was usually the case, marks a major difference from other maundies, and places more emphasis on the specific monarch as Christ figure rather than simply as an anonymous representative of the church. The fact that both Mary and Elizabeth performed the Maundy for women, as opposed to men, as earlier monarchs had done, would also emphasize the sex of the monarch.

Similar to the ceremony of touching, there was something courageous and unorthodox in a young, unmarried, Anglican woman taking on a function that was not only priestly but an act in imitation of Christ himself. The horror over a woman's ordination, mentioned by Fortescue in the fifteenth century, was, if anything, even more potent a century later after the fears and dislocations of the Reformation, and was a view shared by many Protestants as well as Catholics. John Calvin wrote in his *Institutes of the Christian Religion*: "The practice before Augustine was born . . . held that a woman was not allowed to speak in the church, and also not to teach, to baptise, or to offer. This was that she might not claim for herself the function of any man, much less that of a priest. . . . It is a mockery to give women the right to baptise."[79] There are clear parallels in Calvin's thought to both the Reformer Knox and the Catholic Heath. Yet Elizabeth's Maundy ceremonies, which might certainly be construed both to usurp the position of priest and also to retain popish practices, seem to have been highly regarded by many of the English as an imitatio Christi; certainly she retained them throughout her reign, except when disease in London forbade such a public event, and even then alms were widely distributed to make up for the loss of the ceremony.[80] In 1596 Elizabeth took the Maundy seriously enough to eliminate Bishop of London Richard Fletcher from the ceremonial after he had offended her. On April 15, 1595 Fletcher wrote to Robert Cecil, "Contrary to the signification of her Majesty's good pleasure of late unto me for the execution of the Almoner's place at the Maundy, I have this morning a commandment from her Highness, that I shall not deal in it; a thing so grievous that I want words to express it."[81]

The Maundy ceremony also gives us a unique opportunity to learn more about Elizabeth's own religious beliefs. Guzman de Silva wrote to Philip II on the 21 of April 1565 to describe Elizabeth's Maundy.

> The Queen performed the customary ceremony on Holy Thursday. They tell me she did so with great dignity and devotion. . . . After she had washed the poor women's feet she deliberately traced a very large and well-defined cross and kissed it to the sorrow of many persons who witnessed it and of others who would not attend the ceremony, but to the joy of others.

Five days later de Silva reported to the king a conversation he had with Elizabeth about the ceremony.

> I was praising lately to the Queen the ceremony she performed on Holy Thursday . . . and the devotion with which she made the crosses on the feet of the poor women and kissed them . . . to which she answered, "Many people think we are Turks or Moors here, whereas we only differ from other Catholics in things of small importance."[82]

Both the Maundy and the ceremony of touch were so accepted by the English people throughout Elizabeth's long forty-five-year reign that though James I did not want to continue the ceremony of touch when he ascended the English throne, his advisors convinced him it was crucial to do so for the loyalty it engendered.[83] Both the ceremony of touch and the Royal Maundy continued throughout the seventeenth century.

By the sixteenth century the monarch's function was not only politico-religious, but also had a special almost magical quality of the sacred in the minds of many of the people, that of a monarch who ruled by divine providence. In 1462 the thought of a woman performing such sacred functions as touching and blessing was perceived as not only blasphemous but ineffective. Yet by the end of Elizabeth's reign these functions were not only accepted but an important part of a sacred monarchy whose physical body was female. As Steven Mullaney points out, Elizabeth conflated the vulnerability of power with the vulnerability of gender and turned both to her own advantage.[84]

These functions that Elizabeth continued and developed suggest the depth of her religious feelings as well as her view of her role as monarch. As queen, Elizabeth had little fondness for listening to sermons, but this does not demonstrate any lack of piety. It is hardly surprising she disliked sermons given the harangues to which she was subjected by her preachers, and the kinds of limits—to dress simply, to marry, to purify the church according to their guidelines—they wanted to place on her. Camden argued, "Yet was she truly Religious, who every day, as soon as arose, spent some time in prayers to God. She many times said . . . that she had rather talk with God devoutly by Prayer, than hear others speak eloquently of God." In continuing to touch for the king's evil and wash the feet of poor women on Maundy Thursday Elizabeth participated in a way that was important to her and fit in with her religious beliefs and conception of monarchy; she was also well aware that these ceremonies encouraged the devotion of her subjects. Elizabeth truly believed that she was under the special protection of God, who watched out for her for the good of England. She once told the Earl of Shrewsbury "how wonderfully God had preserved her from the malice of her enemies, and to prevent all their wicked practices against her." Elizabeth explained how "having on a time had notice of a man who had undertaken to execute mischief to her sacred person, the stature, and some scars of his face being described unto her, she happened, as she was on progress, amongst a multitude of others to discover that man; yet, not being astonished at the view of him, she called my Lord of Leicester, and shewing the party to him, he was apprehended, and found the same." [85]

Writing at the end of her reign, her surgeon William Clowes prayed for Elizabeth,

> whose long life, much happines, peace and tranquility, let us all (according to our bounden dutyes) continually pray unto the Almighty God, that he will blesse, keepe and defend her Sacred person, from the malice of all her knowne and unknowne enemies, so that shee may forever raigne over us, (if it please the Lord God) even unto the ende of the world, still to cure and heale many thousands moe, then ever she hath yet done. [86]

Clowe's prayer, that Elizabeth might live and rule and cure until the end of the world, projects her not only into the sacred but beyond human into the divine. But we do need to take care how seriously we accept this prayer. In fact, Elizabeth in 1602 was a woman close to seventy years old, who was, in some people's eyes, especially after the Essex rebellion and its

Elizabeth Regina.

2.PARALIPOM. 6.

Domine Deus Ifrael, non eſt ſimilis tui Deus in cœlo & in terra, qui paɛta cuſtodis & miſericordiam cum ſeruis tuis, qui ambulant coram te in toto corde ſuo.

Figure 3. Elizabeth praying, from Richard Day, *A Book of Christian Prayers* (by permission of the Folger Shakespeare Library)

attack on both her person and her monarchy, clearly failing.[87] And while imagery of the sacred was part of the way her people viewed Elizabeth, it was only one aspect of a multi-sided presentation; her gender and questions around her sexuality were also important and possibly troubling aspects of the way the English viewed their queen. Yet for at least some of her subjects the discomfort they may have felt in seeing a woman rule and perform such actions had been lost in appreciation for all Elizabeth had done as a sacred monarch, one who both blessed and cured with a queen's touch.

3. The Official Courtships of the Queen

In 1567 the Spanish Ambassador, Guzman de Silva, wrote to his master Philip II that, "the hatred that this Queen has of marriage is most strange. They presented a comedy before her last night until nearly one in the morning, which ended in a marriage, and the Queen, as she told me herself, expressed her dislike of the woman's part." At about the same time Elizabeth also held a masque for de Silva performed by gentlemen all dressed in black and white. Elizabeth said of the costumes, "those are my colors." This time de Silva apparently did not catch the implication, but in some works on heraldry of the period, black and white are described as the colors of perpetual virginity, of purity and steadfastness.[1]

From the beginning of the reign, as well as the question of religion, the other important issue was whom would the queen marry. Yet, despite repeated behests on the part of Parliament and her Council to marry, Elizabeth claimed she preferred the single state. In Elizabeth's speech before her first Parliament, the queen declared, "And in the end this shalbe for me sufficient—that a marble stone shall declare that a Queene having raigned such a tyme, lived and dyed a virgin."[2] One might suppose, then, that Elizabeth, the Virgin Queen, simply represented the ideal of chastity to her people. But the ways Elizabeth fashioned herself in her public presentations were far more contradictory and complex.[3] For while Elizabeth claimed virginity as her ideal state, and eventually resisted all demands on her to marry, she also loved proposals and courtship. These were not only politically valuable to her, they also seem to have had some deeper emotional resonance. Examining some specific incidents allows us to study the conflicts and contradictions between Elizabeth's self-presentations as virgin and as object of political and sexual desire and marriageability; it is also valuable to examine people's responses to both these images. This chapter focuses on some of the pressures for Elizabeth to marry from the beginning of the reign, and pivotal moments in three different courtships[4]—the mid-1560s and the Archduke Charles, brother of the Holy Roman Emperor, 1571–72 and the Duke of Anjou (the future Henry III), and

Figure 4. Elizabeth being presented with a book by George Gasgoigne
(by permission of the British Library)

the late 1570s and early 1580s and Francis, Duke of Alençon (later Anjou).
As a counterpoint to these official courtships with foreign princes stands
Elizabeth's favorite, Robert Dudley, who also wooed the queen and whose
relationship with her caused such concern over whether it would im-
pede these other negotiations. The complexity of the issue of Elizabeth's

courtships is especially clear when we think of the very word "court." It is the place where the sovereign resides and the center of power. As D. M. Loades argues, the Tudor court was a political institution as well as a cultural center and the place of exchange for patronage and power. But court can also mean the elaborate ritualized form of wooing, of seeking a woman's hand in marriage. Catherine Bates suggests that in the 1560s and 1570s "to court" began to have a distinctly sexual connotation. "By the end of the 1570s, then, the word to court was in general use, with two concurrent senses, the social and the amorous." Moreover, as Norbert Elias points out, in the sixteenth century, among aristocratic court society, sexual life was more concealed, and more ritualized, than previously.[5]

Only with hindsight do we know that Elizabeth indeed never married. Not only did many of her councillors and those at foreign courts hope and expect Elizabeth might marry, she herself at different times appears to have at least considered the possibility, played with the idea, that she might wed.

Camden's version of Elizabeth's 1558 speech to Parliament, where she claims to already be married to England, is often used as an example that Elizabeth from the beginning of her reign had made the decision never to marry.

> I have already joyned my selfe in marriage to an husband, namely the kingdome of England. And behold (said she, which I marvaile ye have forgotten,) the pledge of this my wedlocke and mariage with my kingdome, (and therewith, she stretched forth her finger and shewed the ring of gold.)[6]

But as John King has shown, we have to accept this version of the speech only with reservations.[7] Moreover, in 1604 James I made a similar speech to his Parliament, saying: "I am the husband, and all the whole Isle is my lawfull Wife." Now this is obviously a rhetorical strategy, a statement about the king as body politic, since James was already a husband and a father. Furthermore, in 1624 James elaborated on this metaphor as a means to explain his power. "It is a very fit similitude for a king and his people to be like a husband and wife. . . . It is the husband's part to cherish his wife, to entreat her kindly, and reconcile himself towards her, and procure her love by all means, so it is my part to do the like to my people." Equally, when Mary had addressed the citizens in the Guildhall in February 1554 during the Wyatt rebellion she asserted: "I am your queen, to whom at my coronation, when I was wedded to the realm . . . (the spousal ring whereof I have on my finger, which never hitherto was, nor hereafter shall be left off), you promised your allegiance and obedience unto me." Mary promised to marry only "for the high benefit and commodity of the whole realm." She did not say that since she was married to her realm she could not marry a person. So too we might grant that for Elizabeth to present herself as already married to England is also claiming that her body politic is the spouse of her country; it is not a definitive claim that her body natural will never marry.[8]

Of course, being Elizabeth, and given her deployment of ambiguous rhetorical strategies, in Camden's version of her 1558 speech she is at least implying that she does not need to marry, as she, symbolically, already has. The more authoritative version of Elizabeth's 1558 speech does not give this justification for not marrying but here as well Elizabeth presents her preference for the maiden state. The speech continues, however, by presenting other alternatives. "Whensover it may please God to enclyne my harte to an other kynd of life, ye may well assure your selves my meaninge is not to do or determyne anie thinge wherwith the realme may or shall have juste cause to be discontented. . . . And whomsover my chance shalbe to light apon, I truste he shalbe as carefull for the realme and yow." If however, it "please almightie God to contynew me still in this mynde to lyve out of the state of mariage, yet it is not to be feared but he will so woorke in my harte and in your wisdomes as good provsion by his healpe may be made in convenient tyme, wherby the realme shall not remayne destitute of an heire that may be a fitt governor, and peraventure more beneficiall to the realme then suche ofspring as may come of me. For although I be never so carefull of your well doinges and mynde ever so to be, yet may my issue growe out of kynde and become perhappes ungracious."[9] At the beginning of her reign Elizabeth seemed to show little interest in marriage and children. With a strong lack of maternal feelings, she suggested her own child might be much inferior to her.

But other speeches and statements even more leave open the possibility that the queen was seriously considering marriage and the desirability of children. Elizabeth was under enormous pressure to marry, and indeed in a later speech to Parliament goes much further in her attempts to placate her subjects by offering to wed—if the time were right. In a speech of November 5, 1566, to some thirty members of Lords and thirty members of Commons in the midst of the negotiations with the Archduke Charles, Elizabeth was horrified that Parliament would think she did not care about the fate of England.

> Was I not borne in the realme? Were my parentes borne in anye forreyne contreye? Ys there anye cause I shold alyenatte my self from beynge carefull over this contreye? Ys not my kyngdome here? Whom have I opressede? . . . What turmoyle have I made in this common welthe that I shold be suspected to have no regarde to the same?

Elizabeth protested that

> I wyll never breke the worde of a prynce spoken in publyke place, for my honour sake. And therefore I saye ageyn, I wyll marrye assone as I can convenyentlye, yf God take not hym awaye with whom I mynde to marrye, or my self, or els sum othere great lette happen. . . . And I hope to have chylderne, otherwyse I wolde never marrie.[10]

The pressure on Elizabeth to marry was great, and certainly related to role expectations about her as a woman, in that a king could relieve Elizabeth of the difficulties of rule, or so her councillors fondly believed. But the pressure on all monarchs to marry so that they could provide the country with an heir was intense. This had already been made all too obvious with the murderous, marital antics of Elizabeth's father. And the expectations for what the marriage would accomplish would be clear. In the sixteenth century it was expected that rulers would marry, and royal marriages involved not only providing an heir but bringing to the kingdom honor and perhaps some political and religious advantage. Affection and personal pleasure might be a bonus, but would hardly be the reason for marrying. Jenny Wormald suggests that of all sixteenth century rulers, Mary Stuart was "uniquely" the only one to "put marriage before monarchy."[11]

The expectations that the queen would marry were strong, but there was also the conflict and contradiction that the queen was ruler while a wife was to be ruled by her husband. In 1559 Aylmer in his *Harborrow for Trew and Faithful Subjects* attempted to reconcile these contradictions, but without much success. "Say you, God hath apoynted her to be subject to her husband . . . therfore she maye not be the heade. I graunte that, so farre as perteining to the bandes of mariage, and the offices of a wife, she must be a subjecte: but as a Magistrate she maye be her husbandes heade. . . . Whie may not the woman be the husbandes inferiour in matters of wedlock, and his head in the guiding of the commonwelth." While Aylmer's vision of duty carefully delineated between public and private with Elizabeth as dutiful wife in the domestic circle and head and ruler of the commonwealth in her official role might sound like an ideal solution to the problem of a woman ruler, we can well understand how Elizabeth herself would not be convinced. Delineating the line between what is private and what is public is virtually impossible. In many ways every aspect of Elizabeth's life contained its public element; as she herself once stated, her life was conducted in the open. We might well might wonder if there were any place for Elizabeth to ever be privately the subservient and submissive wife, even if she would choose to be so, which is dubious. And it is highly doubtful that a husband, either a foreign prince or one of her own nobility, could simply accept Elizabeth's domination in the public realm without attempting to interfere.

This question of marriage and what it might mean to her was obviously one that Elizabeth was well aware of throughout her life and reign. We have a number of statements from letters as well as reported events that may give us some insight into how she felt about marriage, and it does seem clear that this is not a monochromatic picture—Elizabeth presented a variety of perspectives on the question of her marriage at different times and in different courtships. We must, however, remember that Elizabeth often was carefully crafting her statements for public consumption, and they reveal not so much what she felt about marriage but what she felt would be politic for her to *say* about marriage.

From the beginning of her reign, Elizabeth's Council and Parliaments beseeched her to marry, and found the idea of an unmarried woman ruling unnatural. William Cecil expounded on this frequently in letters to intimates. For example, in 1561 he wrote to Thomas Radcliffe, the Earl of Sussex, "The Quene's Majestie remanyth still strange to allow of marriadge, wherein God alter her mynde!" The same year he wrote to Sir Nicholas Throckmorton, "I am most sorry of all that her Majesty is not disposed seriously to marriage; for I see likelihood of grat evil . . . if she shall not shortly marry." In letters to his friend, Sir Thomas Smith, Cecil was even more open about the despair Elizabeth's refusal to marry caused him. Writing in 1564 he stated that unless she changed her mind and married, "I assure you, as now thynges hang in desperation, I have no comfort to live." Two years later he was no more sanguine about Elizabeth's single state. "God direct the Quene's Majesty to marriadg in some place, for otherwise her regyment will prove very troublesome and unquiet." Even when he was concerned about the potential marriage partner, as he obviously was about Anjou in 1571, Cecil still considered marriage the best for Elizabeth and the realm. In what he underlines is a *private* letter to Sir

Francis Walsingham, he comments: "I am not able to discern what is best, but surely, I see no continuance of her quietness without a Marriage. And therefore I remit the successe to an almighty God. This that I write privately to your self I trust shall remaine to yourself."[12]

The people around Elizabeth very much wanted Elizabeth to marry. But that is not the sole reason for the various courtships. Despite Elizabeth's supposed dislike of marriage negotiations, she herself encouraged them; she vastly enjoyed the rituals of courtship. Sir Henry Sidney suggested that Elizabeth was "greedy for marriage proposals," a view shared by de Silva. "I do not think anything is more enjoyable to this Queen than the treating of marriage, although she assures me herself that nothing annoys her more. She is vain, and would like all the world to be running after her." At the same time, the actual idea of marriage seems to have been repugnant to her. Elizabeth told the ambassador to the Duke of Württemberg, "I would rather be a beggar and single than a queen and married." She was even more emphatic to the French ambassador. "When I think of marriage, it is as though my heart were being dragged out of my vitals."[13] And there was the question of what would be the role for a husband of a queen. Elizabeth told de Quadra that, if she married, her husband "should not sit at home all day amongst the cinders," a clever allusion to Cinderella, an already well known tale by that time, and one often told about a "poor cinder boy" as well as a girl. But one who did not sit in the cinders might well take over control from Elizabeth. Examining her responses, relationships, and others' responses to the marriage negotiations of Archduke Charles, Anjou, and Alençon can allow us insight into this contradiction of image and purpose.[14]

Adding further to the ambiguity of the foreign negotiations was Robert Dudley's determined courtship of his queen, and his position as her favorite. Elizabeth's relationship with Dudley was very different from those with her foreign suitors. She knew him well, she apparently had intense feelings for him for many years, and his prospects for marrying the queen came not from the suitability of his birth but from Elizabeth's personal affection for him. The rumors about Elizabeth's sexual misconduct that abounded throughout her reign almost entirely centered on her relationship with Dudley.[15] In terms of being English and Protestant, Dudley did have certain advantages as a potential husband. He was, however, also the son and grandson of executed traitors, and deeply disliked as an arrogant upstart. Elizabeth, whatever her emotions, kept them sufficiently under control as to not make such a potentially divisive marriage.[16]

Dudley was clearly Elizabeth's favorite from the beginning of her reign—they had apparently become friends while both were in the Tower in the reign of her sister. Unfortunately (from his point of view), at the time Elizabeth became queen Dudley was already married, though his wife, Amy Robsart, lived in the country away from court, suffering from what was probably breast cancer. Many people suggested that Robert was simply waiting for Amy to die so that he might marry the queen. Others thought he might not simply wait. "I had heard . . . veracious news that Lord Robert has sent to poison his wife," de Feria's successor, Alvaro de Quadra, Bishop of Aquila, wrote home in November 1559.[17] We have no evidence that Dudley contemplated murdering his wife; however, he may well have not regretted the idea of a natural death for Amy in the not too distant future. But Amy did not die of illness peacefully in her bed. Her death was mysterious and disturbing; on September 8, 1560 she was found dead with her neck broken at the bottom of some stairs in the country house where she was living. Her body was otherwise undisturbed with marks of violence. Many people around Elizabeth were desperately afraid the queen would forget everything in a moment of passion and marry Robert Dudley. We truly do not have all the answers to the questions about Amy's death. Was she murdered? The coroner's court said no, but the verdict never quieted the rumors. Perhaps she threw herself down those stairs; she was certainly unhappy enough, though this is a particularly uncertain way to commit suicide. Her maid Pinto had overheard her mistress praying to God to deliver her from desperation. On the day she died, Amy sent everyone out of the house to the Abingdon Fair, refusing to go herself, and was angry when her companion decided to stay at home. We might wonder if she wanted to be alone so that she could kill herself. Indeed, some scholars suggest that she may have simply died accidentally, her spine so brittle from metastasized cancer that even the act of walking down stairs—especially if she stumbled—could have cause her neck to snap.[18]

Whatever the truth, the scurrilous comments about Elizabeth and Robert Dudley disturbed many people. A marriage with Dudley would have been most unpopular. But fear of public opinion may not have been the only reason that Elizabeth declined to marry her favorite. She also did not want to give up her control as monarch, as she surely would if she married. Even though Philip was often an absentee husband, his impact on Mary's reign was profound. While Elizabeth was also emotionally involved with Dudley in a way that was unique, she did not allow him to presume too far on his position. When Dudley tried to discipline her servant, Bowyer, the latter threw himself at Elizabeth's feet and humbly craved for Elizabeth to tell him "Whether my Lord of Leicester was King, or her Majesty Queen?"—a question that could not be better calculated to sway Elizabeth's answer. Elizabeth turned to Dudley and told him, "If you think to rule here, I will take a course to see you forth-coming: I will have here but one Mistress, and no Master." [19]

Robert Dudley did, however, hope to see England with a master as well as a mistress; he tried both overtly and indirectly to convince Elizabeth that she should marry, and that he ought to to be the man. As early as 1560 he confided "that if he live another year he will be in a very different position from now." Of course in fact he was not. Elizabeth was well aware of his maneuvers. In 1565 Dudley sponsored a party as a part of the pre-Lenten festivals. De Silva described the events of the day in some detail to his king.

> We went to the Queen's room and descended to where all was prepared for the representation of a comedy in English, of which I understood just so much as the Queen told me. The plot was founded on the question of marriage, discussed between Juno and Diana, Juno advocating marriage and Diana chastity. Jupiter gave a verdict in favour of matrimony after many things had passed on both sides in defence of the respective arguments. The Queen turned to me and said, "This is all against me." [20]

It is hard to know for how long Robert Dudley seriously thought he had a chance to marry Elizabeth, and when the courtship became a game. Richard McCoy suggests this change happened by the mid-1560s and uses as evidence Dudley's statement (reported in a 4 February 1566 letter from de Silva to Philip) that he did not tell Elizabeth he had abandoned his courtship because "the Queen should not be led to think that he relinquished his suit of distaste for it and so turn her regard into anger and enmity against him which might cause her, womanlike, to undo him." While it is true that Elizabeth and Dudley's relationship did begin to change around 1564, and that Elizabeth seems to have made up her mind not to marry him but neither to diminish her preference for him, we should not necessarily take Dudley at his word here, though of course he may be telling the truth. It is not at all clear that Dudley had yet given up all hope of marrying his queen. We might question whether instead of misleading Elizabeth, he hoped to convince the Spanish ambassador and the English lords who favored the marriage with Archduke Charles. [21] Like

Elizabeth's, Dudley's statements were often calculated for effect and are not trustworthy guides to what he really thought. Susan Doran, in fact, suggests that those in favor of the marriage with the archduke were such a formidable force at Court that Dudley was afraid to show his hostility publicly. "Instead he chose to negotiate secretly with the French ambassador to sabotage it by putting forward first Charles IX's candidature and then his own." Wallace MacCaffrey states of the period between 1562 and 1569 that "Leicester's position was for obvious reasons a . . . difficult one. The prospect of marriage with Elizabeth diminished steadily during these years but he never quite gave up hope."[22]

There were a number of obstacles in the 1560s marriage negotiations of Elizabeth to the Archduke Charles, but it also had a number of attractions for the English. The marriage had been suggested by the Austrians and not taken seriously by the English at the very beginning of the reign, around 1559–60. Despite all de Quadra's attempt to encourage the marriage, Elizabeth then had told the Emperor she had "no wish to give up solitude and our lonely life."[23] Though no one really expected Elizabeth would keep to her "lonely life" at that time, more of the nation supported the idea of Elizabeth marrying an Englishman. By the mid-1560s the situation had changed.

In 1563 the idea of the marriage was one again revived, this time by the English, leading to Vienna sending an Imperial envoy, Adam Zwetkovich, Baron von Mitterburg, in 1565. In the mid-1560s the concerns over a disputed succession were acute, especially after Catherine Grey's secret marriage to the Earl of Hertford and her subsequent disgrace. Mary Stuart's position may have been an even stronger motive. Elizabeth may have felt the need to encourage courtships herself when her Scottish cousin was attempting to negotiate an advantageous marriage. Elizabeth was extremely concerned with whom Mary Stuart might marry for her second husband. "Until 1565, when she finally married her cousin," Susan Bassnett suggests, "the question of Mary's marriage preoccupied Elizabeth as much as that of her own."[24] Mary had made herself available to the Spanish (with hopes of marrying Philip's heir, Don Carlos) and the French (she hoped to marry her brother-in-law, Charles IX, younger brother of her first husband Francis II). Mary even listened to Elizabeth's incredible proposal that she marry Robert Dudley in the hopes Elizabeth would name her as heir as a wedding gift. None of these marriage possibilities worked out, probably due to Mary's own weaknesses as queen,[25] and in the summer of 1565 Mary married her cousin Henry Stuart, Lord

Darnley. Despite Elizabeth's own role in narrowing Mary's choices for marriage partners, and allowing Darnley to go to Scotland, both the English queen and the English people were angry and frightened by the implications of this marriage, since Darnley also had some claim to the English throne through his grandmother, Margaret Tudor. A marriage alliance with the archduke could possibly restore the balance of power lost with Mary's marriage. Among foreign princes there was really none other of comparable status. And a marriage with Robert Dudley, clearly the only domestic candidate by the early 1560s, was unpopular. Elizabeth also recognized that relations with the Hapsburgs needed to be repaired after the ill will that had developed over textile trade between the English and the Netherlands.[26]

Yet whether Elizabeth really wanted to marry is another question. In March 1565 she told de Silva:

> If I could appoint such a successor to the Crown as would please me and the country, I would not marry, as it is a thing for which I have never had any inclination. My subjects, however press me so that I cannot help myself or take the other course, which is a very difficult one. There is a strong idea in the world that a woman cannot live unless she is married, or at all events that is she refrains from marriage she does so for some bad reason. . . . But what can we do? We cannot cover everybody's mouth, but must content ourselves with doing our duty and trust in God, for the truth will at last be made manifest. He knows my heart, which is very different from what people think, as you will see some day.[27]

Elizabeth certainly believed that a woman, at least a queen, could live unmarried, and do it for the best of reasons. We might wonder what Elizabeth believed God knew was in her heart and what truth would someday be made manifest. Was it that she would never marry, but would rule her entire reign as the Virgin Queen? But, as she admitted, she was pressed very hard, and did agree to to seriously negotiate with the Empire over a marriage with Charles.

A large obstacle in the negotiation for the English was Archduke Charles's Catholicism. For Elizabeth herself it was also crucial that she see the archduke before any marriage contract could be signed. It seemed to be an insurmountable difficulty that Elizabeth refused to commit herself before she had actually seen Charles. The emperor's negotiators claimed that Charles would lose his dignity were he to come to England prior to a formal betrothal, but without his coming to England first, a formal betrothal was impossible.[28]

Throughout her reign Elizabeth made the prospect of a successful courtship more difficult by claiming that she could not trust portrait painters. She must see a potential husband before she could decide whether she would marry. De Quadra recorded in May 1559 that "the Queen says that she has taken a vow to marry no man whom she has not seen. . . . And said she would rather be a nun than marry without knowing with whom and on the faith of portrait painters." This ploy was not simply used in the negotiations with the Austrians. For example during the negotiations for Elizabeth to marry the Duke of Anjou (the future Henri III) in the early 1570s, Cecil wrote to Walsingham, who was then her ambassador in France:

> For the Marriage her Majesty caused me privately to confer with the Ambassador, and her Majesty hath willed me to let him know, that you shall make the Answer, . . . her Majesty would have you to let the King and his Mother understand that she cannot accord to take any person to her husband whom she shall not first see.

There were certainly a number of reasons to hold to this position, and Elizabeth had personal experience with some of them. Elizabeth was all too aware of Henry VIII's scathing disappointment when he actually met Anne of Cleves. Her sister's husband Philip, too, had scarcely bothered to hide his contempt for his older queen, despite Mary's passionate love for him. While it was obviously important to Elizabeth that she not be paired with a man she found distasteful, she would also not to place herself in a vulnerable position with a foreign suitor who would not sufficiently appreciate her charms. And Elizabeth's position made sense not only in terms of what would be a happy marriage but in the medical beliefs of the day of what would hasten conception. In the sixteenth-century medical text, *The Methode of Phisicke*, Philip Barrow argues that "unwilling carnall copulation for the most part is vaine and barren: for love causeth conception, and therfore loving women do conceave often." Elizabeth's position also, however, worked effectively to keep a number of marriage negotiations from going further than she wanted them to go. Elizabeth never wavered on this issue, though as we shall see, even if she did see the potential marriage partner, this was not simply a formality, and did not necessarily mean she would marry. Nor did a potential suitor's willingness to come make her agree to a visit.[29]

William Cecil reopened the negotiations with the Empire in 1563, and by 1565 the support for the marriage with Charles included much of the

Council; its most vocal supporters included both Thomas Howard, the Duke of Norfolk, and Thomas Radcliffe, the Earl of Sussex. The fear of a disputed succession was so strong in the Council it overrode the question of religious differences. The promoters of the marriage believed the Hapsburgs to be more flexible about religion than indeed was the case. Cecil was committed to the new religion, but he optimistically believed that Charles would eventually agree to total conformity. Sussex was more realistic about the obstacle of religion but hoped that a compromise could be arrived at where by Charles would attend Anglican church services with Elizabeth and privately hear Mass.[30]

When the negotiations were seriously under way, the open exercise of Charles's Catholicism was the area of greatest dispute. Further areas of disagreement included who should bear the cost of Charles's household in England and Charles's title and role in governing England. De Silva wrote to Philip that the English thought the Imperial stand on the practice of religion "offered great difficulties. . . . They also struck at the clause about the Archduke's expenses, thinking that the Emperor wants to burden them with them. With regard to the Emperor's remarks showing that he wishes the Archduke to be called King and to govern jointly with [the] Queen, Cecil thinks this would be difficult. . . . With regard . . . to the request that in case of the Queen's death without an heir, that the Archduke should remain here with a footing in the country, that is a thing they cannot concede, and will never agree to." While the other issues might have been resolved, Elizabeth was adamant about religion. By the end of August, 1565, Zwetkovich returned to Vienna with Elizabeth's stand and Emperor Maximilian decided "to abandon the matter" unless Elizabeth was willing to modify her position.[31]

Elizabeth, however, did not want to see the negotiations ended, whatever she hoped to finally gain from them, and in May 1566 she sent Thomas Danett to Vienna to ask Maximilian to reconsider his position. Susan Doran speculates that this may have been done to avoid a confrontation with her 1566 Parliament over her marriage and the succession. She may also have wanted to keep Philip's good will, at least for a time longer. Maximilian refused to reconsider, however, and Danett also discovered that Charles was a far more devout Catholic, attending Mass daily, than the English had previously believed. Even this news, however, did not keep Norfolk, Sussex, and Cecil from continue to advance the cause of the marriage. With Parliament pressuring her, Elizabeth agreed to send Sussex to Austria to further discuss the marriage negotiation. Elizabeth kept postponing his departure, however, and "some feared that the embassy was a mere public relations device intended to silence demands that the Queen marry or settle the succession." This was certainly de Silva's interpretation. He believed that in the end the English would make "an excuse that in consequence of religion, the marriage cannot be effected." [32]

Elizabeth finally allowed Sussex to depart; he arrived in Vienna on August 5. He and Maximilian eventually were able to hammer out a compromise that would allow Charles private worship if he also publicly attended Anglican services with the queen. While there were still some differences in interpretations between Sussex and Charles over what this all entailed, Sussex believed that these concessions would clear the way for the marriage and sent Henry Cobham to England. Elizabeth said she could not make a commitment without discussing it with her Council. Norfolk, the strongest supporter, was ill and could not attend, and the opponents to the marriage, Leicester, Pembroke, Northampton, and Knollys, pressed their case forcefully, arguing that a Catholic husband would cause religious and political unrest. They were answered by Cecil, Lord Admiral Clinton, and Howard of Effingham, the Lord Chamberlain, who argued that the dangers of a disputed succession and civil war far outweighed any problems over the marriage.

After listening to the arguments, Elizabeth decided that she could not allow Charles even the right to have the Mass celebrated in private. Nor was there any point in Charles coming to England in the hope of changing her mind, as she was adamant. Elizabeth's letter to Sussex informing him of this ended all hopes for the marriage, despite Sussex's attempts to salvage the negotiations, and he returned to England in February 1568.

Susan Doran argues intriguingly that though it was Elizabeth herself who eventually killed the negotiations, "it would be a mistake to conclude . . . that she had at no point taken the negotiations seriously. . . . By her own admission, she had reluctantly agreed in 1564 to abandon the single life, for the good of her realm, if a suitable candidate could be found. She made it clear, however, from the first, that she would only marry a man who would practise the same religion as her own." Wallace MacCaffrey suggests that "she was probably not entirely insincere when she expressed her willingness to marry for the sake of her realm. But in her own mind this eventuality remained a remote—indeed, almost an abstract—possibility." [33] We might consider, though, if however much Elizabeth might agree that she would marry for the good of England, in 1565–66 on a deeper level the thought of marriage was overwhelming to her. Despite the pressure of some members of the Council toward the marriage, for Elizabeth it was always something to play with but keep at arms' length. An incident that occurred with Zwetkovich and de Silva is illuminating.

When the Imperial envoy arrived in 1565 he observed of Elizabeth that "although she wished to be a maid and single, she had subordinated her will to the interests of the country, and for its sake would also accept in love him whom the country recommended to her." On July 2 he further wrote to Maximilian "that the Queen becomes fonder of His Princely Highness and her impatience to see him grows daily. Her marriage is, I take it, certain and resolved on." De Silva, who had known Elizabeth far longer than Zwetkovich, may have doubted it and put it to the test. On August 13, 1565 Elizabeth was walking with the two men. Zwetkovich noticed a beautiful ring that Elizabeth was wearing. He suggested that Elizabeth give to him the ruby ring as a token for Charles. Elizabeth refused, but she spoke of longing for Charles to come and visit, since then a marriage could be arranged and he would get much more than one ring from her finger. De Silva had already had enough experience with the queen to know her great ambivalence at the idea of marriage, and how often she spoke longingly of seeing a suitor she knew to be safely far away. He decided to tease her, and suggest that Charles was already at Court in disguise.

> I asked her whether she had noticed amongst those who accompanied the Ambassador and me any gentleman she had not seen before, as perhaps she was entertaining more than she thought.

The idea horrified Elizabeth. It was easy to wish for Charles's presence as long as he was far away in a distant country. De Silva described Elizabeth's reception to his hint: "She turned white, and was so agitated that I could not help laughing to see her." Only after she got her breath back was Elizabeth able to try to turn the joke around, saying that indeed would be a good way for Charles to come and "I promise you plenty of princes have come to see me in that manner." [34]

Charles never did come to England; by 1568 he finally refused to continue his courtship with the elusive queen, and eventually married elsewhere. [35] For a prince actually to come, however much Elizabeth claimed this was what she wanted, or her even more outlandish statement that this had happened "plenty" of times, would be pushing the courtship game farther than Elizabeth really wanted it to go. The arrival of a foreign suitor would put the queen in a position where her options would be closed, and make refusing to marry much more difficult. Elizabeth's physical reaction to the possibility of Charles' presence—she apparently nearly fainted—is eloquent testimony to the difficulty of the balancing act she was forever playing.

Certainly throughout these lengthy negotiations she convinced members of her own Council that she was serious about marrying. Sussex and Cecil both believed at certain points that she would marry Archduke Charles. So did Dudley, to his great dismay. Later, during the negotiations with the French, he again believed that Elizabeth might indeed marry, and a foreigner. He wrote to Walsingham in 1571 when the latter was in France negotiating the marriage between Anjou and Elizabeth, "I perceive her Majestie more bent to marry then heretofore she hath been." This may not have been good news to him—a marriage for Elizabeth must have hurt his position as Elizabeth's favorite—as he put in the same letter: "I wish all things to be thoroughly considered of him, that her Majestie may fully understand the condition of his person before hand." A few months later Dudley came to understand that Elizabeth's eagerness for the marriage was pretense. In a subsequent letter to Walsingham, he wrote: "I suppose my Lord of Burleigh hath written plainly to you of his opinion how little hope there is that it [the marriage] will ever take place, for surely I am now perswaded that her Majesties heart is nothing inclined to marry at all."[36]

Around 1569–70 there was again great pressure on Elizabeth to marry, as she was moving into her late thirties. If she were to have a child she needed to do it soon. The English also felt a tremendous fear that Elizabeth might be a target for assassins, and believed this would lessen if she had a child, since with a child her death would not end the dynasty and the gain for the assassins would be that much less. There was also the strong feeling that England was at risk both at home and abroad, and England desperately needed to secure an alliance. The discussion of Elizabeth's marriage to the Duke of Anjou was part of these larger negotiations with France. By the end of the 1560s England's relationship with Spain was highly strained. The Duke of Alva was effectively crushing Protestant resistance in the Low Countries, and refugees poured into England with horror stories and desperate requests for aid. In November 1568, Spanish ships with treasure borrowed from the Genoese for Alva's use took refuge in Devon and Cornwall from pirates. Elizabeth kept the money, claiming it still belonged to the Genoese and that she had as much right as Philip to borrow it. Moreover, Mary Stuart's presence in England presented possibilities for English conflict with both Spain and France. Despite the Scottish queen's French connections, she was soon moving toward a realignment with Spain that further hurt Anglo-Spanish relations.

To Elizabeth's great regret, in February 1568 de Silva requested a new posting, arguing that the English climate was injurious to his health, and that "since things here being quiet, the friendliness of the Queen undoubted, and the Flemish commercial affairs arranged, another person could easily fill my place."[37] De Silva's tact and his genuine respect for the queen helped bridge problems between England and Spain during his four years as ambassador. His replacement, Guerau de Spes, considered Elizabeth a heretic and Cecil an enemy of Spain. One of his first acts when he arrived in September 1568 was to communicate with Mary Stuart. "It was," G. D. Ramsay suggests, "the fateful first step towards an alignment of interests between Philip II and Mary Stuart."[38] De Spes's response to the Genoese loan—he asked Alva to seize all English property and subjects in the Low Countries—brought England and Spain to the brink of conflict. Spain's interest in Mary Stuart and the repression of the revolt in the Netherlands made the French much more attractive allies, particularly if an alliance could neutralize French interest in Mary Stuart and Scotland. Especially after the Rising of the Earls of Northumberland and Westmoreland in Mary Stuart's favor in the fall of 1569, the English saw the serious need for a rapprochement with the French, the alliance also having been damaged because of English aid to the Huguenots.

It is of course impossible to know whether Elizabeth was sincere about this marriage negotiation. MacCaffrey believes that "we can be quite certain that in 1571 she had no intention of taking the Duke of Anjou or anyone else as her husband." On the other hand, Neale argues that "she was probably sincere in her in her resolve to marry, convinced by the urgent reasons for it," but the religious issues—Anjou's Catholicism and his refusal to compromise on his worship—derailed the negotiations. As always, it is impossible to know Elizabeth's own feelings on the subject, as what she said, however sincere it sounded, was not necessarily what she meant.[39]

While Sir Francis Walsingham was in France in 1571 as a negotiator, Elizabeth wrote to him an insightful but carefully constructed letter about her attitudes toward marriage and how they had changed over the course of time. She had by this time been queen for over a decade, had successfully ruled alone, and had also witnessed the consternation and horror her people felt about not having a recognized heir. Elizabeth's letter is certainly interesting, though we must be careful how much credence to give it. The letter may well have hidden more than it revealed, however honest it presented itself to be. At this point it was certainly in Elizabeth's interest to convince Walsingham, so he might convince Catherine de Medici and Charles IX, that she was sincere that *now* she would truly want to wed.

> In the beginning of our Reign, that is not unknown how we had no disposition of our own nature to marry, [or] when we lived but in a private state as a daughter, or as a sister of a King, yet could we never induce our mind to marry, but rather did satisfie our self with a solitary life. . . .

Nevertheless, the letter continues, after some years passed Elizabeth realized

> the continual urgent and frequent solicitations, not only of our Cousellours, to whom we alwaies think meet to give ear, but also of the whole Estates of our Subjects . . . did stir us to some further consideration by the weight of their reasons. . . . And therefore we yielded thus far to their importunitie. . . . we would commend our heart to be directed by Almighty God, to follow that which might be to the comfort of our loving Subjects. . . . So may you for more assurance of our firm determination to marrie, affirm to them that have judged doubtfullie of us.[40]

But despite this "firm determination to marie," this negotiation along with all the others eventually ended with certain short-term agreements between the two countries but no marriage for Elizabeth. And indeed, the proposal that Elizabeth would marry Anjou was part of larger negotiations for amity between the two nations. At the very least, the possibility of marriage could provide some time for the English to strengthen their position. Catherine de Medici was immediately very interested, as she desired royal crowns for each of her children, and Anjou was her favorite. But already Elizabeth's age, and what this might mean for her fertility, was becoming an issue in the negotiations. In 1570 the Lord Keeper Nicholas Bacon wrote a summary of arguments for Elizabeth's marriage, stating the queen should marry without delay. He did, however, express a worry over the marriage: "If the Duke shall not have children by the Queen, and the Scottish Queen should remain unmarried, it might be dangerous to the shortening of Her Majesty's life, lest some insinuation might light in the heart of the Duke to attain to the marriage of the Queen of Scots, thereby to continue possession of the crown of England and conjoin the kingdoms of England, Scotland, and Ireland in his own person."[41]

Cecil felt such conflict over the need for Elizabeth to marry and the difficulties of this particular marriage negotiation with the French that he may even have secretly and privately "by calculating her nativity . . . inquire[d] into her marriage."[42] We do not know whom Cecil found to make the prognostication, but the result is interesting and encouraged Cecil even though "the queen had not much inclination to marriage." Despite this, "wedlock would be very happy to her." The prediction went on to say that Elizabeth would be somewhat older when she entered the state of matrimony—a wise statement on the part of the astrologer, given that she was already in her late thirties by 1570, and that she would marry only once. It also said that while "she should arrive at a prosperous married estate" it would be "but slowly, and after much counsel taken, and the common rumour of it everywhere, and after very great disputes and arguings concerning it for many years, by divers persons, before it should be effected." The prediction was quite specific about her husband: he would be young, had never been married previously, and was a foreigner (obviously ruling out Elizabeth's favorite, Robert Dudley, whose marriage to Elizabeth Cecil had never favored). The prediction was not entirely positive since it suggested, "that (especially towards the middle of her age) she should not much delight in wedlock." Even so, "she should obey and reverence her husband, and have him in great respect." Despite the fact that Elizabeth's husband would be younger, her "husband should die first: and yet she should live long with her husband; and should possess much of his estate." On the most important question of the heir, the astrologer was optimistic, if not so definite. "For *children*, but few, yet very great hope of one son, that should be strong, famous, and happy in his mature age: and one daughter."[43]

From January 1571 onward the marriage negotiations continued. The question of Elizabeth's sincerity in these negotiations was a problem for the English ambassador, Walsingham, who feared the French would take offense at Elizabeth's playing them along. Dudley wrote to Walsingham in March that Catherine de Medici would "doubt much her Majesties intention to marriage, at least, that she had rather hear of it then perform it," and Walsingham wrote to Cecil in April that "I feare that by the next dispatch you shall well perceive that there is no other meaning in the Queen of England but dalliance, and that you and I shall be sorry that ever we waded so far." But there was also a question of sincerity on the

French side. While Catherine and Charles IX were enthusiastic about the marriage, Anjou himself was not, placing the French in a somewhat embarrassing position. Catherine attempted to reassure the English that it was Anjou's Catholicism, not any doubts about Elizabeth's person, which made Anjou reluctant. Catherine assured Sir Thomas Smith that Anjou "knew [Elizabeth] had so vertuously Governed her Realm this long time, that she must needs be a good and vertuous Princesse, and full of honour, and other opinion of her he could not have; but that his conscience and his Religion did trouble him that he could not be in quiet, and nothing else."[44]

When it was clear that the marriage negotiation with Anjou was dead, Catherine suggested her younger son Francis, Duke of Alençon—at seventeen twenty years Elizabeth's junior—urging that if the marriage was to take place it ought to be soon. In a letter to Cecil, Smith reported the conversation with Catherine; she had first told Smith how she wished Elizabeth "quiet from all these broils" referring to the problems with Norfolk and Mary Stuart. Catherine then went on to ask: "doe you know nothing how she can fancie the marriage with my son the Duke of Alanson?" Catherine went on to say she recognized that she had a mother's partiality but she considered Alençon as good a match for Elizabeth as any prince in Europe and "if she should marrie, it were pitty any more time were lost."

Smith reported to Cecil he had responded thus: "Madame (quoth I) If it pleased God that she were married, and had a child, all these braggs, and all these Treasons would soon be appaled." Catherine agreed and suggested that if Elizabeth did not marry into the French royal house, "I cannot see how this League and Amity would be so strong as it is." In a later meeting with Catherine the French queen mother told Smith: "Jesu! doth not your Mistress see that she shall be alwaes in danger untill she marry?" Smith did not have to be convinced. He was always urging marriage on Elizabeth. "Madam (quoth I) I think if she were once married, all in England that had any traiterous hearts, would be discouraged. . . . If she had a child, then all these bold and troublesome Titles of the Scotch Queen, or other that make such gapings for her death, will be clean choaked up." Catherine, perhaps from her own experience, did not think that one child was enough, suggesting to Smith that Elizabeth should have at least two sons, in case one died, and three daughters, so they might make advantageous marriages. Smith, perhaps more realistic given Elizabeth's age and inclination, responded with the desperate hope of any heir: "I would to God we had one."[45]

In the fall of 1571 the English discovered the Ridolfi Plot, a plan for the Duke of Alva to send over a force of six thousand men to join English insurgents who would rise in revolt to rescue Mary Stuart and marry her to the Duke of Norfolk. Catholicism would be restored and Mary and Norfolk would be king and queen of England and Scotland. De Spes was expelled from England in January 1572 for his complicity. The Duke of Norfolk's role in the plot especially grieved Elizabeth, who had already warned him of the danger of involvement with Mary Stuart. Though he was found guilty of treason she continued to postpone his execution, not finally agreeing to it until June of 1572 and no amount of pressure could convince Elizabeth to have Mary Stuart executed for her role in the assassination plot. Elizabeth did, however, abandon any thought of seeing Mary Stuart restored as queen of Scotland under any conditions and agreed to the publication of the Casket Letters. Elizabeth's councillors were worried and distressed by her attitude. Cecil wrote to Walsingham that "the Queens Majesty hath been alwaies a merciful Lady, and by mercy she hath taken more harm then by justice, and yet she thinks that she is more beloved in doing her self harm, God save her to his honour long among us." That the plot also involved the assassination of both Cecil and Elizabeth caused an even deeper sense of panic, and though Cecil was convinced that "truly the more matters are discovered, the more necessary it is seen that her Majestie should marry," the need for some kind of agreement was critical, and the question of marriage was separated from a general agreement. By April 1572 the English and French signed the Treaty of Blois, a defensive treaty against Spain that promised also to keep France out of the affairs of Mary Stuart and Scotland.[46]

Throughout the negotiations, the French Protestants were very concerned that if there were no marriage between Elizabeth and the French royal house their own position might be perilous. In August of 1571 Walsingham had written to Dudley: "My Lord, if neither Marriage nor Amity may take place, the poor Protestants here do think then their case desperate; they tell me so with tears, and therefore I do believe them." Once the amity was signed, Smith and Walsingham believed the Huguenots' position was more secure, and Walsingham wrote serenely about the coming marriage of Henry of Navarre and Catherine's daughter, Margaret. Instead, on St. Bartholomew's Day, August 24, 1572, Catherine de Medici ordered the slaughter of thousands of Protestants. The English who heard about the massacre across the Channel were horrified. The Spanish agent, Antonio de Guaras, wrote to the Duke of Alva, "I have since heard that, whilst the Queen was hunting in company with her principal Councellors, the said post from France reached her and she read the letters at once, whereupon she immediately abandoned her hunting and returned to the palace, so distressed at the news that all the Court was downcast."[47] For those actually in Paris witnessing the slaughter, the experience marked them forever. The memory of the massacre would taint marriage negotiations at the end of the decade as well. The eighteen-year-old Sir Philip Sidney, abroad for his education and in Paris at the time, vividly remembered the massacre years later when in 1579, for the last time, there was again talk of a marriage between Elizabeth and a foreign Prince.

Elizabeth had always claimed that she must see a suitor before she would decide to wed; however, Charles did not come in 1565 nor did Anjou in 1571–72. It was to be twenty years into her reign before a foreign Prince would actually come and woo the queen in person. In the late 1570s the idea of marriage to the French royal house was revived with the potential husband being Francis, Duke of Alençon (or Anjou as he later was). In 1571 Catherine had already mentioned Alençon as a partner for Elizabeth. Again in 1574 there was some discussion of Alençon, and of his coming to England for a visit, but again nothing came of it. In 1579 the suggestion was suddenly taken seriously by Elizabeth. This was the final marriage charade, and perhaps the most difficult to sort out. There were real political reasons for these negotiations—to support anti-Spanish forces in the Netherlands—and this flirtation was one segment of an important element in English foreign policy, one of the crucial turning points in Anglo-Spanish relations.[48] But it also seems that Elizabeth, then in her mid-forties, was actually playing seriously as a woman looking at her last chance at marriage and potential motherhood. MacCaffrey suggests that at the beginning of the negotiations the possibility of marriage was simply a useful means to open discussion, but "what had began as a conventional diplomatic exercise in which—as often before—discussion of a royal marriage was simply a handy vehicle for arriving at some kind of entente, turned into an intense, almost breathless, wooing of François d'Anjou by Elizabeth Tudor."[49] When Alençon's envoy and close friend Jehan de Simier arrived at court, Elizabeth did everything she could to show that she was sincere about the marriage. She even agreed to Alençon's private practice of Catholicism, something she had always before refused to grant a potential husband. While the decade earlier the thought of the archduke's presence almost caused Elizabeth to faint, this time she encouraged Alençon to come in person and fulfill her longstanding condition that she must see any potential marriage partner before a final commitment was made.

Robert Dudley was so distressed by Elizabeth's attitude he expressed the opinion that Simier had caused Elizabeth to fall in love with Alençon through the use of "amorous potions and unlawful arts."[50] Dudley's arguments against the marriage were deflated when Simier learned of his secret marriage to Lettice Knollys and informed Elizabeth. Elizabeth was deeply hurt and outraged, and only Sussex's urgent arguments that one could not imprison someone for entering into the holy state of matrimony may have kept her from sending Dudley to the Tower. She immediately agreed to Alençon's visit.

Alençon came to England twice in the midst of these negotiations, the first time in August 1579, supposedly in secret, for a ten-day visit. He was the first foreign suitor actually to fulfill Elizabeth's condition that she must see a potential husband. Elizabeth expressed her delight with Alençon, but the proposed French marriage caused great dissension in England. The 1572 St. Bartholomew's Day massacre was still a vivid memory.[51] But it was not only fear of Catholicism; after her people had been begging Elizabeth for two decades to marry, now many worried that marriage and potential pregnancy were too dangerous for a woman of Elizabeth's age.

Both these concerns were expressed by John Stubbs in his 1579 pamphlet, *The Discoverie of a Gaping Gulf whereinto England is like to be swallowed*. Stubbs, a Cambridge graduate, a lawyer, and a member of Lincoln's Inn, had Puritan leanings; his sister was married to Thomas Cartwright. Stubbs was also a loyal Englishman who was expressing his love and concern for his sovereign. But both the tone and the argument of the pamphlet infuriated Elizabeth. John Stubbs was convinced that the marriage was so dangerous because a husband could easily dominate a wife. "How much more forcibly shall the stronger vessell pull weak woman, considering that with the inequality of strength there is joined as great or more readiness to idolatry and superstition." Through this marriage to the French "our dear Queen Elizabeth (I shake to speak it) [would be] led blindfold as a poor lamb to the slaughter." Stubbs also discussed "how exceedingly dangerous . . . for Her Majesty at these years to have her first child, yea, how fearful the expectation of death is to mother and child."[52] Worse, Stubbs claimed that Alençon's motives in making such a match must be disreputable and suggested that Alençon hoped Elizabeth would die in childbirth so that England would be ripe for a French takeover.

Elizabeth was furious. MacCaffrey argues that Elizabeth's anger was understandable, since this work "had to be taken seriously." *The Gaping Gulf* was "a literarily respectable piece of work . . . addressed to an educated audience." Her response, however, was brutal. Stubbs, his book-seller, Page, and his printer, Singleton, were all put on trial in October for seditious libel. Stubbs and Page both lost their right hands. Camden was an eyewitness. "I remember (being present therat,) that when Stubbs, hav-ing his right hand cut off, put off his hat with his left, and sayd in a loud voyce, God save the Queene; the multitude standing about, was altogether silent."[53]

In November or December 1579 Sir Philip Sidney also wrote against Elizabeth's marriage to Alençon. As a nephew of Dudley, Sidney wanted to argue the anti-Alençon position not politic for his uncle to present. Also his own experience in Paris during the massacre made the idea of the French match horrifying. Sidney's letter to the queen was circulated in manuscript only, not printed as Stubbs's *Gaping Gulf* was, but a fairly wide circle saw Sidney's composition. Hubert Languet wrote to Sidney in Oc-tober of 1580 that he was "glad you have told me how your letter about the Duke of Anjou has come to the knowledge of so many persons. . . . no fair judging man can blame you for putting forward freely what you thought good for your country, nor even for exaggerating some circum-stances in order to convince them of what you judged expedient." While Sidney's letter was more restrained than the one by Stubbs, Katherine Duncan-Jones argues that it is clear from the parallels that Sidney had read Stubbs with great care when constructing his own argument. Sidney does not, however, argue that Elizabeth would die in childbirth; rather he is diplomatic enough, whatever his real beliefs, to suggest she might marry and have children, but should choose a better partner than "the son of the Jezebel of our age." In fact, Sidney was convinced Elizabeth was far too old to marry, and four years earlier in a private letter to the Count of Hanau had described her as "old and ripe for death."[54] Besides, Elizabeth does not need to marry, argues Sidney, since "truly, in the behalf of your subjects, I dare with my blood answer it that there was never monarch held in more precious reckoning of her people." While Sidney did not suffer the horrific punishment of a Stubbs for his letter, Richard McCoy is probably right that Elizabeth found his advice "presumptuous" and Sid-ney did leave court at that time, though there is no evidence that he was actually banished.[55]

Elizabeth called a meeting of the Privy Council at Greenwich on October 2, 1579 to consider the marriage. The meeting lasted five days, and everyone but Burghley and Sussex opposed Elizabeth's proposed marriage to Alençon or to anyone else from the royal French house. Elizabeth was very upset by their response. Burghley reported:

> She allowed very well of the dutiful offer of their services; nevertheless she uttered many speeches, and that not without shedding of many tears, that she should find in her Councillors by their long disputations any dispositions to make it doubtful whether there could be any more surety for her and her realm than to have her marry and have a child of her own body to inherit, and so to continue the line of Henry the Eighth; and she said she condemned herself of simplicity in committing this matter to be argued by them, for that she thought to have rather had a universal request made to her to proceed in this marriage than to have made doubt of it.[56]

On November 10, 1579, Elizabeth told her Council that she had made up her mind to marry and bade them urge no further objections but instead to consider what was necessary to do to accomplish her purpose. In late January, however, Elizabeth wrote to Alençon that the agitation against the marriage continued, and she could not let the prince return to a people so disturbed. A year later, though, in October 1581, Alençon did return to England to ask Elizabeth for assistance in his war in the Low Countries and to try once more to convince Elizabeth to agree to the marriage. The Spanish Ambassador reports that Alençon and all his company were in entire disillusionment that the marriage would ever take place on November 21. On the 22nd, however, at 11 : 00 in the morning Elizabeth and Alençon walked together in a gallery. The French ambassador entered and told the queen he must write to his master, from whom he had received orders to hear from Elizabeth herself what her intentions were in regards to marrying his brother. "You may write this to the king," Elizabeth startled the ambassador by stating, "that the duke of Alençon shall be my husband." She then turned to the duke and kissed him on the mouth, and drew a ring from her own hand to give him as a pledge. While she had refused Charles a ring, these many years later she did offer one to Alençon. The astonished and jubilant Alençon gave her a ring of his in return. Soon afterward, Elizabeth summoned the ladies and gentlemen from her presence chamber and repeated to them in a loud voice what she had just stated. Alençon was delighted with this turn of events, but Elizabeth grew reluctant, expressing the belief she must remain a spinster until she could "overcome her natural hatred to marriage." The ring, she claimed "was only a pledge of perpetual friendship."

The story is an odd one. Was she so swept away that "the force of modest love amongst amorous talke carried her so farre" and then spent the night "in doubtfull care without sleepe" when she realized what she had done, as Camden suggests? Or did she never really intend to marry him despite this public scene? Maria Perry argues it was Elizabeth's hurt and anger over Dudley's marriage that fueled the relationship with Alençon. "Hurt her ego was. She never forgave Lettice. . . . Alençon's affection was a salve to Elizabeth's wounded feelings." MacCaffrey suggests that, "Whatever we are to make of the scene in the gallery at Greenwich between the Queen and her 'frog,' it is certain that no marriage eventuated." Elizabeth finally lent Alençon some money and he left in February to return to the Low Countries, where the war there was a fiasco. Elizabeth publicly wept at his leaving, but it was said "in her own chamber she danced for very joy at getting rid of him." The following year the French Ambassador told Elizabeth the most important reason to marry Alençon was to save her honor, a reason "of more importance than any, namely, that it was said that he [Alençon] had slept with her." Elizabeth responded that she could disregard such a rumor. Hardly so, said the ambassador, "she might well do so in her own country, but not elsewhere, where it had been publicly stated. She was extremely angry, and retorted that a clear and innocent conscience feared nothing."[57] On June 10, 1584, Alençon died. Elizabeth again wept and wrote to Catherine de Medici that even she as his mother could not feel the loss more deeply than Elizabeth.[58]

This incident with Alençon demonstrates some of the pressures Elizabeth was under, especially as the reign progressed. People begged her to marry—and not to marry. They wished for her to have a child, but feared she was too old. As a public self she was both Virgin and Mother to her people; the private Elizabeth may in her forties at least momentarily regretted that she never had a child of her own. Icon to the ideal of chastity, Elizabeth had to be womanly and yet rule, a hitherto masculine enterprise. By not marrying, Elizabeth refused the most obvious function of being a queen, that of bearing a son. To compensate, Elizabeth presented herself to her people as an symbol of virginity, a Virgin Queen. As we saw in the previous chapter, this proved a powerful resource for Elizabeth in dealing with the political problems of her regime. But this image too was balanced with contradictions.

Elizabeth, wed only to her kingdom and mother to her people, represented many images. She was intensely courted throughout her reign both as a potential marriage partner and the political object of desire in a highly ritualized courtship game that lasted even when the queen was in her sixties. Yet throughout her reign as well Elizabeth was also the Virgin Queen, a secularized version of the Virgin Mary. Many people have chosen to see Elizabeth's public self-presentation as Virgin Queen as a sign of some sexual or psychological inadequacy: we may understand her better, however, if we see it as a political strategy, and one with considerable merit. The possibility of marriage was fraught with difficulties. Years ago Sir John Neale commented that "it must have been a question with Elizabeth whether a woman ruler could ever do otherwise than err in marriage; whether, in fact to be a success as a Queen she might not have to be a Virgin Queen."[59] Unmarried, Elizabeth avoided the role of wife and the risk of being perceived as the inferior partner in the marriage relationship. Also, she need worry neither about lack of fertility and subsequent embarrassment, such as dogged her sister Mary, nor about the risks of dying of disease related to childbirth, as were the fates of two of her stepmothers, Jane Seymour and Katherine Parr. Certainly there were costs as well to this choice, both personal and political, but it was a choice that was also in keeping with Elizabeth's own wishes. With Elizabeth as Virgin Queen, unmarried and ruling alone, England had but "one mistress and *no* master."

4. Wanton and Whore

Elizabeth's contemporary, Henry IV of France, was known for his sense of humor. Henry, originally a Protestant, had converted to Catholicism in 1593 when it was clear that the French country as a whole would never accept a Protestant king. On that occasion he claimed that "Paris is well worth a mass." In the 1590s Henry is supposed to have joked to a Scottish marquis that there were three questions that would never be resolved: the first was, how valiant was Maurice of Orange (a leader in the Dutch resistance against the Spanish) who had never fought a battle; the second was, what was Henry IV's own religion; and the third was "whether Queen Elizabeth was a maid or no."[1] The three topics jokingly mentioned by Henry IV deal with some of the most important facets of the Renaissance princely persona: courage on the battlefield, which often had to do with how honorable a ruler was seen to be; religion, and serving as a religious figure for the people; and the sexuality of the monarch and the reputation for chaste behavior. The first two issues Henry discussed he applied to male monarchs, while the last, sexuality, the French king mentioned as of most concern for the woman ruler. For Elizabeth, however, presenting herself as a courageous leader and a religious figure were as important as the way she dealt with questions surrounding her sexuality. In both these areas gender played a significant role in how Elizabeth both presented herself to, and was perceived by, her people.[2] But the questions about her sexuality were those asked the most intensely throughout her reign. Perceptions of gender and role expectation influenced Elizabeth's public and private images in terms of courage, religion, and, most especially, sexuality, and the ways these images were shaped reflected the insecurity caused by female rule, especially that of a woman who refused to marry yet had many suitors and favorites.[3]

Beliefs about Elizabeth's sexual behavior disturbed many of her own subjects as well as foreigners, but this concern was expressed in terms quite different from those involving the sexuality of a male monarch. While questions, comments, and gossip about Elizabeth's sexual behavior had begun long before she became queen,[4] attention to her behavior intensified once she ascended the throne, and continued throughout her reign, even when she was in her sixties. Nor did it end with her death. This solicitude over Elizabeth's sexual capacity was a means for the people to express their concern over a female monarch, and also a way of expressing the hope she would fulfill her womanly function, and have a child—a son who would reverse the dangerous precedent of a woman ruler. Especially in the last two decades of the reign, when Elizabeth was too old to marry and have a child, the rumors served as a focus for discontent and fear for the succession. Elizabeth was deeply loved by her subjects but her refusal to follow the feminine gender expectations of passivity and acquiescence, her refusal to consider the need of a named heir, caused great fear. Every time the queen was ill the fear over the succession intensified. Comments, questions, and hypotheses about the queen's health and about her sexuality became intertwined as the reign progressed. People wondered if there were some problem about Elizabeth's health that made her refuse to marry and have a child. But if she were to die without a named successor the country could be left in chaos.

By not marrying, Elizabeth also refused the most obvious function of being a queen, that of bearing a child. Nor would she name a successor as Parliament begged her to do, since Elizabeth was convinced this would increase, rather than ease, both the political tension and her personal danger. Until her execution in 1587 Mary Stuart would have been the most logical heir by right of primogeniture. She was, however, Catholic. After she was forced to abdicate the throne of Scotland in 1568 and fled to England the situation became even more problematic for Elizabeth. Elizabeth kept Mary as an enforced "guest," whose freedoms were more and more limited as Mary conspired to have Elizabeth assassinated and herself placed on the throne of England. Elizabeth feared any named successor would be the focus of all potential dissatisfaction. Instead Elizabeth tried to calm fears with vague promises and hoped the future would somehow take care of itself and provide a peaceful succession. She responded to a Parliamentary petition on the succession in 1563 with the statement:

> [I] say and pray, that I may linger here in this vale of misery for comfort, wherein I have witness of my study and travail for your surety: and I cannot . . . end my life, without I see some foundation of your surety after my gravestone.[5]

While time proved her right, the risk to England was horrifying if she should die without a clear successor. As well as believing it was better for the country not to have a named heir, Elizabeth knew it was better for herself. She said in 1561, "Think you that I could love my winding sheet?" Leah Marcus also convincingly suggests that Henry VIII's obsessions and difficulties begetting a male heir and Mary's false pregnancies would have made Elizabeth wary about marriage as a solution to providing a male heir. Why create a situation where failure was such a possibility and which would have so many other risks connected with it?[6]

Elizabeth was effective at conveying her love for her people and encouraging their love for her. Yet many of the English still had great difficulty with the concept of a woman ruler. Elizabeth could not always control the way people responded to her. Together with the love and respect she inspired, one discovers expressions of hostility towards her as an unmarried female ruler whose position transcended the traditional role allotted to women in English Renaissance society. This hostility was expressed in the many rumors that circulated about Elizabeth.

Rumors could be very dangerous and damaging to a monarch's reputation. While this is true of all monarchs, it was especially the case for women in power, and the rumors were so often ones suggesting sexual improprieties. For a woman, her only source of honor is her sexual "credit." Losing it, particularly for a woman in the public sphere, could be devastating.[7] Catherine de Medici made a declaration of this danger during the marriage negotiations between Elizabeth and the Duke of Anjou in 1572, carefully explaining to the English that the future Henry III had not broken off the negotiations because of slanders he had heard about Elizabeth, but rather because of his religious scruples. Catherine repeated to the English envoy Thomas Smith for Elizabeth's benefit a discussion she had had with her son about Elizabeth's reputation.

> And I told him it is all the hurt that evil men can do to Noble Women and Princes, to spread abroad lies and dishonorable tales of them, and that we of all Princes that be women are subject to be slandered wrongfully of them that be our adversaries, other hurt they cannot do to us.[8]

Francis Bacon once wrote that rumors and treasons were siblings, a view that certainly suggests why Elizabeth's government took the rumors about her so seriously. The 1559 Parliament made it treason for anyone not only by "open preaching express words or sayings" to "maliciously, advisedly, and directly say . . . that the Queen's Majesty that now is, during her life, is not or ought not to be Queen of this realm," but also simply to "hold opinion" of this view. Spreading gossip about Elizabeth's claim, even agreeing with gossip, was perceived as very dangerous. The treason act of

1571 reaffirmed this definition of treason. Many of the people arrested in the reign of Elizabeth had gossiped about the queen in malicious ways. There was also a law against sedition that was passed in 1554 in the reign of Mary; Parliament made this law even more stringent in 1581.[9]

During Elizabeth's reign the records of the Privy Council are filled with examples of people charged with the crime of slandering the queen. Over and over again people were arrested for "lewd words" spoken against Elizabeth. For example, at the very beginning of the reign, 1558, a "lewde, Malycious fellowe of Assheforth," was to be examined to determine "whither he uttred the trayterous wordes, or no . . . agaynst the Quenes Hieghnes." The next year the Privy Council sent a letter to "the Keper of the Kinges Benche to kepe in saf warde one Byrche, a priest, that hath uttred lewde wordes of the Quenes Majestie." In 1564 Lord Cobham was asked to investigate "certaine lewde sedytious woordes spoken by some of Tenterden in Kent against the Quenes Majestie . . . that they may be all apprehended and committed." In 1580 Vicar John Pullyver stated that "some did saie that we had no quene," and was placed in the pillory. Some who were found guilty of uttering lewd words were ordered to be put in the pillory and also have their ears cropped or ordered on "the nexte markett daye"—so that there might be maximum publicity—to be put in the pillory "with a paper on his hed having thies words written in great letters therin, 'for lewd and slanderous wordes' and so suffer him stande all the market tyme." Public humiliation was used frequently in Tudor England not only as punishment but in the hopes it would also serve as a public deterrent. Letters from the Council went out to other counties where "lewd and sedicious wordes" were reported, ordering investigation and punishment. People accused included vicars, tailors, laborers, and gentlemen.[10]

And the court as well as the country was a place where rumors spread easily, especially when the ruler was a young unmarried woman who refused to follow advice. At the beginning of Elizabeth's reign Sir Thomas Chaloner wrote a very concerned letter to Cecil on this issue. "As I count the Slaunder most false, so a yong Princesse canne not be to ware. . . . This delaye of rype tyme for Maryage, besides the Losse of the Realme . . . mynistreth Matter to theis lewde Towngs to descant apon, and breedith Contempt." The belief that women are gossips, are most interested in love affairs, and are quick to spread rumors also intensified gender expectations about the spreading of rumors at Elizabeth's court. Referring to the possibility of the marriage of Mary Stuart and the Duke of Norfolk in 1569,

Camden wrote: "Soon after the Rumour of this Marriage came more clearly to Queen Elizabeth's ears, by means of the Women of the Court, who do quickly smell out Love-matters." In 1564 de Silva wrote to Philip about watching a comedy with Elizabeth. Comedies, he observed, generally deal with marriage. Elizabeth then led the talk to the question of marriage between Don Carlos and Mary Stuart. De Silva denied it, claiming that "It is no new thing for great princes to be the subjects of gossip." "So true is that," replied the queen, "that they said in London the other day that the King my brother, was sending an Ambassador to treat of the marriage of the Prince with me!"[11]

As was discussed in a previous chapter, Elizabeth presented herself to her people as an icon of virginity, a Virgin Queen, to bring her people through the break with the Catholic Church and the worship of the Virgin Mary. Elizabeth and her government deliberately took over the symbolism and prestige of the suppressed Marian cult in order to foster a cult of the Virgin Queen. This proved a powerful resource for Elizabeth in dealing with the political problems of her regime.

People did not, however, regard Elizabeth solely as a Virgin Queen. They were also intrigued by her imagined and real sexuality, a speculation that echoed some late medieval questions about the Virgin Mary. People talked about Elizabeth's love affairs, speculating on the one hand, about the number of illegitimate children she had, and, wondering, on the other, whether she had a physical deformity that kept her from consumating a physical relationship. These rumors served the dual purpose of allowing people to openly speculate about the succession of a male heir, while denigrating Elizabeth in a typically misogynist way—by dismissing her as a whore.

The interest in Elizabeth's sexuality was undoubtedly heightened by the many courtships in which Elizabeth was involved. While Elizabeth proclaimed that she hated these negotiations, as we have seen, many believed otherwise. While the previous chapter concerned itself with the official courtships of Elizabeth and responses to them, this chapter instead concentrates on the rumors that she took lovers and had illegitimate children. Her love not only of marriage offers but of the accoutrements of courtship worked to encourage this perception. While it is extremely unlikely that she had any intention of actually satisfying her courtiers, she loved their claims of adoration. As Jonathan Goldberg suggests, "Courting was a metaphor for the desire for power and authority, a metaphor enacted and lived."[12]

Figure 5. Artist unknown, Robert Dudley, Earl of Leicester, c. 1575 (by courtesy of the National Portait Gallery, London)

In the first years of her reign, Elizabeth was seen everywhere with Robert Dudley, whom she eventually created Earl of Leicester. The Dudley family was one that had been been intimately connected with the Tudors for two generations, a connection that had previously led to disastrous setbacks for the Dudley family. Robert's grandfather, Edmund, had ruthlessly squeezed money out of the populace for Henry VII; the young Henry VIII had him executed at the beginning of his reign as a way to court popularity. Robert's father John, Duke of Northumberland, had attempted the coup to place Lady Jane Grey on the throne in 1553 as a means to continue the power he had assumed in the reign of the boy king, Edward. When the plot failed John Dudley was one of the few that Mary immediately had executed. Robert and Elizabeth had known each other since childhood and Elizabeth clearly cared deeply for him. Their friendship may have been further strengthened while both were in the Tower during Mary's reign. Upon becoming queen, Elizabeth sent Robert Dudley to the astrologer/magician John Dee, his old tutor, to discover the most auspicious day for her coronation. Almost immediately she made Dudley her Master of the Horse, the man who chose the horses for her official processions and rode with her, and so had close access to her. She showered him with other gifts and honors.[13] Within a few months of Elizabeth's accession the foreign ambassadors' letters home were filled with references to the close friendship of Robert and the new queen. The Spanish Ambassador, the Count de Feria, wrote to Philip in April 1559 that "during the last few days Lord Robert has come so much into favour that he does whatever he likes with affairs and it is even said that her Majesty visits him in his chamber day and night."[14]

Unfortunately (from his point of view), as we know, at the time Elizabeth became queen Dudley was already married. Many people suggested that Robert was simply waiting for Amy to die so that he might marry the queen. Paolo Tiepolo, the Venetian ambassador in Brussels, heard from England that Elizabeth "evinces such affection and inclination [toward Robert] that many persons believe that if his wife, who has been ailing some time, were perchance to die, the Queen might easily take him for her husband."[15] We know that Amy's mysterious death made Dudley's courtship of Elizabeth far more problematic. Whenever Dudley was mentioned as a potential marriage partner for the queen, people were bound to bring up the rumor that he had murdered his wife.

Whatever the truth, the scurrilous comments about Elizabeth and Robert Dudley disturbed many people. Thomas Lever wrote to Francis Knollys and William Cecil on September 17, 1560 about "the grevous and dangerous suspition, and muttering" in Coventry about Amy's death. Unless these suspicions were allayed, the "displeasure of God, the dishonor of the Quene, and the Danger of the whole Realme is to be feared." The next January de Quadra wrote to Philip about certain preachers who spoke about Amy's death in a way that harmed the queen's honor. The other courts of Europe were rife with gleeful gossip. Mary Stuart, still queen of France and without yet a scandal to touch her, said that "the Queen of

English is going to marry her horsekeeper." Sir Nicholas Throckmorton, the English Ambassador, wrote from Paris that the French gossip about Elizabeth's morals made him wish he were dead. "The bruits be so brim, and so maliciously reported here, touching the marriage of the Lord Robert, and the death of his wife. . . . We begin already to be in derision and hatred, for the bruit only." Throckmorton added, "One laugheth at us, another threateneth, another revileth the Queen. Some let not to say, what religion is this that a subject shall kill his wife, and the Prince not only bear withal but marry with him?" Throckmorton begged William Cecil to discover some method to prevent the marriage. If the queen married Dudley, he predicted, "God and religion will be out of estimation; the Queen discredited, condemned, and neglected; and the country ruined and made prey." [16]

So strong was the belief that Elizabeth would marry Dudley that in November of 1560 de Quadra reported to Philip that the marriage had already taken place. "Cecil has given way to Robert, who they say was married to the Queen in the presence of his brother and two ladies of the chamber." Whether to marry Dudley or not must have caused Elizabeth great anguish. In the same month Elizabeth's servant R. J. Jones wrote to Throckmorton in Paris that "the Queen's Majesty looketh not so hearty and well as she did, by a great deal; and surely the matter of my Lord Robert doth much perplex her." Despite such stories and all her soul-searching, Elizabeth never did marry Robert Dudley, no matter how close she may have felt toward him and how long and intensely he courted her. It was not really until 1575, after he had grandly feted the queen at Kenilworth, that Dudley finally and completely recognized that she would never marry him. In what some saw as a bizarre twist, in 1564 Elizabeth did propose Dudley as a marriage partner for the then-widowed Mary Stuart before the Scottish queen married her second husband, Henry Stuart, Lord Darnley. It was to make Dudley a more acceptable suitor that Elizabeth made him Earl of Leicester. But even at this solemn ceremony Elizabeth tickled his neck. People were on occasion shocked by the affection she showed to him. Yet when Katherine Ashley, Elizabeth's closest confidante when she was in her teens and then one of the ladies of the queen's bed chamber, "covertly commended Leicester unto her for a husband, [Elizabeth] answered in a passion: 'Dost thou think me so unlike myself, and so unmindful of my Royal Majesty, that I would prefer my servant, whom I myself have raised, before the greatest princes of Christendom, in choosing of an husband.'" And when Elizabeth thought she was dying of smallpox in October 1562 she solemnly swore that, though she loved Lord Robert dearly, God was her witness that nothing improper had happened between them, that there was no dishonor to their relationship. She asked, however, that if she died not only should Dudley be made the protector of the realm but his man servant should be given a large salary, which does suggest there were aspects of her relationship with Dudley that she did not want exposed.[17]

Elizabeth's bout with smallpox intensified the already existing fear of a lack of a successor felt by her councillors and the people. What would happen if the queen were to die with no child and no established succession? To add to the sense of popular horror, about the same time that Elizabeth was ill a monstrosity was found in the Lincoln's Inn Fields—"a certaine image of wax, with a great pin struck into it about the brest of it." If Elizabeth's illness was caused by magic how even more helpless her councillors were. They sent urgent messages to John Dee, begging him to "prevent the mischeife," or at least so Dee himself later claimed. Such fear might well engender not only pressure on Elizabeth to marry and name a successor, but also rumors about her that expressed in a more latent fashion some of that fear. Throughout her reign any illness of Elizabeth caused panic and consternation on the part of her councillors. Gossip about the queen's health, which must have heightened the tension even more, was as intense as the gossip about her sexuality, and often intertwined with it. The Venetian envoy reported in June of 1559, "Before leaving London her Majesty was blooded from one foot and from one arm, but what her infirmity is, is not known. Many persons say things which I should not dare write." In March 1561 the Venetian ambassador to Philip II wrote back to Venice that "I am informed on good authority that the Queen of England has become indisposed, and that the physicians greatly fear her malady to be dropsy." Six months later de Quadra was mentioning similar rumors. "What is most important now, as I am informed, is that the Queen is becoming dropsical and has already began to swell extraordinarily. I have been advised of this by three different sources and by a person who had the opportunity of being an eye witness. To all appearance she is falling away, and is extremely thin and the colour of a corpse."[18]

De Quadra's successor, Guzman de Silva, wrote to Philip II in August 1564 that Elizabeth was returning to London from her progress sooner than planned. "She is much in fear of falling ill, which I do not wonder at if they tell her the prophecies that are current about her short life. Everybody is talking of them." In 1571 Cecil again expressed panic over Elizabeth becoming ill in a letter to Francis Walsingham. "This bearer . . . can also tell you of a sudden alarm given to me, specially yesternight, by her Majestie, being suddenly sick in her stomack, and as suddenly relieved by a vomit. You must think such a matter would drive men to the end of their wits, but God is the stay of all that put their trust in him." In 1572 the Earl of Shrewsbury wrote to Cecil, "Five weeks are passed since I had any advertisements from your Lordship, which I think is long; and now especially that it is spoken the Queen's Majesty has been lately sick . . . and as yet no certainty is heard of her Majesty's recovery or perfect health. You may be sure it is no little grief or discomfort to me." News of the queen's health peppered letters to and from Court. The next year Leicester wrote to Shrewsbury, "This is all the news presently worth the writing, save the good and perfect health of her Majesty." Leicester echoed this statement in 1578 as well. "The best news I can write your Lordship is of her Majesty's good and perfect health, which God long continue." There was great concern in 1580. Thomas Bawdewn wrote to the Earl of Shrewsbury, "The Queen our Sovereign, being persuaded by her physicians, did enter into a bath on Sunday last; and, either by taking cold, or by some other accident, did presently fall sick, and so did continue two days together, but now is very well recovered again." And Shrewsbury ended a letter to Walsingham, "Thus, with my daily prayer for the Queen's Majesty's long life and good health, I take my leave." Elizabeth's request to make Robert Dudley protector of the realm would not in any way have reassured her councillors, and their relief must have been enormous that in 1562 they were not called upon to either keep—or break—that promise.[19]

That Elizabeth wanted Dudley to be protector suggests how important he was to her at least at that moment, and one can certainly imagine that their relationship was close, romantic, complex, and ambiguous, and may well have had some sort of sexual component, yet Elizabeth's statement in 1562 (and the way she behaved throughout her reign) makes it doubtful that they were lovers in the traditional sense.[20] What is more important than the possible relationship between Elizabeth and Dudley is the widespread belief about the nature of their relationship. The gossip about the two continued throughout the reign and was carefully gathered up by worried government officials. A generation earlier rumors and scandal about Elizabeth's mother helped to destroy Anne Boleyn.[21]

Implicit in these comments and speculations, which we find in the public records, is a definite thread of malice—the sense that Elizabeth, this unmarried woman of questionable morals, had no business ruling. In 1560 there were several reports that Elizabeth was pregnant. For instance, Mother Anne Dowe was committed to jail for "openly asserting that the Queen was with child by Robt. Duddeley." Mother Dowe had come in one morning to a tailor's shop, saying that there were things going on that no one should speak about—which she immediately proceeded to do. She told the astonished tailor that Lord Robert had given the queen a child. When the tailor responded, "Why she hath no child yet!" Mother Dowe replied, "He hath put one to the making." Three years later Edmund Baxter openly expressed the not uncommon view that Elizabeth's reputed unchastity disqualified her as a monarch, something that had never been said of her father or any other heterosexual male ruler. Baxter's reported words were: "that Lord Robert kept her Majesty, and that she was a naughty woman, and could not rule her realm, and that justice was not being administered." His wife added that when she saw the queen at Ipswich "she looked like one lately come out of child-bed." Though the ability to administer justice should have nothing to do with Elizabeth's sexual behavior, in these subjects' minds, and it was far from an unusual perspective, they were inextricably linked. Even the most private sin would have impact in public rule, and this was particularly the case for a sexual sin. Corruption to the body of the monarch would reflect the corrupting of the whole realm, the body politic. By being called unchaste, Elizabeth was also being charged with not being a good ruler in a way that was directly connected with her sex, especially since the concept of honor and its relation to behavior was markedly different for women and for men in the sixteenth century. For males, honor had to do with keeping one's word and with not being shamed on the battlefield. Women preserved their honor not only through their actual chastity but also by maintaining the reputation of chaste behavior. For a woman to be thought unchaste, even if it were untrue, was a loss of honor. In accusing the queen of sexual improprieties, people were charging her with dishonorable behavior in a way that would not be the case in a similar rumor about a king.[22]

Moreover, accusations of behaving as a "lewd woman," or being called "whore," were among the principal terms of abuse used against women on all social levels of society. By calling their monarch a whore, these people were identifying Elizabeth's gender as the most salient aspect of her entity as ruler.[23] There are parallels to the reaction of the Scottish people toward Mary Stuart, except that Mary's weakness in handling government and her behavior with Darnley and Bothwell were such she was forced to abdicate and fled Scotland after a short reign. The rumors and hostile denigrations of Elizabeth never put the English queen at such risk, nor was she ever personally such a target as Mary was. In August 1562, while Mary was walking with Sir Henry Sidney, the day before he was to depart back to England, a Captain Hepburn "presented her grace a byll," which contained "as ribbalde verses as anye dyvleshe wytte coulde invent, and under them drawne with a penne the secreate members both of men and women in as monstrous a sort as nothynge coulde be more shameful-lye dyvisede." Jenny Wormald points out how "profoundly humiliating and insulting" it was for Mary to not only be "the object of scandal spread about her, but the personal recipient of a direct gesture," and argues no one would have dared hand such a paper to Elizabeth. After Darnley's murder and her marriage to Bothwell, a rebellion forced Mary off the throne. As she was taken back to Edinburgh as a prisoner in June 1567 people cried out, "burn the whore! . . . burn her, burn her, she is not worthy to live, kill her, drown her." [24]

The English never yelled "burn the whore" at Elizabeth, but they did feel free to speculate about her lovers and supposed bastards. The gossip of Mother Ann Dowe and the Baxters may be more comprehensible than the later rumors, since in the 1560s Elizabeth was young, unmarried, and indiscreet in some people's eyes with her public displays of affection for Robert Dudley. Elizabeth herself responded to the various rumors that surrounded her. In 1564 she told the Spanish Ambassador, Guzman de Silva, a man with whom she shared a number of confidences:

> They charge me with a good many things in my own country and elsewhere, and, amongst others, that I show more favour to Robert than is fitting; speaking of me as they might speak of an immodest woman. . . . I have shown favour, although not so much as he deserves, but God knows how great a slander it is, and a time will come when the world will know it. My life is in the open, and I have so many witnesses that I cannot understand how so bad a judgement can have been formed of me. [25]

Two years later, when Elizabeth was upset with Dudley, or at least wished de Silva to believe she was so he would encourage the prospective marriage with the Archduke Charles, she complained to de Silva about Robert's ingratitude, "after she had shown him so much kindness and favour, that even her honour had suffered for the sake of honouring him." William Cecil for one did not have this "bad a judgement," and believed in the virtue of his queen. But he too was well aware of what was being said, and how her honor had suffered. In a letter to his close associate Thomas

Smith in March 1566 he wrote: "Briefly I affirm, that the Quene's Majesty may be, by malicious tongs, not well reported, but in truth she herself is blameless, and hath no spot of evill intent."[26] De Silva also came to believe in the virtue of the queen he observed so closely. He wrote in 1564 to the Duchess of Parma about Elizabeth that "she bears herself toward [Robert] in a way that together with other things that can be better imagined than described make me doubt sometimes whether Robert's position is so irregular as many think. It is nothing for princes to hear evil, even without giving any cause of it."[27]

Yet the gossip about Elizabeth's behavior continued. De Silva heard rumors that Dudley slept with the queen on New Year's day, 1566.[28] In 1570 a man named Marshame was condemned to lose both his ears or else pay a fine of a hundred pounds for saying that Elizabeth had two children by Robert Dudley. Two years later, during the investigations of the Ridolfi Plot, further comments about Elizabeth and her lovers were divulged. Keneln Berney confessed that a confederate, Mather, a supporter of the Duke of Norfolk, had intended to kill the queen, for "yf she weare not kylled, or made awaye, ther was no Waye but Deathe with the Duke." Berney claimed that Mather had described Elizabeth as "so vyle a Woman . . . that desyrethe nothinge but to fede her owne lewd fantasye." The way she would do it would be to ignore the worthwhile nobililty in favor of "Daunsers . . . [who] please her delycate Eye," such men as Dudley and Sir Christopher Hatton. Mather claimed these men "had more recourse to Her Majesty in her Privy Chamber than reason would suffer if she were so virtuous and well-inclined as some [noiseth] her!" According to Berney, Mather had "other suche vyle Words as I ame ashamed to speake, much more to wrytt." Mather asked for mercy, "I confesse further, of mislanguage in seeking to praise the Queen of Scottes, and to slander your Royall Persone. . . . I wholly remit my Cause to your Majestie's Mercie, who beinge a Mirror of Clemencie, will of your Majestie's Graciousnes, deale herein." But despite Elizabeth's reputation for leniency, both Berney and Mather were executed for their part in the Ridolfi Plot, soon after the death of Norfolk.[29] In 1572 Robert Blosse was brought before the Record of London, William Fleetwood, for spreading rumors that Elizabeth had four children by Robert Dudley. That same year Matthew Parker, Archbishop of Canterbury, wrote a very concerned letter to William Cecil about the "most shamefull words against" Elizabeth spoken by a man brought before the mayor of Dover. What the man said about Elizabeth and both Dudley and Sir Christopher Hatton was "a matter so horrible" that Parker would not put it on paper, but instead, he wrote, wished only to speak of it to Cecil when he had the chance.[30]

By 1570 sexual rumors mentioned not only Dudley but Sir Christopher Hatton as well, making Elizabeth even more a whore in the eyes of those who spread these stories. Hatton, like Dudley, had risen to prominence because of Elizabeth's affection for him. Hatton was seven years younger than the queen, and had first captured her attention by his graceful dancing in a court masque. Some people believed that Hatton's rise to power came from his charm rather than his ability. Mather's contemptuous comment about Elizabeth's favor to Hatton is an example of a stereotypical view of a powerful woman—that she could be dazzled by a man's dancing and give him a responsible place. MacCaffrey argues that "Leicester and Hatton were advanced to high office and a share in the royal confidence solely because of their private attraction for the Queen. . . . To promote them from personal intimacy to public eminence was a risky business for any ruler, all the more so for a woman."[31]

In 1564 Hatton had become a gentleman pensioner. Eventually he gained positions of real stature. In 1578 he became Vice-Chamberlain of the queen's household. Nine years later he became the Lord Chancellor. Hatton's letters to Elizabeth express deep feelings for her, but also a fear that they are not reciprocated on the same level. In 1573 he wrote to her, "Would God I were with you but for one hour. My wits are overwrought with thoughts. I find myself amazed. Bear with me, my most dear sweet lady. Passion overcometh me. I can write no more. Love me; for I love you. . . . Live forever. . . . Ten thousand thousand farewells. He speaketh it that most dearly loveth you." Yet Hatton was also aware that his position did not make him an appropriate consort to the queen. In 1580, during the negotiations for Elizabeth to marry Alençon, Hatton wrote to Thomas Heneage, sending him a ring for Elizabeth that she should wear for good health and referring to the differing status of himself and the French prince. Hatton spoke of his feelings for "Our mistress, whom through choice I love no less than he that by the greatness of a kingly birth and fortune is most fit to have her. I am likewise bold to commend my most humble duty by this letter and ring, which hath the virtue to expel infectious airs, and is, as is telled to me, to be wearen betwixt the sweet dugs,—the chaste nest of more pure constancy." Hatton's reference to Elizabeth's dugs—her breasts—suggest some level of at least emotional intimacy, though they are described as "chaste." Hatton's supposed influence over Elizabeth led to an assassination attempt in 1573 by a fanatic

Puritan, though Peter Burchet mistook Sir John Hawkins for Hatton on the London streets; luckily Hawkins was not hurt seriously. Elizabeth's fury at this attack, and her concern over Hatton when he was ill, certainly fanned rumors that he was her lover. And the stories persisted.[32]

In the 1560s and 1570s the rumors of Elizabeth's pregnancies and illegitimate children continued to crop up, especially among hostile foreign Catholics. Writing in 1564, Luis Roman, the secretary to the former Spanish Ambassador de Quadra, commented on plans for Elizabeth to go to the North of England. "Some say she is pregnant and is going away to lie in." A decade later Antonio de Guaras, acting Spanish agent in London, reported that there would be a marriage between the son of Catherine Grey and "a daughter of Leicester and the Queen . . . who, it is said, is kept hidden, although there are bishops to witness that she is legitimate." In December of 1575 Nicholas Ormanetto, Bishop of Padua and Nuncio in Spain, heard the rumor that Elizabeth had a daughter. He suspected that Sir Henry Cobham, whom Elizabeth had sent to Spain to negotiate with Philip II, spread the rumors. "I am assured that he has let it be known that the pretended Queene has a daughter, thirteen years of age, and that she would bestow her in marriage on someone acceptable to his Catholic Majesty. I have heard talk before of this daughter, but the English here say that they know nought of such matter." The pope took the possibility of Elizabeth having a marriageable daughter seriously and saw it as a way to "bring the realm back to the Catholic faith" without the hazards of war. In 1578 there were rumors on the continent that Alençon, the French king's younger brother, would marry, not Elizabeth, but her niece or daughter. It is interesting and revealing that the pope and some of the Spanish not only took seriously the idea that Elizabeth had a child, but despite her probable illegitimacy (if she had in fact existed), they were willing to consider negotiating a marriage. For Catholics, after all, Elizabeth herself was not legitimate and was still the ruler of England. Seemingly they were willing to overlook these technicalities if England could thus be brought back to the Catholic faith.[33]

But some Catholics were less forgiving. Cardinal William Allen also used these stories in his 1588 *Admonition to the Nobility and People of England*, a propaganda tract to gain support for Philip II's proposed invasion. Allen argues that Elizabeth was damaged even from her birth, since she was "an incestuous bastard, begotten and born in sin." Not only was Henry married to Catherine of Aragon at the time, but more shockingly, Allen implies that Anne Boleyn was Henry's own daughter since "he did before unnaturally know and kepe both the said Anne's mother and sister." Elizabeth proves herself the true daughter of such parents by how she acts as queen. "She sells laws, licences, dispensations, pardons, &c., for money and bribes, with which she enriches her poor cousins and favourites." The chief favorite is Dudley, whom "she took up first to serve her filthy lust." Allen repeats every damaging comment about Dudley that he can. "To have more freedom and interest, he caused his own wife to be murdered, as afterwarde, for the accomplishment of his like brutish pleasures with another noble dame, it is openly known he made away with her husband." But, according to Allen, Dudley is not Elizabeth's only lover, and the older she gets, the more debased is her court. With "divers others, she hath abused her bodie against God's lawes, to the disgrace of princely majestie, and the whole nation's reproache, by unspeakable and incredible variety of luste . . . shamfully she hath defiled her person and cuntry, and made her court as a trappe, by this damnable and detestable art to intangle in sinne, and overthrowe the yonger sorte of her nobilitye and gentlemen of the lande." Elizabeth's behavior has made her "notorious to the worlde . . . [with] the whole worlde deriding our effeminate dastardie, that have suffered such a creature almost thirty years together to raigne both over our bodies and soules." Allen explains that the reason Elizabeth never married is "because she cannot confine herself to one man." He describes how she has "unlawfule, longe concealed, or fained issue," and claims that "she forced the very parliament to give consent to a law, that none should be named for her successor, savinge the natural, that is to saie, bastard-borne child of her owne bodie." [34] Allen's attack on Elizabeth's rule is centered around her supposed sexual behavior. His claim that she took lovers demonstrates how her female identity and the beliefs about appropriate womanly behavior determined the attacks on her monarchy. Such an attack on a king—that he had lovers and was thus unfit to rule and somehow monstrous—would be laughable, unless, of course, the king's lovers, like Elizabeth's, were male. Allen's tract, the most inflammatory of all his works, was a great embarrassment once the Armada failed. Most copies were destroyed, but the scandal invoked continued to be repeated.

Of course there was no child born of her body, but the rumors of illegitimate children eventually brought forth someone who did claim to be her child. In 1587 a young Englishman in pilgrim's garb was arrested in the north of Spain on suspicion of being a spy. He was sent to Madrid where Philip II's English secretary, Sir Francis Englefield, examined him. The young man claimed to be Arthur Dudley, the illegitimate son of

Robert Dudley and the queen. His first name is an interesting choice—the Tudors had attempted throughout the century to demonstrate strong ties to the King Arthur legend, and Henry VII had named his eldest son Arthur. It was only his premature death that had allowed Henry VIII to become the heir. James V of Scotland (son of Henry VIII's older sister, Margaret) also named his son Arthur; this boy too died in his youth and so did not ascend the throne. "Arthur Dudley" gave Englefield a detailed account of his childhood in the household of Robert Southern, who had told the boy his real identity on his deathbed.[35] Dudley described meetings he had had with important members of Elizabeth's government before he finally successfully fled the country in the mid-1580s to wander the continent in the company of disaffected English and Elizabeth's enemies. Arthur Dudley proposed to Englefield that Philip II take him under his protection and utilize him in the coming attack on England. Though at first inclined to believe Dudley's story, Englefield came to believe that Dudley was actually "a simple instrument in the hands of Elizabeth herself." Englefield suggested to the Spanish king, "I am of the opinion that he should not be allowed to get away, but should be kept very secure to prevent his escape. It is true his claim at present amounts to nothing, but . . . it cannot be doubted that France and the English heretics, or some other party, might turn it to their own advantage." Alarmingly for Dudley, Philip added the notation to the letter that it would be "safest to make sure of [Dudley's] person until we know more about it."[36]

Though Dudley's story has enough plausible details to suggest that he had been well coached, its basic premise is impossible. We know that Elizabeth was seriously ill in 1562 with smallpox; this was not a cover for her having given birth to a child. And, as Martin Hume pointed out, "It is. . . . beyond belief that a boy in the condition represented would have been allowed to run about the world at his own free will." Hume believes that Dudley was a spy who used this story to try and gain access and to save himself when caught. Elizabeth Jenkins adds that he may well have been willing to spy for either side. After Philip's notation, "Arthur Dudley" disappears from the records, certainly kept safe by the Spanish, never to be heard from again.[37]

The rumors about Elizabeth's illegitimate children became even more intense in the last two decades of Elizabeth's reign, as did attacks on her rule. By the late 1570s and early 1580s Elizabeth, already in her late forties, was playing out the final marriage negotiations of her reign with the young Duke of Alençon. Critics such as John Stubbs outraged the queen by arguing against the marriage in part on the grounds that Elizabeth was now too old to bear a child. And Elizabeth still refused to name a successor. At Court people worried desperately about her health, and reassurances became even more intense.[38] In the countryside, these worries took on a different form. The rumors about her illicit children, often coupled with the suggestion that these children had also been destroyed, reflect on another level the fears over the succession and the antagonism toward a queen who refused to provide for her people's future. In 1577 Mary Clere, an Ingatestone spinster, declared Elizabeth was base born and Mary Stuart had a better claim to the throne. She was brought to trial and executed. Soon after, Randall Duckworth, a laborer in the village of Bradwell, stated that "this is no good government which we now live under and it was merry England when there was better government and if the queen die there will be a change." He was made to stand in the pillory with a paper on his head.[39]

In 1580 an Essex laborer, Thomas Playfere, stated that Elizabeth had two children by Lord Robert; he had himself seen them when they had been shipped out at Rye in two of the queen's best ships. The next year Henry Hawkins explained Elizabeth's frequent progresses throughout the countryside as a way for her to leave court and have her illegitimate children by Dudley—five all told. Said Hawkins of the queen, "She never goethe in progress but to be delivered." At the end of the decade, in 1589, Thomas Wendon claimed that "Parson Wylton spake openly in church . . . that the Queen's Majesty was an arrant whore" since "the Queen is a dancer, and Wylton said that all dancers are whores."[40]

The next year a widow named Dionisia Deryck claimed that Elizabeth "hath already had as many children as I, and that two of them were yet alive, one a man child and the other a maiden child, and the others were burned." We do not know exactly how many that was meant to be since the records do not state how many times Deryck herself had given birth. The father of the queen's children, claimed Deryck, was Dudley, who had "wrapped them up in the embers which was in the chamber where they were born." The same year Robert Gardner or Garner told a similar story; Leicester "had four children by the Queen's Majesty, whereof three were daughters alive, and the fourth a son that was burnt." Both Deryck and Gardner stood in the pillory for their indiscreet comments.[41]

In 1598 Edward Fraunces, of Melbury Osmond in Dorsetshire, attempted to seduce Elizabeth Baylie by telling her the queen had three bastards by noblemen at court, two sons and a daughter. Why should not

Baylie have a sexual relationship without marriage, he asked her, when "the best in England, i.e. the Queen, had done so." Elizabeth Baylie's refusal made Fraunces angry not only with her but with the woman he had urged on her as a model. He called the queen "base born," and he added, "that the land had been happy if Her Majesty had been cut off twenty years since, so that some noble prince might have reigned in her stead." Elizabeth Baylie testified about this conversation before the magistrates, as did some of her neighbors. Frauncis attempted to bribe the witnesses, offering the men twice the money he offered the women. The witnesses, however, were outraged enough by his slander of the queen to refuse. Fraunces further amplified his misogyny when he attempted to discredit Baylie's testimony with the statement that "women are base creatures and of no credit."[42]

There are several more reports of infanticide in 1601. The most interesting version is from Hugh Broughton, who again wove together the themes of Elizabeth's lack of chastity, hostility toward her rule, and destruction of the potential heir. According to Broughton, a midwife was taken to a secret chamber where she was told to save the mother (Elizabeth, of course) at whatever cost to the child. The midwife was too skilled; she saved them both.

> And after [delivering] . . . a daughter, [the midwife] was brought to another chamber where there was a very great fire of coals, into which she was commanded to cast the child, and so it was burnt. This midwife was rewarded with a handful of gold, and at her departure, one came to her with a cup of wine, and said, Thou whore, drink before thou goest from hence, and she drank, and was sent back to her house, where within six days after she died of poison, but revealed this before her death.[43]

By this time the story has become absurdly melodramatic. If one wanted to keep someone from revealing information, one surely would not use a poison that took six days to take effect.

In Playfere's story of 1580, the children were shipped away. Closer to the end of the reign, in the rumors spread by Deryck, Gardner, and Broughton, the children are actually destroyed. Elizabeth had therefore not only dishonored herself by being a whore, but had destroyed, literally burned up, her succession. Gardner, for example, insisted that although Elizabeth's supposed daughters survived, the son, the potential king, died horribly. We cannot simply label these stories of Elizabeth's sexual misconduct as male discomfort at female rule, since women also participated in this gossip.

There is another possible example illustrating the difficulty many English people early in Elizabeth's reign had in accepting her refusal to follow the traditional role of a woman as wife and mother. In these years there were a larger number of reported monstrous births than earlier in the century. Stories of monsters were immensely popular throughout the sixteenth and seventeenth centuries. It seems as if childbirth, and the fear around it, were on the minds of many people. It is possible that for some people having as ruler an unmarried woman who refused to have a child or name an heir was unnatural and frightening. Especially with the religious situation causing such uncertainty, they may have believed that the only progeny possible from such an unnatural situation was monstrous. There were at least a dozen broadsides describing these monstrous births in the 1560s, five in the year 1562 alone.[44]

The rumors about Elizabeth's illegitimate children and the use of these rumors to discredit her continued after her death. In 1609 *Pruritanus*, a Catholic book in Latin published in France and smuggled into England, caused James I's government a great deal of concern. The book was highly critical of Henry VIII, Elizabeth, and James. Of Elizabeth it said that, though she styled herself head of the Church and a Virgin, she was an immodest woman who had given births to sons and daughters. It claimed that Elizabeth prostituted herself with men of many backgrounds and nationalities, "even with blackamoors." The book repeated the rumor already circulated by William Allen, that Henry VIII had had an affair with Anne Boleyn's mother, and thus Anne was actually his own daughter, making Elizabeth the child of incest.[45]

From a very different perspective and a half century after Elizabeth's death, Francis Osborne referred to stories that "she had a son bred in the state of Venice, and a daughter, I know not where nor when." Osborne, however, dismissed these stories as "fitter for a romance than a history." Wistfully, he added that after considering the straits to which Elizabeth's successors, the Stuarts, had brought England, he wished that she had left "the smallest chip of that incomparable instrument of honour, peace, and safety." Osborne did not care if such a child were legitimate or illegitimate.[46]

At the same time that some people were whispering about just how many illegitimate children Elizabeth had, others were doubting whether she was capable of conceiving a child or of even consummating a sexual relationship. The Spanish Ambassador, de Feria, told Philip II, "for a reason they have given me, I understand she will not bear children." His successor, de Quadra, believed the same. "It is the common opinion confirmed by certain physicians, that this woman is unhealthy and it is believed that she will not bear children." Early in her reign, foreign ambassadors bribed the women of Elizabeth's bedchamber for intimate information about her life, and their reports home are filled with such details as Elizabeth's light and irregular periods. The Venetian Ambassador heard that she had been bled in the foot in an attempt to correct this problem. Later the Nuncio in France heard rumors that Elizabeth flowed from "an issue in one of her legs" since "she has hardly ever had the purgations proper to all women." One of Elizabeth's physicians, Dr. Robert Huicke, apparently encouraged Elizabeth's desire not to marry, which greatly angered members of Parliament. Camden reported that the 1566 Parliament "cursed Huic, the Queen's Physician, as a Disswader of her marriage for I know not what womanish Impotency." Elizabeth probably felt comfortable with Huicke's advice; he was eventually appointed chief physician to the queen. Elizabeth may well have had some fears of pregnancy. Camden certainly believed this. "The perils by conception and child-bearing, objected by the physicians and her gentlewomen for some private reasons, did many times run in her mind, and very much deter her from thoughts of marrying."[47]

There were also rumors that Elizabeth had an impediment that would prohibit regular sexual relations and thus make conception impossible. Mary Stuart referred to these rumors in a vitriolic letter she wrote to Elizabeth (which William Cecil apparently suppressed). Claiming Bess of Hardwick, the Countess of Shrewsbury, as her source, Mary Stuart wrote, "she says, moreover, that indubitably you are not like other women, and it is folly to advance the notion of your marriage with the Duke of [Alençon], seeing that such a conjugal union would never be consummated." This opinion was probably widespread. After Elizabeth's death, Ben Jonson made a similar remark, suggesting that Elizabeth had a membrane that made her incapable of intercourse, though despite that "for her delight she tryed many." At the time of the proposed marriage to Alençon, Jonson claimed, a French surgeon "took in hand to cut it, yett fear stayed her." These statements suggest that one way to minimize the power of a woman such as Elizabeth was to describe her as "different from other women," less than them in the most fundamental sense of the ability to be wife and mother. In 1566, however, the queen's physician assured the French ambassador if Elizabeth married the French king she would have ten children at least, although how much this was based on any real diagnosis and how much on wishful thinking is another question. William Cecil always assumed that Elizabeth would be able to produce a child.[48]

By being "wed to England," as she so often claimed, Elizabeth could present yet another image to her subjects, that of a mother.[49] The many godchildren she sponsored encouraged the concept that all the English were in some sense her children.[50] At the very beginning of her reign, when the House of Common beseeched the queen to marry, Elizabeth had responded,

> And doe not upbraid me with miserable lacke of children: for everyone of you, and as many as are Englishmen, are children, and kinsmen to me; of whom if God deprive me not . . . I cannot without injury be accounted Barren.[51]

In a letter to his wife Sir John Harington referred to Elizabeth when he feared that she was dying as "our deare Queene, my royale godmother, and this state's natural mother." John Jewel, bishop of Salisbury, in 1567, referred to Elizabeth as "the only nurse and mother of the church of God." In 1578 a person representing the city of Norwich told Elizabeth in a pageant to celebrate her coming: "Thou art my joy next [to] God, I have no other, My Princesse and my peerlesse Queene, my loving Nurse and Mother." This image was repeated throughout the week of Elizabeth's stay, and when she left she was told, "Farewell, oh Queene, farewell, oh Mother dere." Yet Elizabeth's self-presentation as mother was not always successful. In 1566 one member of the House of Commons, Paul Wentworth, Peter's younger brother, suggested that if Elizabeth did not designate a successor "she may be reckoned of, not as a Nurse, not as a Mother of Countrye, but as a Step-mother, nay as a Parricide of her Countrey, which had rather that England, which now breathed with her Breath, should expire together with her than survive her." The concern over the succession was rational; had Elizabeth died in the first decade of her reign the problems for the country could have been horrific—disrupted succession and religious civil war. The way the anger is expressed here, however, may suggest not just a subject to his sovereign, but a child disappointed by his mother and rejecting her.[52]

By not marrying, by being both no-one's mother and everyone's, and by presenting herself as both a virgin to be revered and a sensuous woman to be adored, Elizabeth exerted a strong psychological hold on her subjects. In 1600 a sailor, Abraham Edwards, was arrested for sending the queen passionate love letters and drawing a dagger in her presence.

Officials were convinced that though apparently mad, "greatly distracted" Edwards had no wish to harm the queen, rather that he was "transported with a humour of love." Described as "very bare and in pitiful case," Edwards was placed in Bedlam. In the seventeenth century, Francis Osborne advised his son about the dangers of passionate attachments; he described the "voluptuous death" of a tailor, who "whined away" for love of Elizabeth.[53]

Certainly there were rumors about male monarchs as well. As de Silva said to Elizabeth in 1564, "It is no new thing for great princes to be the subjects of gossip."[54] During the reign of Henry VIII there many prophecies contending the king would die. In late 1537 people in Kent, Sussex, Northamptonshire, Berkshire, and Oxfordshire were repeating rumors that Henry VIII was dead. Those the authorities were convinced were the worst scandalmongers were put in the pillory. The next year Norfolk was filled with rumors that Henry was dead after Mabel Brigge performed a black fast, also known as a "Saint Trinian's Fast," against him. Henry lived another eight years but Brigge was executed for treason. At about the same time there were also rumors that Henry would impose a "horn tax" on every head of cattle; this rumor especially concerned authorities who were afraid it might lead to an uprising.[55] In 1590, William Cecil's grandson and namesake wrote to Lord Talbot that Philip II was dead, adding for good measure that before his death "he had sent to the Pope to obtain licence to marry his own daughter." Philip did not die until 1598 and, though he had a penchant for marrying cousins, his marriage plans were not as bizarre as Cecil indicated.[56]

And many of the rumors spread about Elizabeth did not have to do with her sexuality. During Elizabeth's reign a wide variety of rumors about her spread throughout Europe. In 1576 the Venetian envoy had to assure those back in Venice that Elizabeth was well and in good health since the city was rife with rumors that she was dead. At the time of the Armada some people believed that England had been "subdued, the Quene taken and sent prisoner over the Alpes to Rome, where, barefoote, she should make her humble reconciliation." Don Barnardino de Mendoza, the Spanish Ambassador who had been expelled from England and was now in residence in Paris, so believed this that he entered "into our Ladie Church, (Notre Dame) advancing his rapier in his right hande, and with a loud voice cried, 'Victorie! victorie!' and it was forthwith bruted, that England was vanquished. But the next day, when truth was knowne of the Armada's overthrowe. . . . Mendoza, being much dismayed, obscured himself, not daring to shewe his face." But the rumors about her sexuality were particularly intense and widespread, suggesting they resonated far more than other rumors. Coupled with the concerns and rumors over her health they express some of the terror over a future for which she had not provided her country.[57]

Though the way Elizabeth behaved may have fostered these rumors they might well have surfaced even if she had not enjoyed and encouraged the ritual of courtship and favorites. Her sister Mary I in no way mirrored this behavior; she was the epitome of virgin and then chaste wife. Moreover, she was clearly infertile in her reign. Her marriage to Philip yielded only a false pregnancy that ended in humiliation and despair. Despite this a rumor surfaced during her reign that she had an illegitimate child by Stephen Gardiner, the bishop of Winchester, a most improbable combination. Here as well this rumor represented both denigration of the queen and wish fulfillment.[58]

The belief in Elizabeth's lovers, in her illegitimate children, and the sexual interest in her suggest how significant and complex gender constructions and sexual issues were in the minds of Elizabeth's subjects and the important part they played in shaping the way English men and women regarded their queen. Though there were often comments about the personal lives of male monarchs, they were of a different nature, and served very different functions. With a king, the need for an heir was equally important, but it was the *wife* of the king who was there to produce the heir, and, as Henry VIII demonstrated all too clearly, if the wife did not adequately perform this role, if she did not have healthy sons, she could always be replaced. With Elizabeth, the question of the queen marrying and producing an heir was much more serious, since she herself was both ruler and potential producer of the heir. Elizabeth's councillors and Parliament felt a deep need to insure the legitimate succession in order to safeguard the peace of the nation. In the Parliament of 1559, one member maintained that "nothing can be more contrary to the public [interest] than that such a Princess, in whose marriage is comprehended the safety and peace of the Commonwealth, should live unmarried, and as it were a Vestal Virgin." But perhaps there were also other more obscure motivations behind the repeated behests to Elizabeth to marry. This nation of men at times found it both frustrating and degrading to serve a female, especially one not under the control of any man. William Cecil, for one, prayed that "God send our mistress a husband, and by time a son, that we may hope our posterity shall have a masculine succession."[59]

Elizabeth was queen to a people unused to female rule, a people who were just getting over the dislocation of the break with the Catholic Church. Elizabeth, unmarried and refusing to name an heir, was both Virgin and Mother; queen and prince. The very real adoration most of her people felt for Elizabeth made her even more the focus for their distress. The gossip about Elizabeth allowed her subjects to express their ambiguous feelings about her anomalous position in a patriarchal culture as a female ruler who took the unprecedented step of refusing to assume the roles traditionally allotted to women as wives and mothers. Instead, Elizabeth ruled with great success—establishing a broadly based religious policy and a long peace as well as presiding over spectacular cultural developments. Elizabeth was not only politically astute but truly loved her subjects and revelled in their love for her. Yet with all her varied self-presentations, she was still an unmarried woman instead of a king. She could not overcome either her sex or the decision she made not to provide England with a king-consort and an heir of her body or to name any other successor. The comments about her sexuality were one way for her people to come to express their ambivalent feelings about her position as ruler, and also to come to terms with it.

5. The Return of the King

In January 1575 Matthew Parker, Arch[bishop of] Canterbury, learned from [the dean of Westminster of a young man named W]illiam Cartwright. Cart[wright, a "vain young stripling," claimed in a fren]zy that he was the right[ful heir to the lands of the realm and that Eliza]beth kept him from his [proper place. Cartwright was temporarily lodg]ed in the gatehouse at [Westminster ... ask]ed what should be done about him. [While some of Park... wanted to send] him to the Privy Coun[cil, Parker felt this was unnecessary. Desc]ribing Cartwright in a [letter to Burghley as one whose] "wit is so foolish and so simple," Parker [suggested the best way to handle ... unt]il Cartwright's wits re[turned ... to have him committed to Bridewell] or Bedlam unless his [friends, under bond, would ...] him [... a]t home. Parker wanted [to ... knew ... of the delicate] political ramifications [to this case because ... wright happened to be the] brother of the Puritan [Thomas Cartwright. It was ... impo]rtant that "his brother, [...] [...] hardly with this young [...] sake, whose opinions [...] treatment meted out [...] all see in this chapter. [...] years later, in his last [...] Cartwright provided [...] "be kepte from wan-[...]

[...] ciously kept from his [...] le Elizabeth was rul-[... the fact of] a woman on the throne might lend itself to such a delusion.

The view that a woman could not legitimately rule was so strong it could have led a foolish, simple person to believe that he, as a man, had the better claim. Thomas Cartwright's criticism of the religious settlement might well have added to his brother's belief in Elizabeth's illegitimacy. In

Figure 6. Artist unknown, Tudor family group, 1597 (by permission of the Art Institute of Chicago)

the medieval and early modern period the "mock king" appeared often in festivals and riots and served both as a safety valve for discontent and as an element of inversion that could be used to express disatisfaction in a culturally accepted mode. William Cartwright's delusion took the idea of the mock king one step further, into an individual's fantasy life.[2] While Cartwright claimed to be the true king, he did not express an identity to go along with it. But in the reigns of both Mary and Elizabeth a number of people claimed that Edward VI had survived, and in each reign at least one man appeared claiming to be Edward. What follows is an examination of certain related aspects of the insecurity caused by women's rule, especially in a time of religious upheaval: rumors of the survival of the last Tudor king and male impostors and incidents that did not name Edward VI but also suggested the lack of legitimacy of the female sovereign.[3]

I am not arguing that these rumors and impostures appeared only in the reigns of women rulers. There were similar occurrences at other times in English history, when kings were on the throne. They do, however, appear with some regularity at times when the legitimacy of the sovereign is in question. Given sixteenth-century beliefs in the sanctity of the king, the fact of a queen regnant was in itself enough of a departure from what was perceived to be the proper form of rule to bring about such phenomena. The desire for a king was a very powerful emotion. We can see it in the problems of the succession in the Middle Ages, and in the religious aspects of monarchy in the medieval and early modern period.

The pressure on both Mary and Elizabeth to marry and have a son, or at least (in Elizabeth's case) to name a male heir, was intense. Mary attempted to fulfill these expectations; she married (though disastrously) and pathetically hoped for a child, a son. Elizabeth, however, refused this role. By not marrying, Elizabeth refused even to attempt to accomplish the most obvious function of a queen, that of bearing an heir. And, despite other great pressures, she also refused to appoint a successor. Fear over the succession and distress over the legitimacy of the monarch were especially intense in the last years of Elizabeth's reign, when she was too old to conceive a child and the charade of marriage proposals had finally been exhausted. Even in the final decade of her reign she still refused to name an heir. No doubt the insecurity this created prompted the whisperings of King Edward VI's survival, which had occurred in Mary's time, to be heard again. The religious upheaval of the sixteenth century added to the feelings of tension and insecurity and may also have played a role in motivating some of the impostors and their followers. In Tudor England the need for security in terms of both ruler and religion was enormous, the more so when both seemed threatened. However effective a ruler Elizabeth in particular might be, the fact that she was a woman was insurmountable—and thus in part cause of the longing for the king that was manifest in the belief of Edward VI's survival.

The motif of the woman ruler, the generalized sense of insecurity, and the consequent appearance of a male impostor pretending to be the supposedly dead king had occurred previously in thirteenth-century Flanders. In the 1220s the Countess Joanna ruled under the domination of the French. The people of Flanders, in the midst of famine and wishing to throw off French influence, were in an uneasy state. Rumors began to circulate that Joanna's father, Count Baldwin, killed on a Crusade twenty years before, was not really dead. After years of wandering, he would return home to free his people from bondage. With wild delight many people recognized a wandering hermit as the returned count. He admitted his "identity" and then proposed to take Flanders by force from Joanna. After losing in battle Joanna fled, and "Baldwin" was crowned with great ceremony. It was seven months before he was identified as a serf, Bertrand of Ray, and executed. Yet Joanna was spoken of with hatred for generations for having caused her "father"'s death.[4]

We can see the link between perceived lack of legitimacy of the ruler and belief in rumors of survival and pretenders in earlier periods of English history as well. Such rumors occurred after the depositions of both Edward II and Richard II, in each case where the new ruler was seen as not the legitimate ruler.[5] The most famous impostors of the Tudor period, Lambert Simnel and Perkin Warbeck, appeared in the early part of the reign of Henry VII, when the legitimacy of the king was again questioned.[6] The appearance of Simnel and Warbeck was understandable, even to be expected. Henry VII had become king after thirty years of civil war, and his claim to the throne was weak. By mid-century, however, the question of the succession was rather different. Even though Henry VIII tightly controlled the kingship, the only way for his line to continue, he believed, was to have a son. Despite the success of his wife Catherine of Aragon as regent early in his reign when he was fighting in France, Henry gravely doubted a woman could rule, leading to the crisis of the 1520s over the Divorce.[7]

Yet in 1547 when Henry died, despite all his marital adventures, he had only one son; all the other close heirs were women. With Edward's death in 1553, queenship became a reality.[8] In the mid-sixteenth century the English people not only had to deal with the new phenomenon of a woman ruler, but had to deal with it at a time of great religious unrest. At the same time as this religious confusion came queenship. Women were to rule in England for the rest of the century, and one of the many results of this change in the sex of the monarch was the rumor that Edward VI was not really dead. Concurrent with the rumors were the impostors who claimed that they were the king and other impostors who threatened the legitimacy of the sovereign.

Sex and gender as well as legitimacy appear to be significant factors in the emergence of pretenders. Yet the issue is an exceedingly complex one, and sorting through the belief patterns of people from earlier centuries is difficult. For example, although during Mary's reign the rumors and impostures all centered on her brother Edward, Mary herself had once been the object of such an impersonation. In 1533 in the north of England, an eighteen-year-old woman, Mary Baynton, was arrested and examined for impersonating Mary. She had gone around begging money so that she might use it to seek the protection of Emperor Charles V. She explained to her listeners that her aunt and namesake Mary, the French queen, had once read a book of prophecies and had told her, "Niece, Mary, I am right sorry for you, for I see here that your fortune is very hard. Ye must go a-begging once in your life, either in your youth or in your age." Temperamentally inclined to get something unpleasant out of the way immediately, she decided to do it in her youth. It is not clear from the examination whether Mary Baynton really believed she was the Lady Mary or had merely figured out a clever scheme for gaining money, but she was apparently successful enough at finding people to accept her claim to bring her to the attention of the magistrates. The year 1533 was, of course, a particularly stressful one not only for the Lady Mary but for those who believed in her cause: Archbishop Cranmer had finally declared the marriage between her parents invalid, and Henry as a free man had publicly announced his marriage to Anne Boleyn, who later that year gave birth to Elizabeth.[9]

In the sixteenth century identity had a fluidity and uncertainty inconceivable today. This was strikingly so in the French case of Martin Guerre, where the returned impostor lived as Martin for three years and the question of his identity led to a court case.[10] The drama of the late sixteenth/early seventeenth century was filled with plot devices of characters returning after presumed dead, such as Hermione in *The Winter's Tale*, and kings who leave to return in disguise to see what is happening in their realm, such as the duke in *Measure for Measure*. The idea of a king returned from the dead to care for his people in need resonates with both Christian overtones and elements of fairy tales and folk stories. Clearly people then as now could distinguish between fiction and reality, between a folk story and their everyday life, and they knew that what they saw on stage was fantasy yet these motifs provided a context for a belief system that could accept a dead king's return.[11]

When Edward died, despite the provisions of Henry's will there was not a smooth transition to Mary. Encouraged by the Duke of Northumberland, who had been ruling England in Edward's name, the young king had made a will of his own, disinheriting both his sisters in favor of his cousin Jane Grey, who had just been forced into a marriage with Northumberland's youngest son, Guilford Dudley.[12] Without the force of

Parliament, this new will was patently illegal. As it happened, it was also dynastically unsound, since even if Edward's sisters were excluded, Jane's mother Frances was still alive. People rallied quickly around Mary, who had adroitly escaped capture despite Northumberland's attempts to trap her. Northumberland had, in the king's name, asked Mary to come to London, claiming that the boy king wanted to die in his sister's arms. Luckily Mary had been warned that this message was a trick and that Edward was already dead. She fled to Framlingham in Suffolk and proclaimed herself queen. Elizabeth too received warnings that the message was false and stayed where she was. As Mary was the true heir, even many Protestants supported her. In fact, Northumberland was so disliked that Mary began her reign with an abundance of goodwill. Londoners were desperate to reverse Northumberland's coup; they were delighted to repudiate Jane and proclaim Mary their queen.[13] The fact that her rival—the figurehead Northumberland was forced to use—was also a woman no doubt contributed to Mary's success; thus the sex-gender issue was mitigated by the circumstance.

In August 1553, Mary triumphantly entered London as the first queen regnant since the Conquest. The distant failure of Henry I's daughter, Matilda, to hold her position as ruler in the twelfth century was forgotten. Yet by November, when it was known that the queen would soon marry the hated Philip of Spain, people were saying that Edward was still alive.

In 1908 Margaret Cornfield suggested that the rumors of the king's survival may have had something to do with the mystery surrounding Edward's death and with Protestant fears of a Catholic ruler. Northumberland had kept Edward's death secret for a few days while he attempted to lure Mary and Elizabeth to London. The confusion this caused, as well as the bizarre treatment Edward may have received at the hands of the quacks hired in a desperate attempt to keep him alive when the royal physicians believed he was clearly dying, produced rumors that Northumberland had had Edward poisoned. This was the last thing Northumberland would have done in the circumstances; events were already moving too quickly for him.[14]

It is not at all clear how the rumors of poison would eventually lead people to believe that Edward was not dead at all. Yet within a few months this was exactly what happened. In November 1553, three men, Robert Tayler, Edmonde Cole (or Coles), and Thomas Wood, were brought before the Privy Council for their "lewde reportes" that Edward was still alive. Wood was a servant, and the other two were dealers in textiles—men of the tradesman class. After their appearance before the Council they were ordered to appear before the Star Chamber, so the Council obviously viewed these rumors with some seriousness. In January, Tayler was forced to pay 500 marks in good behavior so that he would be available if called upon. Coles was later asked to pay £500.[15]

These rumors were beginning to appear at a time when Mary's government had a number of other disturbances about which to worry. For example, a mysterious wailing wall prophesied against Mary; only later was it found out that a carefully coached child was inside. Mobs broke up sermons and threw daggers at preachers. Libelous pamphlets and ballads were available on every street corner. The belief in Edward's survival appears to have been part of a larger crisis in the people's confidence about the queen's rule. This belief in the king's presence was a fundamental attack on Mary's legitimacy. If Edward were still alive, she had no business claiming to be queen.

It was distressing enough to Mary's government that men of the tradesman class would repeat such a rumor. The response to Robert Robotham "of the wardrobe of the robes" shows even more alarm. Even though he was himself a part of Mary's government, in January 1554 he repeated talk that could have drastically undercut it. "For his lewde talk that the kinges majestie deceased shulde by yet lyving" he was committed to the Fleet as a close prisoner. But the rumors continued to spread. The very next day Johan Wheler "for hir devellishe sayeng that King Edward was styll lyving" was committed to the Tower. Her husband, Thomas, "for his scaunderous reporte and concealing of the brute of the late Kinges being on lyve" was committed to Marshalsea, yet another prison. Cornfield suggests that they may have been sent to different prisons to keep them isolated from each other, in an attempt to stop the rumors. Certainly none of them were publicly punished by being put in the pillory, which may have been the government's way of trying to keep these rumors from spreading.[16]

The isolating of prisoners apparently was effective for a while. For more than a year after this the rumor does not appear in any official records. During that time Thomas Wyatt attempted his futile rebellion against the coming Spanish marriage and died on the scaffold before Philip came to England. The Spanish marriage was solemnized with great ceremony in 1554, and by the end of October of that year Mary was convinced she was pregnant. Despite all the upsets earlier in her reign which had been aimed against the Spanish marriage and the restoration of

Roman Catholicism, "the news of [her pregnancy] had a strangely calming effect on the turbulent citizens of London," Loades states. "Any child born to Philip and Mary would have been three-quarters Spanish but the evidence all suggests that English people were prepared to welcome such a child." It may not be so strange that news of Mary's pregnancy would have a calming effect, since that would mean continuation of the line. This was even more important than the fact that a child by Mary would mean the continuation of Catholicism in England.[17]

When it became painfully obvious the next May and June that this was a false pregnancy, there was another rash of disturbances, including rumors of Edward's survival and an impostor claiming to be the king. This time it was impossible for Mary's government to keep the matter quiet. Realizing this, they tried different means of suppression. The reaction over Mary's false pregnancy was especially acute because on April 30 rumors had spread all over London that Mary had been safely delivered of a son. The celebration turned to sullenness when it became clear that this had not occurred. Carolly Erickson suggests that, "In London disillusionment . . . led to mounting agitation. New libels against Mary were thrown into the streets every few days, stirring up fears and encouraging rebellion . . . . Seditious talk was everywhere—in taverns, in the streets, anywhere gentlemen met to eat and gamble."[18]

In mid-May 1555, two men were apprehended in Essex for spreading rumors of Edward's survival. Also at about this time a young man actually claimed to be Edward. Instead of simply passing along a rumor that Edward was still alive, eighteen-year-old Edward (or William) Featherstone, alias Constable, son of a miller and sometime lackey to Sir Peter Mewtas, claimed that *he* was the king. He was brought before the Council at Hampton Court for examination but when asked for an explanation of his behavior "counterfetted a manner of simplicitie, or rather frensie, and would make no direct answer." He was committed to jail at Marshalsea as a "lunatike foole," though historians writing thirty years later believed this to have been feigned as a defense. The Council wondered if there were more important people behind Featherstone coaching him. Though this seems quite likely, it was never proved, and none of the people mentioned in connection with Featherstone were particularly significant. Loades argues, "It is hard to avoid the suspicion that determined intriguers were making use of Constable's little weakness." Erickson's suggestion that Mary's failed pregnancy encouraged sedition is supported by

Stow's history. On the same page Stow reported that Mary "neither had childe, nor great hope to have any," and the story of Featherstone.[19]

Featherstone's case gained enough notoriety for the London citizen Henry Machyn to record it in his diary. Apparently Featherstone had found a number of people willing to express belief in him, whether genuine or not. The Venetian Ambassador Michiel reported, "Being believed to be such, both in the country and here . . . he raised a tumult amongst the populace." Michiel concludes, "Nor is this a novelty in England, as of youre there was a similar impostor who represented himself as one of the sons of Edward the 4th, . . . which I mention that your Serenity may comprehend what strange fancies prevail amongst these people, and how much their ideas differ from those of other nations."[20]

If the government had decided to keep earlier rumors about Edward's survival quiet, they took a different approach with an actual pretender. On May 22, 1555, Featherstone was driven through London in a cart wearing a fool's coat with derisive statements attached to it. After being thus paraded he was whipped and had his ears cropped. When this painful and humiliating punishment ended he was banished from London.[21]

Yet in January 1556 more rumors were heard, and hand bills were circulated in London and the countryside. One such handbill, in effect inciting rebellion, assured readers that Edward was alive and well and waiting in France for a demonstration of support that would enable him to recover his crown. At least some of these communications could be traced back to Featherstone, who had certainly not learned his lesson. In fact, his supporters were keeping very busy. "One Laurance Trymmyng of Grenewich committed this day at the Towre for a seditious bill conteyning King Edward to be alive" that had been delivered to him by Constable.[22] The same month William Cockes, one of the officers of the Pantry, was arrested, relieved of his office, and commanded to appear before the Council on a weekly basis simply for "receiving a lewde bill surmysing that King Edward was still lyving." Michiel for one considered the matter "ridiculous and unimportant," but assured the doge that Mary's Council "viewed it in a different light."[23]

After Featherstone's followers distributed his handbills, he again made an appearance claiming to be Edward. "Many persons both men and women were troubled by him." This time there was no leniency. He was arraigned at the Guildhall in London, found guilty, and condemned to be hanged, drawn, quartered, and beheaded. This grisly sentence was carried out on March 13, and as a stern reminder his head was set on London Bridge. By this time Mary and her government would show no leniency. Nor were there further rumors or impostors during her reign, to judge from the official records. "The affair is consigned to silence," Michiel correctly wrote to the doge.[24]

The rumors that had disappeared by 1556 surfaced again nearly twenty years later, well into the reign of Elizabeth. Their reappearance might at first glance be surprising, since such allegations should have ended in the reign of Catholic Mary if religion had been the motivating factor in their development, as Cornfield has suggested. True, Edward had been a Protestant, and Mary was enforcing Catholicism at a time when there was great confusion over religious belief, and a good many people resisted the return of English allegiance to the pope. Religious uncertainty might well have encouraged the emergence of rumors concerning Edward's survival. If this were their whole motivation, however, one might question why the rumors emerged again in the reign of the Protestant Elizabeth. Religious insecurity was still very much a problem in her reign, especially with Catholic Mary Stuart as the alternate possibility for ruler; in their Protestantism, however, as opposed to their sex, Edward and Elizabeth were very similar. Yet the fact of a woman's rule is not enough to explain the re-emergence of these rumors and impostors, since for the most part this did not happen until late in her reign. The crucial factor was that by the time the rumors of Edward's survival resurfaced, the problems of a successor for Elizabeth were acute. With Mary Stuart an enforced "guest" in her country, the queen still refused to name a safe Protestant heir. Moreover, Elizabeth was finally too old to marry and have a child, which would have solved the succession problem in the most acceptable way.

Howard Dobin suggests that the beginning of Elizabeth's reign was conspicuous with prophecy as England faced rule by a young unmarried woman.[25] Another period of even more intense belief in prophecy, however, was the late 1580s and 1590s. With the fears brought on by an uncertain succession, there was more and more interest in the reassurance of prophecy. The concern for a potential Spanish invasion and the economic problems of the last decade of the century exaggerated this phenomenon. There was enough concern in the late Elizabethan period over prophecies in general and the rumors of Edward VI's survival in particular for John Harvey to write in 1588:

> Alas, what fond and vaine expectation hath a long time rested in the minds not of one or two, or a few, but of great multitudes of the simpler sort in

England about King Edward the Sixt, as though they were sure either of his arising from death, or his returne from I know not what Jerusalem, or other strange land. . . . And what counterfet suborned marchants of base parentage, have sithence ranged a brode in the countrie, presuming to term themselves by the roiall name of king Edward? Such is the rath and blind credulitie of the common people, and such is the desperate insolencie of some brainsicke presumptuous runnagates.[26]

We know about one of the "runnagates" to whom Harvey referred. He was Robert Blosse, who used the name Mantell or Mantle while trying to find supporters for his claim. This alias is a curious one since in sixteenth century usage a mantle was not only a cloak but could mean to cover and conceal, to obscure or enfold, and certainly Blosse was obscuring his own identity when he claimed to be Edward VI. One supporter who believed this claim was Elizabeth Vessie, who had her fortune told by Jane Standlie around 1570. The future foretold for Vessie was certainly an impressive one—nothing less than that "she should be the chief instrument in reinstating, 'the king' of this realm" to his proper place. We notice here that the wily Mistress Standlie did not mention who this king was to be. She did, however, add the warning that while her efforts would bring Vessie into great favor with the king, they would cause her serious problems with the queen and her counselors.[27]

Mistress Standlie did not tell her patron exactly when all this would come to pass, but she did give her a grisly way to mark the time, by enumerating the many children and servants Vessie would bury before the king's return. By 1577 Vessie had apparently buried enough. In London she met a stranger calling himself Mantell, who, she was convinced, was the person to whom Standlie had referred. Vessie asked Mantell who he was, at the some time confiding Standlie's prophecy to him. Mantell admitted he was indeed Edward VI; he had not died in 1553 after all. Mantell then "made much of her, calling her ever after 'sister.'" Elizabeth Vessie was apparently a far better sister to this "Edward VI" than Elizabeth Tudor was. While Mantell did not mention to Vessie his past legal problems, they may explain how she had been able to recognize him; he had already been brought before Robert Fleetwood, Recorder of London, in 1572 for spreading rumors that Edward VI was still alive, and also that Elizabeth was the mother of four children by Robert Dudley.[28]

According to Fleetwood's 1572 examination, Blosse, alias Mantell, was actually born in London, the son of a goldsmith, and had been educated by John Bale, prior of the white friars in Ipswich. As a young man, Mantell had married the daughter of Mr. Egelden, the town clerk of Sandwich, and served as a gunner in the royal ships during the reign of Edward VI. Mantell and his wife did not get along well, however, and he left her.

Mantell told Fleetwood that sixteen years before (in the year 1556) a man named Walker, who was a scholar at Oxford, told him that Edward VI was alive and living in Flanders, eventually to return to England and his true position. This obviously impressed Mantell as "he saith, that ever sithence he hath nourished in his mind that lewd and false matter, and hath reported it for a truth." Mantell was arrested when a man named Norris overheard him and reported the matter to the authorities. Fleetwood did not know just what should be done with Mantell. He wrote to Burghley:

> I had studied all the statutes of treasons, and could not find him within the letter or meaning of them; and for that the fellow, which was executed in queen Maries time, did offend in saying, that he himself was king Edward; therefore I noted that cause to be treason: but not so of Blosses cause. I therefore yesternight did argue the cause Mr. Attorney General by the space of an hour and more. And he resolved it for a clear case to be no treason. . . . And therefore by the statute he ought to be set at liberty.[29]

Some years later Mantell took the rumor another step and claimed that he was himself the king.[30] Some of the people he informed of this were much less sympathetic than Vessie. Mantell was brought before the Essex Assize in August 1577 on the charge that at a variety of places he "did give out and saye that Kinge Edward was alyve, that he (meaning the said Robert) was King Edward the Sixth, and that if he could finde one that was trusty he could disclose that which should rejoice them all; howbeit he could never yet fynde suche an one."[31]

Elizabeth's government regarded Mantell as the victim of "frenzies," and he was sentenced to a year's imprisonment at Colchester gaol. Despite his frenzies he managed to escape in 1578, perhaps with the connivance of Vessie, who visited him soon before the event, and the widow Symonds, who was also a prisoner there. The escape upset Elizabeth's government. Richard Kinge, deputy of the Colchester gaol, was indicted for treason for "feloniously and treacherously" allowing Mantell to escape. Kinge pleaded not guilty to treason but did admit to negligence.[32]

Cynthia Chermely suggests that Mantell was far more attractive to women than to men, almost a "cult" figure.[33] It is certainly true that Mantell had a number of women who supported him. One of these was Jane Kilden. Like Vessie, Kilden was married, but in neither case did the husband share the same involvement with the cause. Vessie and Kilden even convinced a Mistress Swallowe to kneel before Elizabeth to beg for Mantell's pardon, but to no avail. For her part, Vessie herself was arrested and imprisoned. Elizabeth's government, like Mary's, viewed a repeated offense far more seriously than a first one. Mantell was recaptured in 1581 after he again claimed that Edward was alive, and, like Featherstone, he was executed as a traitor. Only after Mantell's execution was Vessie finally released for good behavior. Not all who turned against Mantell did solely out of loyalty to the queen. Mr. Collins of Essex, who informed against him, did so at least partially in hopes of receiving special privileges in his trade as victualer.[34]

Mantell's execution did not end the rumor. There are several other reported cases. John Tusser, described as a gentleman, was indicted for publishing false prophecies in 1583. One prophecy was that "there shall comm into England one that was dead . . . and the dead man shall sett the crownes of England on his hedd." This might have referred to Edward, especially as the prophecy also stated "a lyon, a horse, a liberd shall crowne E." In 1587 William Francis, a smith of Hatfield Broad Oak, claimed that Edward was still alive. In a discussion with some people on the street Francis told them that "there is one in the Tower which saith he is King Edward." Edmund Earle responded that Edward was dead. Francis argued "I dare not saye soe." In fact, he said, he personally knew the man who carried Edward "in a red mantell into Germany in a shipp called the *Harry*." Francis's acquaintances pointed out to him that Edward was buried; that in fact his grave was with the rest of the kings. Not so, said Francis. Edward's elaborate tomb, he claimed, was really empty. "Ther was a pece of leade buryed that was hollowe but ther was nothing in it and that it was but a monument." His audience was shocked. "These are naughty words which awght not be spoken," he was told. Speaking them certainly did Francis no good; brought before the Essex Assizes he was found guilty of seditious speech. (It is interesting in symbolic terms that the ship supposed to have carried the boy king to safety should bear the name of his father.) The same year a Leicester embroiderer named Edward Sawford suggested the possibility of Edward's survival, referring to Merlin's prophecies. In March 1588, a Francis Nevell returned from serving in the Low Countries and while discussing preparations for possible invasion with his drinking companions confided to them that Edward VI was still alive. They were sufficiently surprised by this information to pass it on to the Justice of the Peace. When questioned in a more sober state, Nevell explained "that he had heard [King Edward] was alive by a thousand of his fellow-soldiers in the Low Countries some of whom said he was in France and some in Spain," either of which would be a dubious sanctuary for a Protestant king.[35]

The anxiety of the English people during the period immediately before the Armada manifested itself in a number of similar cases.[36] One of these, which is related to those we have been discussing, is that of Miles Fry, who called himself Emanual Plantagenet. He claimed in a 1587 letter to Lord Burghley that he was the son not only of Elizabeth but of God, and was an ambassador from God to his mother. According to Fry, after his birth he was taken from his mother the queen by the Angel Gabriel and brought to Mistress Fry to be raised and kept. For thirty-five years he was known as Miles Fry, the son of John and Joan Fry. But "the time of this keping is ended: and God my father hath sent me unto her Highnes to declare unto her that I am her sonne." Fry begged Burghley to allow him to speak to his mother the queen, for "[I] am in great extremiti and redi to perish for lak of helpe." Fry had already written to Walsingham four years previously, yet despite what he assumed were promises of help nothing had happened. "I am yet so far from helpe of my Ladi that I have not the favor of a subject in her relme though I be her sonne." Fry assured Burghley, with his "diing hand," if he did not get to see the queen, he would perish, and "then will God punish this land." It appears that Burghley and Walsingham did not consider Fry a danger, and no one else seems to have been convinced by his fantastic obsession, since this is the only mention of him in the official records. We might wonder why Fry was so easily dismissed by Elizabeth's Council while others were taken much more seriously. Perhaps Fry was unable, unlike Mantell, to convince anyone else. He may not have even tried, but instead limited his obsession to writing desperate letters. Fry's delusion is an interesting subtext on Elizabeth's presentation to her people as their "mother," a Virgin Queen who substituted for the worship of the Virgin Mary. For poor Miles Fry, Elizabeth's self-presentation was all too successful.[37]

About the same time, in 1586, Edward Burges, a vicar, also claimed close kinship with Elizabeth when he asked people to pray for the queen as his "right Reverend syster." Asked what he meant by such a statement, Burges made the claim that "the Queenes Majestie was his syster. . . . that he was Kinge Henryes sunne and that the Queene was his syster both by her father and mother." Though Burges was arrested for seditious comments, what happened to him is unknown.[38]

A strange case that had implications for understanding the restrictions of gender also occurred around the time of the preparation for the Spanish Armada in August 1587, though of course the Armada was actually delayed for one year. A woman named Anne Burnell came to the attention of authorities for claiming that she was the daughter of Philip II of Spain, and that on her back had magically appeared the arms of the kingdom of England. Her family had already seen its share of trouble. The previous year her husband, Edward, had been imprisoned for a time, possibly for some connection with the Babington conspiracy or perhaps for debt. Whatever the cause of Burnell's imprisonment, it made him wary of getting into more trouble, and caused him to seek advice about his wife's delusions. What seemed to trigger them was the news that Sir Francis Drake had just captured the Spanish ship the *San Felipe* in the Azores and brought its wealthy cargo back to Plymouth.[39] When Drake returned to England, people wondered if perhaps his exploits would delay the coming of the Armada Philip was threatening to send.

Anne Burnell's claims that she was Philip's daughter came to the attention of the Privy Council, and they asked James Dalton to examine Anne and the people with whom she and her husband had spoken. Dalton may have been chosen for this task since he already knew her. In fact, he and his wife Mary had Anne Burnell live with them for several weeks so she would be under safeguard and observation.

Dalton may also have been chosen because he was well respected and trusted. He is described as one of the Counsellors of the City and was treasurer of Lincoln's Inn, as well as serving as a Member of Parliament for most of Elizabeth's reign, where he spoke frequently. In a 1579 description of lawyers he was called "well practised, welthy." From the records of Lincoln's Inn he was a busy and successful lawyer throughout the reign of Elizabeth. Dalton was a committed enough Protestant that he had been expelled from Lincoln's Inn in May 1558 for suspicion of heresy, but after the death of Mary he was subsequently re-admitted. Twenty years later, in May 1578, his colleagues thought so well of him they voted that "the note in the Black Book touching Mr. Dalton's expulsion . . . must be utterly blotted out and putt to perpetuall oblyvion, and yett that he shalbe so adjudged of the Fellowship of this House as though he hadd bene never expulsed." The year before, in the absence of the Lord Mayor, Dalton read the letter of appreciation from Elizabeth after the thanksgiving in the city when the Babington conspirators had been apprehended. He also gave a speech of his own that ended, "God confound all such traytors and preserve her Highnesse long to live and raigne over us." Dalton's loyalty to Protestantism and the queen were beyond question. Some years subsequent to this examination, in 1594, Burghley helped him to receive the office of Under-Sheriff of London.[40]

One question that greatly concerned the authorities was whether Anne Burnell claimed to be the daughter of Philip *and* Mary, thus making her (in her own eyes) legitimate and the actual queen of England, or whether she claimed to be only the daughter of Philip. John Warner testified that Edward Burnell had come "unto the house of this examinate request[ing] to speake with him." That Drake had brought the Spanish treasure ship to England made Anne, claimed her husband, convinced that King Philip "would not be longe after & further that she was the daughter of king Philip and it mighte be Queene Mary was her mother and she had the armes of England on her bodye." John's wife Avis was present during the conversation and affirmed the truth of her husband's report.[41]

But people who had spoken with Anne herself gave a slightly different story. Johan Fenton, wife of John Fenton, testified that about six weeks previously "she hearde the said Anne Burnell say that she was king Phillips child but she denyeth that she heard her say that she was Queene Maryes daughter." Her husband added that "the said Anne Burnell hath toulde them that she had on her bodye the marks of the Armes of England." But on "veiweinge the body of the said Anne [he] could perceive no such thing." Elizabeth and Thomas Bradeshawe each testified at Anne Burnell's request. Elizabeth had heard Anne "saye that she was kinge Phillips child but she denieth that she heard her say that she was Quene Mary's daughter." Anne had told the Bradeshawes as well about the marks on her back but neither claimed to have actually seen them.

Dalton also publicly and for the record examined Anne Burnell herself. She claimed to be king Philip's child but "denied that ever she said Queen Mary was her mother or it mighte be she was her mother or any . . . [and] she thanckd God she never had so litle witt as to thinke it possible." Anne also affirmed as she had told others that she had the arms of England on her back. It is interesting that while Anne was certainly delusional, her perceptions were not so irrational as to allow her to think that she was the daughter of the late queen. To her the belief about Philip made perfect sense—though one might wonder why, if she was the daughter of Philip but not Mary, she would have the arms of England rather than Spain on her back? We might wonder too why the assertion of her parentage was not enough for Anne, and why she had to believe that there was a physical manifestation of her specialness. Though Anne called herself a Spanish king's daughter, her deepest need may have been to demonstrate her connection to English royalty. In her own world view, Anne was not only rational but aware of what would not be rational behavior and beliefs.

Dalton asked Anne what it was that first put the idea she was King Philip's child into her head. She explained that eight years earlier she was visiting her mother-in-law in the county of Nottingham and while there had spoken with a woman known as the witch of Nuttall. This witch informed Anne that she was "a Spaniarde birde & that she had marks above her, which would appeare hereafter & that she did not knowe her owne father for it was a wise childe that did." Anne was so impressed with this intimation that she gave the "said witch a bande that was about her necke & a bracelett of amber from her arme." Later when she was in London she happened "to be in company of a gentleman that was said to be very well learned who falling in talke with her said she was proude but if she knewe her self she would be the proudest woman in the realm." This made Anne call to mind what the witch of Nuttall had said to her and she told this to the wise man. The fortune teller made Anne promise she would never reveal him and, with this assurance, "then he toulde her that the best spaniard that euer came in England was her father & toulde her that she had markes aboute her yt should appeare greater hereafter." Anne "from that time she took the veiwe hereof in a glass" and began to see the marks promised her. Burnell's story is somewhat reminiscent of Elizabeth Vessie. Just as Jane Standlie had assured Vessie of her importance—"She should be the chief instrument in reinstating 'the king' of this realm," so too did the "wise man" tell Anne if she but knew who she was "she would be the proudest woman in the realm." This language was the stock and trade of fortune tellers, witches, and "wise men," and we can imagine that many people heard similar prognostications and shrugged them off. We might wonder what it was about Vessie and Burnell that made them so susceptible to such suggestions that they altered their entire lives as a result of them.

According to Anne's testimony, her husband Edward was not very sympathetic to her claims. "Since Witsontide her husbande upbradeinge her with the basenes of her parentage her father beinge one Kirkall a Butcher in Eastcheape in London who died xiiii yeares past & her mother long before." Anne responded that she might be more of a gentlewoman than any Burnell in England and told him to look on her back and this

would prove it to him. Anne's delusions may well have reflected her unhappy marriage and the inferior status she felt within it. At first, however,
all Edward could see on Anne's back were veins. Later he had a different,
but even more derisive, response. "Aboute a fourthnight after he looked
on her backe & she asked him why he laughed & he said because she was
branded on the backe as one of the Queene great horses was on the
Buttocke."

Anne claimed that she had been told eight years previously that she
was the daughter of Philip of Spain, but she did not announce it until 1587.
We might wonder what had happened to cause this delusion so to come
to the fore. It certainly was not the death of her actual father, for he had
died, according to her testimony, fourteen years before and her mother
had predeceased him. It may have been the imprisonment of her husband
the previous year as well as the uncertain political situation. Perhaps what
caused Burnell's delusion is less significant than the concern such a delusion caused the Privy Council.

James Dalton's wife, Mary, was far more sympathetic to Anne than
Edward Burnell was. Mary said she thought Anne was a gentlewoman and
that she had "a good likinge of her both for her modest & good behaviour
& also her gentlewomanlye qualities." Even before the Privy Council had
ordered Anne to stay at the Daltons, Mary explained that "before this time
very often & many times . . . [she] hath invited her into her house." Mary
did testify that Anne claimed to be the daughter of Philip but "beinge
demanded wheather ever she hearde her saye Quene Mary was her mother
or the like words she sayeith she never hearde her saye any such wordes
nor toulde that to be her meaninges: but that if she were his childe she
was a bastard." This should have mediated some of the danger of what
Anne Burnell said. Philip fathering bastards while king consort of England
may have demonstrated his potency but hardly his loyalty to Mary. And a
bastard child had no legal standing. Though Anne insisted she was Philip's
daughter, and claimed the English royal arms, she never asserted that this
made her queen.

Anne kept her word and did not reveal the name of the "wise man"
to the authorities, but he was apparently Thomas Watson, later a friend of
Christopher Marlowe and possibly a Catholic sympathizer. While Anne
had not named her "wise man," one of her friends, Elizabeth Bradshawe,
did. Dalton examined Watson, but while he agreed that he and Burnell
had talked eight years ago, when she had told him the witch's prophecy of
her good birth, he denied he had told her anything, or that she had

claimed to be Philip's daughter. Watson was thus dismissed. Charles Nicholl says of Watson's role in the incident, "This is a story of an unscrupulous young man and an unfortunate old woman. Watson's actions are amusing on one level, a jape, but they have a hard edge. He trades on his learning, on the mystique it has for those who lack it. There is the overtone of charlatanism, of phoney magic and mumbo-jumbo. It is a piece of theatre, with Watson giving his best in the role of the 'soothsayer.' The whole thing plays like a comedy, but the comedy has a victim."[42]

James Dalton himself tried to do the best he could for Anne Burnell. He was asked to furnish his opinion of the "behaviour of the gentlewoman & likelyhoode of the truth of the matter." Dalton explained that he "ever thought very well of her for her modestye & good behaviour." While Dalton could not deny Anne's claims that she was Philip's daughter, he agreed it was unlikely that she had claimed to be Mary's as well. Dalton also suggested that Anne's wits had become disordered because of her worry "about her husband being for a time a prisoner in the kinges bench," and the "evell acquaintaunce" she had made at that time. Dalton proved a strong advocate for Anne, explaining that "since she came to my howse her behaviour hath bin very good & vertuous much given to prayer & abstinence & to good gentlewomanlye exercises all the day without resorte to her of anye or goeing abrode but in my wiues company." Dalton was certainly concerned about her, both for her own sake and for the possibility her delusions could be used by others for political reasons. "She seemeth much enclined to melancholye & I am not without doubte of worse effectes of that humor specially if she should come amonge such evell people as woulde feede her humor as amonge such it seemeth she hath bin to much alreadye." Melancholy was, of course, *the* diagnosis for mental illness at the end of the sixteenth century.[43] The possibility that Anne's delusion could be used by people trying to attack Elizabeth's government may well have been the real danger. Dalton only felt pity for Anne herself. "It semeth that her wittes be troubled & through great misery & penury . . . [and] are greatelye decayed: she is weake & taketh no rest a nightes: And this is all that I can as yet enforme yor honors of her."

Apparently Dalton's explanation and advocacy carried the day and nothing was done to Anne Burnell at the time. Five years later, however, the response was much less benign. Reginald Sharpe has argued that the continuation of the war and the threatened renewal of a Spanish invasion in 1592 imposed a great strain on the citizens of London and that Anne Burnell's delusions are one example of this strain, though it does not appear that Sharpe was aware of Burnell's problems in 1587.[44] Certainly it appears by 1592 her delusion had hardened and she was again investigated by the Privy Council.

By now Anne's husband was dead; he had died in 1587, the year of her earlier examination.[45] We can only speculate on what impact being a widow had on her mental state. Word was sent to the Lord Mayor of London "to cause the said An Burnel to be carefullie viewed and seen by som discreet and experimented phisicion and surgeon, whether the armes of England and Spain be naturallie upon . . . her back or otherwize, and thereupon to make true certifcat unto us what shalbe found." The Council considered very seriously what to do if her claim proved false, showing concern not only about Anne herself but about whoever else might be either misled by her or would use her delusions for their own ends. "For yt is meant (if the matter shall apeare to be false or that there hath bin . . . practis therein) that due punishment shalbe inflicted both on the said An Burnel and on such as are parties thereunto. And therefore yt were good for the better bolting owt of the truth your Lordship be verie circumspect herein, carefullie examining such persons as may probablie be suspected to be privie and acquainted herewith upon oath or otherwize."[46] In the last decade and a half of Elizabeth's reign there were many seditious comments, threats against the queen, and unrest. The delusional Anne Burnell might be perceived as dangerous if others supported her claims.

The Council was soon convinced of Anne's culpability, but the only other person they also blamed was her young maidservant Alice Digges. Digges is the one person who claimed she indeed did see the English arms on Anne's back. "She hathe affirmed that she sene uppon the back of Ann Burnell the picture of a lyon with certeine redd crosses adjoyning to the same. Both were ordered to be whipped through the streets of London." Though the Council did not show mercy or understanding towards Anne Burnell, they did towards Alice Digges when they learned that, instead of "a woman servant of some more yeares" she was "but a yong gerl of thirteen yeres and the daughter of a gentlewoman in Kent, and [not] likly to be participant of the practice of the said Ann Burnell." They suggested to the Lord Mayor that "you shall doe well to cause notice to be given to her parentes that they may appoynt some fitter place for her educacion then with a woman of such impudencie and infamie as the said Ann Burnell is."[47]

Anne Burnell was whipped through the streets of London in December 1592 as punishment and warning. Her case received enough interest and publicity for a ballad about her to be registered that same month,

published by Edward White: "shewinge how a fond woman falsely accused her self to be the kinge of Spaines daughter and beinge founde a
lyer was for the same whipped through London the xiiijth of december
1592 beinge known to be a butchers daughter of London, a ballad." The
punishment of Anne Burnell is also recorded in the 1615 edition of John
Stow's *Annals*.[48] The only real danger Anne Burnell might have posed
would have been if she were the focus of others' dissatisfaction, and clev-
erer, saner minds had made use of her. But the only one ever to believe
her was a thirteen-year-old servant maid. Anne herself never asserted that
her royal parentage should give her political position. Though earlier in
the century a butcher's son had risen to be Cardinal and Archbishop of
York, in the 1590s there was no leniency for the delusional Anne Burnell,
who was only a butcher's daughter. We might wonder if it was simply the
generosity of James Dalton that kept Anne Burnell from being punished
this way in 1587, but it does seem that by 1592 Elizabeth's government was
that much more sensitive to any such perceived threat. It is suggestive that
only the year before, in 1591, William Hacket's delusions had been treated
with utmost severity—he had been executed as a traitor.

On July 16, 1591, two gentlemen with Puritan sympathies, Edmund
Copinger and Henry Arthington, went out into the streets of London
proclaiming William Hacket to be the new messiah, Jesus Christ, and the
King of Europe. It was an especially anxious time for Elizabeth's government because of its decision to suppress the Puritan movement and the
subsequent trial of nine Puritan ministers before the High Commission
and the Star Chamber. The connections between the Hacket affair and
the Puritans are ambiguous; Copinger certainly felt great concern over the
fate of the Puritan ministers, had corresponded with them and visited
them, and it was fear over what the Star Chamber might do that seems to
have precipitated his actions. In May 1591 Copinger reported to Hacket
the news of the nine ministers being brought before the Star Chamber.
Copinger planned to attend the next session. "And I fear if sentence
with severity shall be given, I shall be forced in the name of the great
and fearful God of heaven and earth to protest against it." But despite
Copinger's strong identification with the nine, Thomas Cartwright and
the others had not really encouraged Copinger, and it seems that Richard
Cosin, dean of the Court of Arches and an active high Commissioner,
John Whitgift, archbishop of Canterbury, and Richard Bancroft, future
archbishop, publicly emphasized the connection in order to discredit the
Puritan movement.[49]

Though it was Hacket who proclaimed himself messiah, it seems to have been Copinger who was the real instigator. Copinger was deeply concerned about godly ministers and the cause of the Presbyterians. He believed he had a calling from God to accomplish reform in both the political and religious arenas. He and his friend Arthington attended sermons and prayed and fasted together. Keith Thomas argues it is significant that, while both were gentlemen, Copinger was a younger son without a share in his father's estate and Arthington was in debt. Both men were thus under a financial strain which may have made Hacket and his cause much more appealing for them.[50] In May 1591 the two men met Hacket, a man of much lower class standing, and Hacket crystallized in Copinger's mind the need to reform both church and state and free the nine ministers.

Hacket's background before his meeting with Copinger and Arthington is rather obscure. Though Cosin provides an early biography of Hacket in his *Conspiracie for Pretended Reformation* (1592), Curtis Charles Breight observes that what Cosin says of Hacket is "unsupported by other documents and hence, given its bias, of dubious historicity." Cosin's description of Hacket as a drunkard, lecher, would-be rapist, and probable highwayman appears to be formulaic and borrowed from other recent accounts of traitors. One of the most horrifying, if unlikely, of the stories about Hacket appears in Camden's history. Camden states that it "irketh me to remember" Hacket and then tells how he was so "insolent, fierce, and . . . eager upon revenge, that he bit off his honest Schoolmasters Nose as he embraced him." Such an image would help make Hacket utterly unsympathetic. Whether it was true is another matter. We do know, however, that prior to coming to the capital Hacket had apparently already been whipped and expelled from York and several other provincial towns for his claims to be a second John the Baptist. We might notice that by the time he had arrived in London he had promoted himself to Jesus Christ. He could pray with great vividness and theatricality, and people said that he seemed to be addressing God face to face. What probably made Hacket so dangerous is that he prayed out in the streets to the people, and Arthington apparently wished him to pray before Elizabeth herself "in a bizarre kind of public ceremony."[51]

What the authorities described as most dangerous about Hacket and his supporters were not his religious delusions per se but their political implications. Cosin claims that "their last & most damnable designment of al was the deprivation of her sacred Maiesty from her Crown & dignity, & the destruction of her Royal person." That Hacket claimed to be not only Christ but also king or emperor of Europe appears to have put him in a different category. Copinger told Arthington that Hacket was a greater person than Elizabeth, "and indeed, above all the princes in the world." In contrast, earlier in Elizabeth's reign, in 1562, William Geffrey publicly claimed that John Moore was Christ. Both Moore and Geffrey were whipped and imprisoned for over a year, quite a severe punishment, but far less than what was done to Hacket.[52]

On the morning of July 16 Copinger and Arthington appeared at Hacket's lodgings and groveled at the foot of his bed in imitation of courtesies owed a royal figure. Arthington wanted to anoint Hacket "King of Europe," but Hacket said it was unnecessary. "Taking Coppinger by the hande, [Hacket] saide: You shall not neede to anoint me, for I have beene alreadie anointed in heaven by the holy Ghost himself."[53] Instead he told Arthington and Copinger to take his message into the streets:

> Goe your way both . . . and tell them in the Citie, that Christ Iesus is come with his fanne in his hand to iudge the earth. And if any man aske you where he is, tell them he lies at Walkers house . . . & if they will not beleeve it, let them come & kill me, if they can.[54]

Arthington and Copinger started toward Cheapside calling out as they went, "Repent England, Repent." They went to Cheapside because it was very wide street and also a busy market place. Royal proclamations were ceremonially pronounced at the market cross. Elizabeth passed by there as part of her precoronation entry. Interestingly enough, it was also a location of both official and unofficial executions. Breight points out that, "Arthington and Copinger selected Cheapside not only because it offered a ready-made audience, but also because it was associated with official discourse and ceremonial spectacle."[55] The men did not simply want to proclaim their message from the streets. What they really needed was a stage. When they got near the cross "they got them up into an emptie cart which stoode there, and out of that choise pulpit . . . made their lewde and traytrous preachment unto the people." As well as telling the crowd that Hacket was Christ

> There was then and there furthere delivered by them, or by one of them, that Hacket was king of Europe, and so ought to be obeyed and taken: and that all Kings must holde of him, and that the Queenes Maiestie had forfaited her Crowne, and was worthie to be deprived.[56]

Copinger's harangues to the crowd caused a riot. "This strange accident being quickely blowne through the Citie, all was in a buzze, and a kinde of astonishment, what to thinke of the matter." The Privy Council sent two men to investigate leading to the arrest of Hacket, Copinger, and Arthington. Before their arrest Arthington addressed Hacket as "King of the earth" and said of Elizabeth that she was "no longer Queene."[57]

The three men were tried on July 26, 1591. At the trial, when Arthington "sawe Hacket presently [he] fell downe groveling upon his face on the ground And honoured him" while Copinger "behave[d] himselfe as a man distracted of his wits." Copinger confessed he had said Elizabeth was not queen "for Hacket is the onely King of the worlde." As for Hacket, the Justices "could get nothing out of the counterfeit Jesus Christ but 'I am that I am.' 'That I have said I have said,' 'Men shall bear witness of me.'" Also damning, was witnesses' testimony that while Hacket was lodging at the house of a man named Kaye he "was mooved thereunto inwardly by the Spirit" to deface the queen's arms and "put out the Lyons and the Dragons eyes in the Armes." Even more disturbing, Kaye and his wife testified that Hacket "boil[ing] . . . with cruell hatred against the Queene" took "a certaine picture of the Queenes Maiestie, and did maliciously, and traiterouslie thrust an iron instrument into that part of the saide picture that did represent the breast and hart of the Queenes Maiestie." The Kayes were so upset that Hacket was forced to find other lodgings. Hacket reminded people of the Anabaptists earlier in the century. "Men talk of it, and resemble it to that matter of John of Leyden . . . and this mad fool plotted some such kingdom as these prophets might have assembled." Breight argues that, "In essence, the main offenses for which Hacket was found guilty of treason were attacks on official modes of representation. . . . Hacket's curious attack on the royal arms also smacks of image magic. He put out the eyes of the lions and dragons presumably in order to blind the queen and facilitate the removal of 'her whole power of her authoritie.'"[58]

This kind of image magic greatly disturbed the authorities. It is reminiscent of a case over a decade earlier in August 1578. According to the Spanish Ambassador, "A countryman has found, buried in a stable, three wax figures . . . the centre figure had the word Elizabeth written on the forehead and the side figures were dressed like her councillors . . . the left side of the images being transfixed with a large quantity of pig's bristles as if it were some sort of witchcraft. When it reached the Queen's ears she was disturbed, as it was looked upon as an augury." The Privy Council was afraid that what had been "discovered [was] a practice of that device very likely to be intended to the destruction of Her Majesty's person."

Four witches were arrested, tried, and executed.[59] There is certainly the suggestion that Hacket too was practicing image magic and was either "a conjurer or witch." Similarly, in 1591 Brien O'Rork was arraigned in Westminster. One of the charges against him was that he "had commaunded the Queenes Picture painted in a table, to be hung at a horse tayle, and hurried about in scorne, and disgracefully cut in pieces." O'Rork, like Hacket, was executed as a traitor.[60]

Hacket was found guilty as well of "intending the deprivation and deposing our said Soveraigne Ladie Elizabeth from her honor and royall name" and was ordered to be executed July 28, 1591. At his execution he "fell to rayling and cursing of the Queenes Maiestie. . . . hee beganne to pray this most passionate, blasphemous, and execrable prayer. . . . Then turning towards the Executioner, he said unto him, Ah thou bastards childe, wilt thou hange William Hacket thy king?" Copinger apparently underwent a fast and starved himself to death in prison, or so authorities claimed. In his *Conspiracie* Cosin went to great pains to show that Copinger had "fallen into starke madnes" but of Hacket "there can no furie or madnes bee justly noted . . . rather, notable hyposcrisie, craft, and dissembled holines."[61] Arthington spent a year or so in Bridewell before he was released upon writing a suitably apologetic narrative, *The Seduction of Arthington by Hacket,* that he dedicated to the Privy Council. In his apology Arthington claimed that Hacket had bewitched him. Arthington's book served as a warning of the dangers of Satan.[62] Collinson suggests of the Hacket incident that "nothing more convenient to Whitgit's party could possibly have happened. . . . With the ingenuity of the natural investigator [Bancroft] was to claim that if Cartwright did not actively encourage Copinger's attempt neither did he discourage it."[63]

Some people at the time did wonder whether the government took the matter too seriously. Thomas Phelippes, Sir Francis Walsingham's confidential secretary, wrote of Elizabeth, "she is more troubled with it than it is worth." Writing in 1592, Francis Bacon attempted to show the loyalty of Londoners to the queen by minimizing Hacket's appeal. Bacon compared Hacket and his followers to "blisters in some small ignoble part of the body, which have soon after fallen and gone away." Instead of attracting a crowd, "Hacket, who must needs have been thought a very dangerous heretic, . . . could never get but two disciples . . . a dangerous commotioner, that in so great and populous a city as London is, could draw but those same two fellows, whom the people rather laughed at as a may-game, than took any heed of what they did or said." Keith Thomas argues that usually Elizabeth's government dismissed such religious fanatics as "brainsick" and "frantic," but when they perceived political consequences of such enthusiasm they were quick to act. Brieght, however, takes his analysis further than Thomas does. He sees visual ceremony as an official strategy used by an insecure government to serve as a severe warning. He argues "the authorities understood the necessity of producing not just Hacket as Jesus, but especially Hacket as King of Europe." Hacket's claim that he was king and that as a result Elizabeth had no right to rule went to the heart of the Elizabethan regime. By putting a piece of iron through the breast of the portrait of the queen, Hacket was cutting her at the most vulnerable place, a point that Cosin seems to appreciate as suggested in his language: "This Noble heart, which thereby hee so trayterously despited, God of his infinite mercy long blesse . . . within her Maiesties sacred breast." In the Elizabethan period "breast" could be used particularly to refer to women or to the area of the body near the heart for both men and women. The possible emphasis on the breast as both female and also the most vulnerable place to attack the queen is paralleled by a crude woodcut denigrating Mary I during her reign, which showed her having many breasts that were used to suckle bishops, priests, and the Spanish. Hacket, as well as Mantell in his claim to be Edward, threatened the position of the legitimacy of the queen, and it is no wonder Elizabeth's government responded with severity.[64] While Burnell's claim was not as serious, she too was publicly punished and humiliated. As a woman she *could* not make a claim that would be perceived as equally dangerous.

The 1590s saw not only the rumors of Edward's survival and such strange impostors and claimants as Anne Burnell and William Hacket, but a generalized sense of dismay at women's rule in the accounts of people arrested for making seditious statements about the queen. This last decade appears to have the most arrests for such comments, though they begin to be noticeable around 1585 as the fear of invasion, the recognition Elizabeth will now never marry, and concern for the succession begins to become acute. Only the 1560s, the first decade of Elizabeth's reign, comes close to the number of seditious statements.[65] A few examples demonstrate this desire for a male rule and, for at least a few of her subjects, disdain for the queen.

In April of 1585 Jeremy Vanhill, a laborer, publicly stated, "Shyte uppon your Queene; I woulde to god shee were dead that I might shytt on her face." Vanhill wished "that the Queene were as sicke as Peter Aveger then was." Aveger was so ill he died that same night. The authorities took

Vanhill's ravings seriously; he was hanged for what he said, a far more serious punishment than was usually given.[66] In 1586 Joan Lyster of Cobham argued that "the Counsayle makes a foole of the Queenes Majestie, and bycause she is but a wooman she owght not to be governor of a Realme." In September 1589 Cecily Burche, a spinster of London, was sentenced to stand in the pillory for publicly saying that "she trusted in god to see the blodd run thorrowe the streetes as water runneth in the Thames. And she trusted to see a newe prince to raigne over us."[67]

In 1591 John Feltwell, a laborer of Great Wenden, wanted to "pray for a king." John Thurgood asked Feltwell why as "we have a gracious queene already, wherefore would you praye for a kinge?" Feltwell's answer expresses some of the same disenchantment we have seen in Hacket. "The Queene was but a woman and ruled by noblemen. . . . so that poore men cold gett nothinge. . . . We shall never have a merry world while the Queene lyveth, but yf we had but one that would ryse, I would be the next, or els I wold the Spaniards wold come in that we maye have some sport." Feltwell spent two hours in the pillory on market day for these comments. Henry Collins, a servant, was committed to prison in the Marshalsea in 1592 for saying he would kill Elizabeth. Another prisoner there, Gratian Brownell, said that there were many prisoners who felt that way, and "some one would make an end of her one day, and then all those commitment would be void, and all would be well." On November 10, 1596 Edward Ewer said that it "would never be a merrye worlde till her majestie was dead or killed." Perhaps to make his world more merry in the meantime, three weeks later Ewer stole a horse. He was sentenced to hang, though whether it was for larceny or seditious words is not clear. Two years later in October 1598 the laborer, Thomas Farryngton, publicly stated that "the Queenes majestie was Antechrist and therefore she is throwne downe into hell." Farryngton was placed in the pillory and his ears were cropped. In 1598 Edward Fraunces also made a remark that connected misogyny and sexual politics. Fraunces called Elizabeth "base born," and wished "that Her Majesty had been cut off twenty years since, so that some noble prince might have reigned in her stead."[68] In 1599 Patrick Doffe was accused of calling Elizabeth "a Jezabel." In 1600, echoing Hacket, Nicholas Knyght claimed he "was above the Queen, for she carried the sword in her left hand but he in his right hand, and she ruled in temporal causes but he in spiritual." Lord Chief Justice Popham wrote to Robert Cecil of his concern over Knyght; "I see he is of a more puissant spirit," suggesting that Knyght possessed power and potency that would make his claim appealing. Yet, with all these seditious comments we might remember that they also occurred in great number in the seventeenth century. At least from the Essex court records F. G. Emmison concludes, "the sudden sprouting of seditious statements after Elizabeth's death was much thicker than at any time during her life. . . . The outburst of treasonable sayings by Essex folk after the accession of James I is a remarkable posthumous tribute."[69]

Along with all the other seditious comments, the rumor of Edward VI's survival made its last appearance in Elizabeth's reign in 1599. Thomas Vaughan claimed that a child had been put to death as a substitute for Edward, who had been safely spirited off to Denmark, where he married the queen and "now is king there." Recently, Vaughan asserted, Edward, though King of Denmark, had been in Ireland, and had saved the poor in England, Wales, and Ireland by giving them corn and provisions. Vaughan volunteered the names of others whom he claimed had told him about Edward's survival as many as eight or nine years previously. With touching faith in family feeling, Vaughan added that "he heard that her Majesty did say she would gladly hear whether her brother King Edward were dead or alive." The examiners said of Vaughan that "the man is a very simple person, a common wanderer against the law, and little better than a natural." By 1599 Edward was almost a mythic religious figure who provided for his people in need. Accounts of the rumor in the seventeenth century are far more vague; for the most part, when Elizabeth died, the belief in her still-living brother died with her.[70]

Although the rumors of Edward VI's survival were much rarer in the early Stuart period, there appears to be more to this development than the mere fact that there was now a male sovereign. The timing of these rumors under Elizabeth may provide a clue to the social and psychological functions they served. They appeared for the most part in the late 1570s, 1580s, and 1590s, reflecting not only doubts over female rule but uncertainty concerning a woman who would soon be leading her country to war with Spain, who was too old to have a child of her own, and who yet refused to name her heir. The recurrent rumor that Elizabeth herself had one or more children is analogous.[71]

We can only speculate why these people made such claims. Mantell's announcement that he was Edward VI gave him high status, at least with his followers. As for Elizabeth Vessie, it allowed her to be valued as a "king's sister." Anne Burnell paid dearly for her delusion, but it again gave this "butcher's daughter" a voice she never had before. Hacket died horribly, but he died with the words on his lips "wilt thou hange William Hacket thy king?" Catherine Belsey has argued that for women accused of witchcraft, their time of execution "offered women a place from which to speak in public with a hitherto unimagined authority which was not diminished by the fact that it was demonic."[72] One might argue that these impostures also gave both women and men of lower class the same chance for a public voice, though at sometimes horrific cost. Christopher Hill has suggested that "madness itself may be a form of protest against social norms, and that the 'lunatic' may in some sense be saner than the society which rejects him."[73] But the chance of a public voice and the move beyond expectations of class and gender were not the only reason such rumors of the returned king spread.

The belief in Edward VI's survival and the actual appearance of pretenders were only aspects of a very complex system of beliefs that flourished in the second half of the sixteenth century, all reflecting the uncertainty of having a woman ruler. Moreover, the rumors were most frequent, and were coupled with the appearance of an actual impostor, in Mary's reign after it was evident that she would not have a child. In Elizabeth's reign, for the most part, the rumors of Edward VI's survival did not emerge until well into her reign.

The rumors and pretenders of the 1580s and 1590s reflect the people's sense of instability over not only the rule of a woman but over the rule of an elderly, childless woman who refused to name a successor, a woman without a direct heir, ruling at a time of great change and potential crisis. For the fifty years preceding, the state had kept changing the official religion back and forth between Catholicism and different forms of Protestantism. The English could look to their neighboring countries such as France and see the ravaging effect of religious civil wars. Mary Stuart's presence in England until her execution in 1587, and the attendant assassination plots against Elizabeth, made it clear to many of the English people how close they were to political chaos. And though Mary Stuart's death removed one danger, Philip II's threatened invasion of England in a holy war provided another. Though the English felt victorious over the defeat of the Armada in 1588, the threat of further Spanish invasions intensified the strains of the 1590s. The disastrous harvests, especially in 1595, intensified economic problems, as did taxation, inflation, and excessive food prices.

Mary and Elizabeth never had to face a pretender with an army behind him, as Joanna of Flanders did. Neither Featherstone nor Mantell had great support, nor did the queens evoke commensurate hatred for refusing to accept an impostor as their brother. Nonetheless, for the English people in the second half of the sixteenth century, a woman ruling in her own right—and without a son of her own to succeed her and reestablish the male order—was unsettling. These male pretenders were one example of the insecurities the English people felt. There never was a tradition envisioning a savior queen. The pattern of the male monarch as savior echoes through sixteenth-century England, so that the fears caused by female rule manifested themselves in a longing for the safety and tradition of the king.

6. Elizabeth as King and Queen

Probably the most vital question for Elizabeth at her accession and throughout her reign was whether as a woman she could rule successfully.[1] This question echoes through the pressure on her to marry, through her religious role as sacred monarch, in the rumors around her sexuality, and in the belief in male pretenders. At the beginning of her reign Nicholas Heath, Archbishop of York, argued against Elizabeth becoming Supreme Head of the Church because she was "a woman by birthe and nature." Yet his speech had another component that in many ways undermined this argument; he also stated that by the "appointment of God she [is] our sovaraigne lord and ladie, our kinge and quene, our emperor and empresse." In this section of his speech, at the very beginning of the reign, Heath described Elizabeth as having two identities simultaneously, one male and the other female, both incorporating sovereignty.[2] Though female, Elizabeth was also in part "kinge." In some ways Heath echoed the 1554 Act Concerning Regal Power, in which Parliament during Mary I's reign made clear to all "malicious and ignorant persons" that despite the fact that "the most ancient statutes of this realm being made by Kings then reigning, do not only attribute and refer all prerogative . . . unto the name of King," a woman could rule in her own right, that "the regality and dignity of the king or of the Crown, the same [was] the Queen." Constance Jordan suggests that this act states of the queen that "politically she is a man." The construct implies something a bit more complex than that, however. Rather, it is stating that a woman as queen has the same rights as a male monarch. It may mean that politically she is a man or that she is a woman who can take on male rights. She may be both woman and man in one, both king and queen together, a male body politic in concept while a female body natural in practice. There are several possible interpretations. Yet the act does seem to suggest an aura of monarchy that goes beyond traditional representations of power as only male. A queen has as much right as a king to rule. "The same all regal power, dignity, honour, authority, prerogative . . . belong unto her Highness . . . in as full, large, and ample manner as it hath done heretofore to any other her most noble progenitors, kings of this realm." The Act of 1554 may be suggesting that when a woman is on the throne she is both king and queen, an idea more explicitly stated by Heath.[3]

We might well understand Heath's speech as the encapsulation of the medieval concept of the king's two bodies. The construct was current in the later Middle Ages and lawyers and theologians gave it new meaning in the reign of Elizabeth. The idea grew out of the difficulty of separating the body politic from the person of the monarch. While individual kings died, the crown survived. With a woman on the throne, the importance of separating the individual sovereign from the ideal of king became more difficult and more crucial. In the Elizabethan age the theory was presented in a newly gendered fashion, though we must be careful not to overstate the theory of the king's two bodies as a totally accepted political truth. Marie Axton reminds us that it "was never a fact, nor did it ever attain the status of orthodoxy; it remained a controversial idea." Axton argues that by 1561 the English common lawyers found it necessary "to endow the Queen with two bodies: *a body natural* and *a body politic*. . . . The body politic was supposed to be *contained within the natural body of the Queen*. . . . The Queen's natural body was subject to infancy, infirmity, error and old age; her body politic, created out of a combination of faith, ingenuity and practical expediency, was held to be unerring and immortal." Joel Hurstfield argues that some references to the theory during Elizabeth's reign "cannot establish for it any strong claim on the outlook or interests of Englishmen of the 1590s." To further complicate the question of gender and power, Renaissance political theory often presented the tyrant as effeminate, or womanish.[4]

The theory of the two bodies proved useful to some of Elizabeth's councillors both in justifying her to foreign courts and in their own dealings with their often recalcitrant queen. In explaining Elizabeth's shifting views on marriage to Alençon, Walsingham hoped the metaphor was of value so that Alençon would not feel insulted by Elizabeth's decision not to marry him. Her body natural cared for him, Walsingham explained, but her body politic saw all too clearly the dangers of losing her subjects' love through an unpopular marriage. What is interesting in this passage is that the two bodies Walsingham posits both seem distinctly female—and both very much Elizabeth. As David Starkey has pointed out when discussing the concept of the king's two bodies, "in practice, as contemporaries usually stressed, both bodies fused in the actual person of the king," or, in this case, in the person of the queen. Walsingham wrote to Cecil, "I thought it very necessary . . . to assure him that the allegation of the said impediment grew not for want of good will in her Majestie, for when she did with the eye and affection of her natural body, look into his constant love born towards her . . . [her Majesty] grew to have so great a liking, as she rested greatly afflicted and perplexed in mind." The problems instead concerned her "pollitique body (which did so greatly import her, as the alienation of her Subjects good will from her, in case her Majestie should be accompanied with a War) she could not proceed as she did desire."[5] Walsingham in no way implies Elizabeth's "pollitique body" is any less female than her natural one, and still it incorporates all sovereignty.

No one could look at the queen from the moment her reign began and have any doubt that she was female. But though the English knew she was a woman, she was also, in some sense and certain contexts, their king. The power of this image for the English is clearly expressed in a private letter of advice the Earl of Shrewsbury sent to his son, Gilbert Talbot (1 January 1574/5). "I hope you will be faithful, loyal, and serviceable, to the Queen's Majesty, my Sovereign, who to me, under God, is King of Kings and Lord of Lords." And though William Cecil in his correspondence overwhelmingly referred to Elizabeth as "queen" and "her Majesty," on occasion she was "prince" to him too. In a letter justifying his loyalty, Cecil protested, "My actions . . . truly have no other foundation than upon the service of God and my Prince, without any particular respect of offence against any" (Burghley to the Earl of Shrewsbury, 1 January 1575/6). The Earl of Essex also expressed this doubled view of the queen in 1591. "I wish your Majesty to be the greatest and happiest Prince, the kindest and constantest Mistress that ever was; and I will be ever your Majesty's most humble, affectionate, and devoted servant."[6] One of the most complex relationships Elizabeth had in the last part of her reign was that with Essex. He used love imagery most extravagantly, and, as it turned out, all the more falsely, but the reason Essex called the queen his mistress was that he also recognized that she was his prince.

This concept of two bodies had a particular value to the queen. If a kingly body politic could be incorporated into an actual natural female body—her natural self—how much more natural right Elizabeth had to rule, and to rule alone. This theory resonates not only in some of the legal and political treatises of the time, but also in the multi-layered levels of meanings in the speeches of Elizabeth herself, who played on her femininity as much as on her "kingly" style. This chapter further explores some

Figure 7. Thomas Cecil, *Truth Presents the Queen with a Lance*, c. 1625 (by permission of the Mansell Collection)

of the issues—particularly courtship, marriage, and sexuality—developed earlier in this study. It analyzes them from the vantage point of how relating Elizabeth's use of language to describe herself and the ways others describe her resonates with the way gender, power, and sexuality were used in the drama of the time. The view of the king's two bodies is echoed and paralleled in the drama that presents—often to the monarch as audience—the player king on stage. Anne Righter (Barton) argues that, "Not only is the actor on the stage committed in the world of illusion to play the king, but the living monarch may see in the player's performance a true dimension of kingship itself. At the point where the distance between the world and the stage might seem the greatest—between the king in his majesty and the poor player with his imitation crown—the play metaphor in fact operates most powerfully, bringing illusion and reality into a juxtaposition that is both poignant and enormously complex."[7]

It seems easiest to assume that, if there are two images of the queen, one male, the other female, then the male image is the one with power while the female image lacks it. I would argue, however, that Elizabeth not only redefines the limits of these traditional gender expectations, but that the male image has at least the possibilities both of powerlessness and danger. We might see this as an underlying theme of a joke between Scots Ambassador Sir James Melville and Elizabeth.

In 1564 Melville was at the Court of Elizabeth to negotiate with the English queen about whom she would agree would be an acceptable marriage partner for Mary Stuart. Several times already the chance of the two queens meeting face to face had evaporated. Elizabeth expressed to Melville how much she wished that she might see Mary at some convenient place. Melville replied with the rather startling proposition.

> I offered to convey her secretly to Scotland by post, clothed like a page; so that under this disguise she might see the Queen . . . telling her that her chamber might be kept in her absence, as though she were sick. . . . She appeared to like that kind of language only answered it with a sigh, saying, "Alas! if I might do this."[8]

Though this story may be apocryphal (some of the material in Melville's *Memoirs* is historically questionable), the suggestion connotes a complicated image: Elizabeth in male garb, but as a male with no power, a page under the protection of a foreign ambassador. Melville's suggestion can be read as a mirrored but fractured image of the king's two bodies—a body natural and a body politic—that had been re-expressed and refined in the reign of Elizabeth. Elizabeth as queen regularly used male language to present herself. She was a "prince" and "king." But Melville's joke also suggests the fragility and potential lack of power of the queen, the woman, as male. Though of course we do not believe that Elizabeth ever seriously contemplated secretly leaving Court disguised as a boy for a rendezvous in Scotland, the image is a delicious one and reminds us of a number of Shakespeare's heroines who indeed did very comparable actions. Rosalind stole away from Court in *As You Like It*. Viola was shipwrecked in *Twelfth Night*. Both these women characters used a male disguise to hide their vulnerability. I am not suggesting that Shakespeare was aware of Melville's frivolous suggestion, but that his drama reflects the fact that a powerful, unmarried woman ruling opened up both the possibility of expanding gender definitions and recognition of the limits of those definitions.[9] Even Elizabeth herself, despite her effectiveness in using language to present herself as both queen and king, was still sometimes confined by the limits of role expectations. Whatever she might say, and however she might behave, for some of her councillors, she was a woman they were attempting to control, however unsuccessful they might be at it.

The image becomes even more confusing when one connects it with some of the drama of the time, where girls disguised as boys, played by boy actors, could be exciting objects of an ambiguous sexuality. A boy actor playing a female disguised as a male could be either a powerful professional young man, like Portia as Balthazar in *The Merchant of Venice*, or a sexually attractive but powerless boy, like Jessica in her male disguise as she elopes with Lorenzo in the same play. And we might consider that Elizabeth's own sexuality was not expressed in a traditionally acceptable female fashion. This is not to imply that Elizabeth was anything but a heterosexual woman—her interest in Robert Dudley as well as Christopher Hatton and possibly the Duke of Alençon had clear sexual components—but that as queen she did not play the traditional female role in her relations with them. Instead she took on what might be perceived as the male role, certainly the position of power, controlling the courtship and intimacy.

Indeed, cross-dressing sometimes represents not power but a sexual freedom that delimits autonomy and power. It is said of Lady Mary Fitton that she disguised herself as a boy to keep an assignation with the Earl of Pembroke. She bore him a son, but the earl refused to marry her, putting her in a most vulnerable, rather than powerful, position. Such disguise for romantic intrigue was not uncommon and not simply the creation of dramatists. In 1605 Sir Robert Dudley, after he lost his bid to be declared the legitimate son of the Earl of Leicester, fled England for Italy with his nineteen-year-old cousin, Elizabeth Southwell, disguised as his page. The fact that he was married at the time made the elopement even more of a scandal, and the two never returned to England.

There were a variety of reasons why women cross-dressed. Some did it for romantic or sexual reasons, while others saw it as a means to challenge traditional attitudes about women's roles. The fact that there actually were women who paraded the streets of Elizabethan and Jacobean London in male garb did definitely upset some men, including James I himself when he became king. In 1583 Philip Stubbes in *Anatomy of Abuses* describes mannish women as the cause of the downfall of society. He expressed his shock for women who wear the "kind of attire appropriate onely for man, yet they blushe not to weare it; and if they coulde as well chaunge their sexe, . . . I thinke they would as verily become men indeed as now they degenerat from godly sober women." In fact, they are really not women at all: "Wherefore, these women may not improperly bee called hermaphroditi, that is, monsters of both kindes, halfe women, halfe men; who if they were naturall women, and honest matrones, would blush to goe in such wanton and lewd attire, as is proper onely to man." In many ways Stubbes's argument is a precursor of anti-feminist arguments of the twentieth century. In 1588 William Averell also refers to women who "yet in attire they appeare to be men" as "indeede neither" men or women but "plaine Monsters." The controversy became even more intense in the seventeenth century with the *Hic-Mulier* pamphlet war about women in men's clothings, and James I ordered his ministers to preach against women who would dare dress as men.[10]

R. Mark Benbow has discovered that many of the women arrested in public wearing men's clothes between 1565 and 1605 were accused of being prostitutes. Of course, one wonders if what they were arrested for was indeed prostitution, not cross-dressing, and what their background was. Jean Howard asserts that "It is tempting to speculate that if citizen wives of the Jacobean period assumed men's clothes as a sign of their wealth and independence, lower-class women may well have assumed them from a sense of vulnerability, with an eventual turn to prostitution merely marking the extent of that vulnerability." So, in part depending on class, some women who cross-dressed were more vulnerable, some less.

We might at first see cross-dressing as means to power for Shakespearean heroines, paralleling Elizabeth's use of language to present herself as male; however, when we look closely at Elizabeth's rhetoric we see a more complicated strategy, especially as the reign progressed. Elizabeth not only presented herself as king, but was more comfortable with being a powerful *woman* who ruled. In the same way we might read the cross-dressed heroines as a means to power, but in such later comedies as *Twelfth Night* and *Much Ado About Nothing*, it is the non-cross-dressed heroines who expand gender definitions—who *as women* act in powerful ways that might, like the actions of the queen, be called "male."

Shakespeare was certainly aware of what was going on at Court, and the plays he wrote were sometimes performed there at the express invitation of the queen. As a Londoner, he also had the opportunity to see

Figure 8. Elizabeth in procession, from Anthony Munday, *Zelauto* (1594) (by permission of the Bodleian Library, Oxford)

the queen in her processions through the City. Londoners especially but people in the rest of England as well were very aware of their queen, an awareness Elizabeth deliberately cultivated as a means to promote loyalty. Not only were there public processions and progresses, but especially after 1585 Elizabeth's speeches to Parliament were copied and sometimes printed for wider distribution, though the printed versions were not always the same as the Parliamentary ones.[11] Elizabeth's speeches were deliberately distributed as widely as possible—copied and printed in chronicles and in separate editions. Her proclamations were officially read aloud throughout the kingdom, and those that were printed were posted as well.[12] Elizabeth not only was aiming her rhetoric at Parliament but was looking for a much wider audience.[13] It is hardly surprising that critics see connections and parallels between Shakespearean characters and the queen.

Leah Marcus suggests that "there are remarkable correlations between the sexual multivalence of Shakespeare's heroines and an important strain in the political rhetoric of Queen Elizabeth I."[14] It is worth examining and analyzing some of these statements by the queen to see how they parallel speeches of the heroines of Shakespeare's comedies. These are hardly one-to-one equations, but rather suggest a fluidity and confluence of ideas of the Court and the drama that express some of the changes in views of gender in the English Renaissance. Dramas were frequently performed at Court, and as we have already seen, particularly in the sacred/religious aspects of rule, the Renaissance monarch was perceived as an actor on stage, with the "theatrical apprehension of sovereign power," as Steven Mullaney puts it. Righter further argues, "Moving about his realm in the midst of a continual drama, the ruler bears a superficial resemblance to the actor."[15] Thus the connections we can perceive between Court and drama become that much more interesting, particularly when we consider that only male actors appeared on stage and how some of the plays were staged when played at Court. Sometimes the queen's seat was itself placed on the stage. Stephen Orgel suggests that "there were, properly speaking, two audiences and two spectacles. . . . At these performances what the rest of the spectators watched was not the play but the queen at a play." Elizabeth often felt "on stage" in much of what she accomplished. She said in 1586 with some discomfort, "We princes, I tell you, are set on stages, in sight and view of all the world." While still King of Scotland, James VI expressed a similar view. In *Basilikon Doron* James wrote, "It is a trew old saying, that a King is as one set on a stage, whose smallest actions and gestures, all the people gazingly doe behold."[16] Dudley Carleton echoed this idea when James became king of England: "The next day the king was actor himself, sat out the whole service, went the procession, and dined in public with his fellow knights, at which sight every man was well pleased."[17] Jerzy Limon further makes the point of how masques were performed "not within the illusionistic stage but in front of it," thus involving the monarch more.[18]

In 1600 Ben Jonson even attempted to have Elizabeth appear on stage as a character in *Every Man Out of His Humour*, but he was forced to change his text.[19] While Elizabeth did not appear as a character on stage in her own lifetime, soon after her death she was the heroine of John Heywood's 1605 *If You Know Not Me, You Know Nobody*. At the very end of Shakespeare's *Henry VIII* (c. 1610) she is presented as a baby brought out on stage. Cranmer presents her to the king as a promise of something marvelous to come. For the audience watching, the speech is a reminder of what the ruler had been.[20] Cranmer proclaims of the baby Elizabeth that

> She shall be
> (But few now living can behold that goodness)
> A pattern to all princes living with her,
> And all that shall succeed.
>
> *   *   *
>
> She shall be loved and feared. Her own shall bless her
> Her foes shake like a field of beaten corn.
>   (V.iv. 20–23, 30–31)

That England's enemies would tremble at Elizabeth suggests her kingly attributes; the promise of this on stage reflects again the confluence between political and dramatic performance.

The idea of play, presentation, and performance as the essence of public life and sense of self has been carefully articulated by Stephen Greenblatt, who presents this self-consciousness as peculiar to the Renaissance. A good example is the advice that Henry Percy, Earl of Northumberland, offered to his son: "If everyone played his part well that is allotted him the commonwealth will be happy; if not then will it be deformed." Lacey Baldwin Smith comments on this passage: "'Play his part': no metaphor was so common in Tudor England as 'all the world's a stage,' and the higher the actor's rank, the more public and demanding his performance."[21] One gets a further sense of role playing in Viola/Cesario's comment to Olivia in *Twelfth Night*: "I am not that I play" (I.v.182). Elizabeth as the highest in the realm had not only the most exacting part to play, but in fact many different roles, some male/kingly ones. Even in her most casual, seemingly spontaneous remarks, Elizabeth was playing a role, aware of how her audience would respond. Patricia Fumerton contends that, "Each of her gestures toward sincere self-revelation is self-concealing, cloaked in the artifice of politics." While there may well have been some genuinely open, unpolished, and uncensored remarks to her intimates, what we have recorded as evidence of Elizabeth's speech shows the queen in control, masking what she may be thinking, never telling us completely who she is. Beryl Hughes argues of Elizabeth that "no other English monarch had such an obsession with her own stage management."[22]

The fact that males played Shakespeare's heroines adds to gender extension and ambiguity during the English Renaissance. I would certainly agree with such critics as Jean Howard that Renaissance audiences on some level simply accepted boys playing women and thought of them as female characters. Otherwise there would not be an emotional identification with what was occurring on stage. But it is also true that on the stage women could be presented symbolically, a man in women's dress, but a woman as herself could not appear. We might consider the irony of this at a time when a woman was ruling but felt that to most utilize her power she often had to present herself symbolically as male, as king, rather than as woman.[23]

Elizabeth attempted carefully to fashion the way people perceived her and to present herself as king as well as queen of England; to promote this she used male analogies with which to compare herself, and presented herself in a dramatic fashion. We can see this from the very beginning of the reign, in the processions the day before her coronation. As Elizabeth moved through London, the entire city, according to the contemporary tract that described it, became "a stage wherein was shewed the wonderfull spectacle, of a noble hearted princesse toward her most loving people, & the peoples exceding comfort in beholding so worthy a soveraign." The kingly connotations for Elizabeth's rule were established early. A child from St. Paul's school delivered an oration in Latin comparing Elizabeth to Plato's philosopher-king. And Elizabeth herself continued this male identification. *Holinshed's Chronicle* reports that during her coronation procession she stopped to pray at the Tower, where she had lately been a prisoner. In her prayer she compared herself to Daniel, rather than using a female Biblical reference. "I acknowledge that thou hast delt as woonderfullie and as mercifullie with me as Thou diddest with thy true and faithfull servant, Daniell thy prophet; whome thou deliveredst out of the den from the crueltie of the greedie and raging lions: even so was I overwhelmed and only by thee delivered." Certainly there were female Biblical references she might have used. Aylmer's 1559 *Harborrowe* frequently compares Elizabeth to both Judith and Deborah. Ironically, in *The Merchant of Venice* Shylock also compares Portia to Daniel when he thinks she is the lawyer Balthazar, though of course this "Daniel come to judgment" does not in the end help Shylock.[24]

*   *   *

Although neither Melville nor Elizabeth would ever have assumed that she would take seriously his suggestion that she would disguise herself as a page, for Elizabeth the physical representation of herself dressed in hose and garters might well have been an amusing image. Melville's banter fit in well with the insights he had already gained from observing Elizabeth. He recognized certain truths her own councillors refused to admit. As we have seen, for many years they hoped to negotiate a marriage for Elizabeth. Melville, however, told her he could see that she would never marry since if she did she would be but queen of England, whereas now "she was both king and queen." We know that Elizabeth enjoyed *toying* with the idea of marriage; but courtship was one thing, while actually to marry and have someone else in control would have been quite another. Elizabeth often described herself as "prince," though she sometimes referred to her cousin Mary Stuart as "princess." This usage is not uniform, however, and we must be careful not to overstate the position. In 1566 Cecil referred officially to Mary as "a prince with whom her Majesty's is in good amity." Also, it is not completely accurate that Elizabeth referred to herself as "princess" early in the reign and "prince" as she became more established, as Marcus suggests. In some versions of her 1593 speech before Parliament (in many of her speeches, there are, of course, variant versions) she does call herself a "princess," which would lead one to assume that her self-representations as both male and female were used throughout her reign depending on their usefulness in particular situations and with particular audiences. Elizabeth's view of herself at the end of her reign is obvious in one of her dealings with the 1601 Parliament. In a report back to the members the speaker explained that Elizabeth "said her kingly prerogative (for so she termed it) was tender."[25]

Certainly others also perceived that there were both parallels and clearly expressed differences between Elizabeth's perception of herself and her Scottish cousin. The dichotomy between them was expressed in a whimsical letter with a serious underpinning that Sir Nicholas Throck-

morton wrote to Robert Dudley in 1560 soon after the death of Mary
Stuart's first husband, Francis II.

> Me-thinketh it were to be wished of all wyse men and her Majestie's good
> subjects, that the one of these two Quenes of the ile of Brittaine were trans-
> formed into the shape of a man, to make so happie a marriage, as therbie ther
> might be of an unitie of the hole ile.[26]

Though Throckmorton does not say which queen he would choose to
become a man, one can hardly imagine Elizabeth not taking the position
of "husband" rather than "wife." In fact, in a conversation in 1564 Elizabeth made much the same point. It was the first time she met Guzman de
Silva, the newly arrived ambassador from Spain, and she asked him about
Philip II's widowed sister Juana. De Silva wrote to Philip:

> After asking after your Majesty's health she took me aside and asked . . . about
> the Princess [Juana], saying how much she should like to see her, and how
> well so young a widow and a maiden would get on together, and what a
> pleasant life they could lead. She (the Queen) being the elder would be the
> husband, and her Highness the wife.[27]

We are not meant to take this request seriously, and it is clear that neither
Elizabeth nor de Silva did at the time, but as a window into how Elizabeth
regarded herself it is extremely interesting. This is not to suggest that
Elizabeth wished for a female partner. I do not believe this would have
seriously occurred to her either politically or personally. The only way she
could conceive of herself in marriage, however, was by being still in control and in the powerful position, and that meant playing the husband. It
is hardly surprising that Elizabeth never married and that she resented that
comedies always ended, like fairy tales, with marriage.[28]

The Shakespearean comedies filled with disguise and sexual ambiguity are odd echoes of Elizabeth's joking comment about Juana. We think
of Olivia passionately in love with Cesario who is really Viola, or, less
sympathetically drawn, of Phoebe in love with Ganymede who is really
Rosalind. Olivia's case is especially interesting, as she is possibly older
than Viola/Cesario. Malvolio describes Cesario as "Not yet old enough for
a man, nor young enough for a boy. . . . one would think his mother's
milk scarce out of him "(*Twelfth Night*, I.v.156–57, 160). While Viola may
look younger dressed as a boy than she would in her female garb, this is
the presence that attracts Olivia. Certainly Olivia is of higher rank than

the page of the Duke Orsino; Viola/Cesario tells Olivia in response to the question: "What is your parentage? / Above my fortunes, yet my state is well: / I am a gentleman" (I.v.275–76). Olivia, however, is the daughter of a Count. It is only in the final act that Duke Orsino says of Sebastian (and thus also Viola) in almost a throw-away line, "right noble is his blood" (V.i.263). In the issues of both age and rank Olivia has turned gender expectations for courtship upside down, thus giving herself as a woman more chance of equalizing the power balance of the potential relationship. Olivia is also clearly the aggressor, falling in love with Cesario immediately upon his coming to sue for the Duke.

> How now!
> Even so quickly may one catch the plague?
> Methinks I feel this youth's perfections
> With an invisible and subtle stealth
> To creep in at mine eyes.
> (I.v.304–8)

It is Olivia who sends after Cesario to make sure that he comes to visit her again. It is Olivia who woos the reluctant Cesario (III.i, iv) and considers what to bestow on him.

> Here, wear this jewel for me, 't is my picture.
> Refuse it not, it hath no tongue to vex you.
> (III.iv.219–20)

At the court, wearing the miniature of the queen was a sign of loyalty and signal favor. A miniature was also far more personal than the formal large oil portraits. The miniatures were representations of people in private relationships to those who carried them. According to Eric Mercer, oil paintings represented "a statesman, a soldier, a court favourite in all his regalia" while the miniature was "a lover, a mistress, a wife, an intimate friend." Patricia Fumerton concludes, "Even the queen's limnings (at least up into the 1580s) were personal in opposition to her public portraits: representations more of love mistress than of royal queen." By the 1580s many people—both at Court and throughout the country—wished for pictorial images of Elizabeth that they might wear. While courtiers wore jeweled cameos, other poorer subjects expressed their loyalty wearing base-metal medallions. Of course the very coin in one's hand was an im-

Figure 9. Artist unknown, Sir Christopher Hatton holding a jewel
of Elizabeth I (by courtesy of the National Portrait Gallery, London)

age of the monarch, a reminder of one's allegiance. Allison Heisch suggests that Elizabeth's subjects wearing her miniature is comparable to
Catholics wearing holy medals.[29]

The reference in Olivia's speech to the tongue is also interesting—
a recognition perhaps that to a (supposed) man, the image, which is
silent—more controllable—is preferable to the person, who might say
what she wishes. Patriarchal structures particularly saw talkativeness as a
female weakness and silence as the preferred female mode, one to be imposed if necessary. "What restraint is required in respect of the tongue may
appear by that ivory guard or garrison by which it is impaled," Richard

Brathwait argued in his 1631 conduct book, *The English Gentlewoman*.[30] Leonato tells Beatrice in *Much Ado About Nothing* that "thou wilt never get thee a husband if thou be so shrewd of thy tongue" (II.i.18–19). Olivia may be admitting that in speech she is not following the traditional female admonitions to be not only chaste and obedient but silent. Her powerful speech and actions ally her to a queen who also refused to follow these dictates. Elizabeth herself was ambivalent about this "female" characteristic. In 1598 she told an ambassador who congratulated her on her skills in foreign languages that "It was no marvel to teach a woman to talk; it were far harder to teach her to hold her tongue."[31] Yet Elizabeth was proud of her verbal skill, and in 1598 might have believed praise of that more readily than praise of her beauty.

The young men at Court, such as Raleigh and Essex, sought the queen's favors with formulaic expressions of love and wonder, and compared Elizabeth, then in her sixties, with Venus.[32] We might consider Viola's speech when she first meets Olivia as an echo of that hollow praise that was given to the queen.

> Most radiant, exquisite, and unmatchable beauty—I pray you,
> tell me if this be the lady of the house, for I never saw her;
> I would be loath to cast away my speech, for besides that
> it is excellently well penned, I have taken great pains to con it.
> (I.v.175–78)

Olivia's response to the attempted speech, "It is the more like to be feigned: I pray you, keep it in," may also make us think of the queen. Elizabeth too must have recognized the emptiness and ritualism of her courtiers' praise; it came painfully home to her when she compared what Essex wrote to her ("I have preferred your beauty above all things") and his comment to his intimates: "the Queen was cankered, and . . . her mind had become as crooked as her carcass."[33]

The parallel between Elizabeth and Olivia is not an exact one. Olivia *believes* she has fallen in love with a boy—not a younger girl. And it is only the fact that Viola has a twin brother that allows the romance to end happily. Yet it is Olivia, not the man she is to marry, who arranges the wedding ceremony with Sebastian. Leah Marcus has written perceptively about how the crossed-dressed heroines in some sense represent Elizabeth, who presented herself as male as well as female. But I would argue that in *Twelfth Night* it is the powerful Olivia, the woman who is described as one who can

> command her followers,
> Take and give back affairs and their dispatch
> With such a smooth, discreet, and stable bearing
> (IV.iii.17–19)

and who takes the male role of actively seeking the partner she desires, who echoes Elizabeth far more than the crossed-dressed Viola. Stephen Greenblatt notes that Olivia "appears to enjoy ruling her household. . . . One extraordinary woman in the period provided, of course, a model for such a career, lived out to its fullest—the virgin queen, aging and heirless and very dangerous." Jean Howard suggests that, "The political threat of female insurgency enters the text not through Viola, the cross-dressed woman, but through Olivia." While I agree with Howard in this regard I am not so convinced when she continues, "The play seems to me to applaud a cross-dressed woman who does not aspire to the positions of power assigned to men and to discipline a non-cross-dressed woman who does." The discipline comes, Howard argues, in seeing Olivia punished "comically but unmistakably" by being made to fall in love with a man who is really a woman. Howard equates this with the humiliation of Titania magically forced to fall in love with an ass. In *As You Like It* Phoebe is perhaps "punished" for falling in love with a woman dressed as a man (the portrayal of her is not kind), but even here she ends the play with a man who, though not her choice, loves her deeply.[34]

I am far from convinced that Olivia is punished in *Twelfth Night*. She is a powerful woman who concludes the play achieving her own ends. Her "Most wonderful!" (V.i.224) upon seeing both twins sounds like a rapturous triumph. It may be problematic: her husband is a stranger and not the person whom she thought she was originally marrying. Olivia, however, appears not only satisfied but delighted. Olivia, a powerful woman who stays in her female dress but stretches the boundaries of gender expectation, gets what she wants. Olivia is certainly not a direct and complete parallel to Elizabeth, but the queen's presence and example allowed Shakespeare sympathetically to present—and his audience to accept—a powerful, articulate woman who retains the accoutrements of femininity but demonstrates traditionally male characteristics. Olivia, like Elizabeth, does not need to cross-dress to be powerful.

One can certainly argue, as Susan Shapiro does, that the fact of a woman ruler, and one who presented herself as king as well as queen, might well both encourage some women to dress as men for the freedom it afforded them. The hostile response to the cross-dressed women may in part be shaped by the fact that a woman who used male language was ruling and was a potential model for many sorts of unwelcome behavior. On a number of occasions, both formally as well as conversationally, Elizabeth denigrated her female aspect and expressed a desire to be male. In 1565 the queen told de Silva when she heard of Turks defeating Christians that "she was very sorry, and said she wished she was a man to be there in person."[35]

In *Much Ado About Nothing* Beatrice passionately echoes this statement. In the pivotal church scene Beatrice cannot be distracted from her concern over her cousin Hero despite her love for Benedick. "I am sorry for my cousin" (IV.i.273) she says before confessing "I love you with so much of my heart that none is left to protest." Yet when Benedick then encourages Beatrice to ask him to do something to prove his love, she is back to thinking of her cousin and bids Benedick to "Kill Claudio," the man who has wronged her cousin as well as having been Benedick's friend. Benedick's refusal ("Not for the wide world") leads Beatrice to rail against her female state: "O that I were a man! . . .—O God, that I were a man! I would eat his heart in the market place" (IV.i.302, 308). And later she laments not only her gender limitations but also what the definitions of maleness really are and have been. "O that I were a man for his sake! or that I had any friend would be a man for my sake! But manhood is melted into courtesies, valour into compliment, and men are only turned into tongue, and trim ones too; he is now as valiant as Hercules that only tells a lie and swears it.—I cannot be a man with wishing, therefore I will die a woman with grieving" (IV.i.318–25). Dramatically, the scene ends with Benedick convinced: "Enough, I am engaged; I will challenge him" (IV.i.332).

Beatrice in this scene is passionately intense, much more so than Elizabeth, who is forever playing with de Silva over questions of marriage, sexuality, and gender expectations—saying things she knows are not true and could not be true. One can hardly believe that Elizabeth truly wished to be a male and out on the battlefield in the way that Beatrice heartily wished to be able to defend her cousin's honor. Yet Shakespeare's Beatrice cannot be entirely serious either. Hero is not dead. She is still in love with Claudio and wishes to marry him if the question of her honor can be clarified. It would be disastrous for Claudio to be killed—it would turn comedy into tragedy. And Beatrice must know this. Still the words ring with deep sincerity. Elizabeth also, despite all she could accomplish as queen, was aware of what she could not do. Her inability to breach the world of the battlefield left her vulnerable to courtiers/adventurers who might be successful in war and heroes at home.

Elizabeth did not want war because of the expense, because of hating to go to Parliament for the money and leaving herself open to their demands, and perhaps because she truly disliked war. She preferred instead the reputation of being a peaceful ruler. But certainly one of her reasons for disliking war was that it gave others a chance at glory at her expense. At the very beginning of her reign John Aylmer stated as one of the reasons people did not want a woman ruler was that "She is not mete to go to the wars." Though Aylmer refutes this with the argument that "some women have gonne and sped well," certainly this issue plagued Elizabeth throughout her reign.[36] The example of Joan of Arc, well known by Elizabethans as a woman who went to war with demonic aid, would hardly have been a comforting analogy.[37] We can understand her fury at Essex's wholescale ennobling of his followers in Ireland. Knighted by the earl, would they be more loyal to him than to the queen? As Susan Bassnett argues, "The closed world of the army where fortunes could be made by those in command was beyond Elizabeth's powers, try as she might, and this was principally due to her being a woman."[38]

The monarch on the battlefield during the early modern period held great symbolic significance that went far beyond any king's actual military abilities and leadership. Polydore Vergil, writing in the reign of Henry VIII, describes him arguing with his Council that he must go to France in 1513 and personally take command though they consider this to be dangerous and that the king is needed at home to rule. Henry convinces them by explaining about

> the many triumphs over their enemies won by his ancestors when they were leading their armies in person, and, on the contrary, the losses sustained many times by the English state when battles had been fought without the King's presence.[39]

As David Starkey points out, "Henry (or better, Polydore) was not necessarily making great claims for the quality of royal generalship, rather he was talking of the psychological effect of the king's presence on the troops." For Henry one of the prime functions of monarchy was that the king could be on a battlefield, which was one of the reasons he was so appalled at the idea of a female heir. The battlefield, he said at one point, was "unfit for women's imbecilities."[40]

Writing in the early seventeenth century, Fynes Moryson argues that

"Where a king fights in the head of his Army, such braue Soldiers as ours were could not haue suffered want." He goes on to make the point more clearly one of gender and to personalize it to Elizabeth. "Guicciardine writes that the Popes are more abused in their musters of Soldiers then any other prince; which may be true compared with the frugall Venetians, and the States of the lowe Countryes, and with Armyes where the Prince is in person. But I will boldly say that Queene Elizabeth of happy memory, fighting by her Generalls, was incredibly abused in the musters of her Army."[41]

As war with Spain became more and more likely in the later 1580s, Elizabeth's rhetoric also became more powerful and subtle as she attempted through language to imbue herself with the psychological advantage of the brave king on the battlefield. In 1587 she said "that although she was a woman and her profession was to try to preserve peace with neighboring princes, yet if they attacked her they would find that in war she could be better than a man."[42] This statement expands Elizabeth's view of gender. Though she presented a traditional view of what a woman should do, she also suggested *she* could do much more, and in this case no longer wished to be male, but instead asserted that her female self would be more effective than any man. We might think back to *Twelfth Night* and the first time Viola/Cesario sees Olivia, telling her: "I bring no overture of war. . . . I hold the olive in my hand: words are as full of peace as matter" (I.v.215–16).

Elizabeth expressed the ambiguity of being both female and male a number of times very effectively in public presentations. And it seemed to have worked well. In what was obviously not a friendly perspective, one of the Spanish informants in London wrote in 1587 that there were rumors of Spanish ships being sighted off the English coast. He added that "while everybody seemed much alarmed and confused, . . . the Queen had shown a stouter heart than any of them." Earlier in the reign as well, Elizabeth's enemies feared her because of her fierce and "kingly" stance. In 1570 George Lord Seaton went to the Duke of Alva asking for aid for Mary Stuart. Seaton described Elizabeth as "that Woman [who] will, by so great an increase of her Empire, and having secured all at home, grow dreadfull to Neighbours; and her manly Courage, and Sex ambitions of Command, will easily invent ways to imbroil Spain in a long War." The courage Seaton ascribed to Elizabeth was "manly" but the "Sex ambitions to Command" is a description of a woman who causes others to fear her because of her unwomanly attributes. It appears that Seaton was hoping to gain Alva's support with an image that had both male and female elements.[43]

The confusion over Elizabeth as a weak female—and yet also a powerful male—appears as well in John Stubbs's *Gaping Gulf*. We know that Elizabeth was furious about Stubbs's attack on her potential marriage to the Duke of Alençon, and that one reason Stubbs was convinced the marriage was so dangerous was that a husband could so easily dominate a wife since she was "weak." But like Heath, who made the argument against Elizabeth as supreme head because she was female, and then undercut it by calling her "king and queen," so too did Stubbs identify the monarch Elizabeth with male imagery and title. He referred to the French sending to England a

> serpent in the shape of a man, whose sting is in his mouth, and who doth his endeavor to seduce our Eve, that she and we may lose this English paradise. Who because she is also our Adam and sovereign Lord or Lordly lady of this land, it is so much the more dangerous, therefore he so much the more busily bestires him.[44]

Yet obviously for Stubbs Elizabeth being Adam as well as Eve and Lord as well as Lordly lady did not make her any stronger in her relationship with the French interloper, it only made *him* the more dangerous. And one wonders about the perception of any marriage or sexual encounter for a monarch who was both male and female, king and queen.

A bizarre fantasy that also demonstrated both the sexual interest in the queen and the extension of gender boundaries comes from Richard Topcliffe, a man of dubious integrity and strange reputation.[45] An occasional Member of Parliament, and of Puritan sympathy, he was employed by Lord Burghley and described as one of her Majesty's servants. For twenty-five years he zealously hunted and examined recusants, Jesuits, and seminary priests whom, in a 1578 letter to the Earl of Shrewsbury, he referred to as "lewde Popishe beasts." Topcliffe actually had a rack in his own house, and was given authority to examine priests there, where he could do what he wished without being called to account. His rack was of his own invention, and he boasted that, compared to his, others were like child's play. Topcliffe carried his pursuit to extremes, even seducing the daughter of the man in whose house Robert Southwell was hiding to gain information. Many Protestants were horrified by his excesses and he was several times briefly imprisoned for exceeding his instructions. He gained so much notoriety for his actions that putting someone on the rack became known as a "Topcliffian custom," and in court slang to hunt a recusant was to "topcliffizare."[46]

Thomas Portmort, a seminary priest, was one such person hunted.

Portmort was born in Lincolnshire and fled abroad where he was educated at the College at Rheims and later at Rome. He became a priest and was sent back to England to work for its conversion. He was arrested in October 1591 and lodged in Topcliffe's house, where he was racked and pressed hard to give information about Catholic designs on England.[47] According to Portmort, during the course of these examinations Topcliffe proclaimed that "he himself was so familiar with Her Majesty that he hath very secret dealings with her," and had not only seen her legs and knees but felt her belly, saying it was the "softest belly of any womankind." Topcliffe claimed that he was so intimate with Elizabeth that "he many tymes putteth [his hands] betweene her brestes and pappes . . . [and had] his handes above her knees." Elizabeth had said to him, "Be not these the arms, legs and body of King Henry?" To this he had answered "Yea."

Portmont also said that Topcliffe boasted that, if he wanted Elizabeth, he could take her away from any company, and that she had given him such gifts as white linen hose wrought with silk. But she did not save her favors for Topcliffe alone, he maintained: "she was as pleasant with anyone she loved." Topcliffe, outraged, denied having said any of this. Portmort was executed February 21, 1592 for treason. For two hours before his execution, Portmort was forced to stand in his shirt on a very cold day while Topcliffe harangued him to recant his story. Portmort refused, and thus went to his death.[48]

We will never know who invented this story—Topcliffe or Portmort—though it is undoubtedly an invented story, and it was taken for one at the time. John Hungerford Pollen suggests that "Portmort did not allege Topcliffe's words were true. The charge was that he did utter them."[49] If Portmort appears more believable, it is because Richard Topcliffe in general was so untrustworthy. But out of whoever's imagination this came, it is significant in showing Elizabeth as an object of sexual interest. Furthermore, the words put in Elizabeth's mouth, "Be not these the arms, legs and body of King Henry," have a curious ring. Elizabeth did frequently base her rule on the fact that she was her father's daughter, and reminded people often of the similarities between them. Holbein's striking portrait of Henry VIII hung in the Privy Chamber at Whitehall, a reminder to all that she was his daughter.[50] Wrote one visitor, "The King as he stood there, majestic in his splendour, was so lifelike that the spectator felt abashed, annihilated in his presence." Despite the fact that their personal relationship must have been fraught with pain and difficulties for the child Elizabeth during his lifetime, and with horrific flashes of memories for the woman Elizabeth after his death, politically the connection was

Figure 10. Queen Elizabeth and the Defeat of the Spanish Armada
(by permission of St. Faith's Church, Gaywod, King's Lynn)

crucial for her; and it was one that she publicly reiterated throughout her reign. She had her father's red hair, in the form of wig when her own hair faded; she summoned his image often in her speeches; but, as woman and daughter, she did not have his body.[51] Yet Elizabeth really did present herself in ambiguous gender terms—as king as well as queen, as another Henry as well as Elizabeth. Particularly at the crisis of the Armada the image of king was a powerful one for Elizabeth to use.

The feared Spanish invasion was one the most significant crises of Elizabeth's reign. When she went to Tilbury to rouse the troops, she is described as dressed in breast plate, mounted on a charger, with Leicester on one side and the Earl of Ormond, carrying the sword of state, on the other. Her page followed her carrying her helmet.[52] According to eyewitness James Aske, Elizabeth, a "sacred Generall," "marched King-like" as she surveyed the ranks of her soldiers.[53] Camden's account of Elizabeth looking over the troops at Tilbury is more complicated in using both genders simultaneously. He described her "riding about through the Ranks of Armed men . . . with a Leader's Truncheon in her Hand, sometimes with a martial Pace, another while gently like a Woman, incredible it is how much she encouraged the Hearts of her . . . Souldiers by her Presence and Speech to them."[54]

We see the same doubling of genders in Thomas Deloney's ballad, "The Queenes visiting of the Campe at Tilsburie with her entertainment there," which was registered on August 9, the day after the event. Deloney referred to Elizabeth's greatness as coming from the fact that she was "King Henryes royall daughter." He also referred to her "Princely eyes," and described how "came the Queene on pranceing steede / atired like an Angell bright."[55] Elizabeth's description of herself at this moment of national crisis also demonstrates the double image she had of herself as both woman and king, this time presented visually as well as verbally.

> My loving people. . . . I have always so behaved myself that, under God, I have placed my chiefest strength and safe guard in the loyal hearts and good will of my subjects; and therefore I am come amongst you, as you see, at this time . . . being resolved, in the midst and heat of battle, lay down for my God, and my kingdom, and for my people, my honour and my blood, even in the dust. I know I have the body of a weak and feeble woman, but I have the heart and stomach of a king, and of a king of England too, and think foul scorn that Parma or Spain, or any prince of Europe should dare invade the borders of my realm; to which, rather than any Dishonour shall grow by me, I myself will take up Arms, I myself will be your General.[56]

In this statement, unlike the one of the previous year, she said that being a woman made her "weak and feeble," at least in body, and that the person who would herself take up arms and be a general for her people was in spirit a king, not a queen.

This speech was apparently read and reread aloud the next day by officers and by Leonel Sharp, chaplain, to all the soldiers who had not been able to hear Elizabeth, adding even more to the levels of ambiguity. A rather different version, for which Susan Frye makes a persuasive case, was published in 1612, from a 1601 sermon by William Leigh. In this version Elizabeth claimed, "I have beene your Prince in peace, so will I be in warrre . . . come and let us fight the battell of the Lord, the enemie perhaps may challenge my sexe for that I am a woman, so may I likewise charge their mould for that they are but men." Leigh describes Elizabeth's "Princely power, spirit, and praier."[57] Aske's version is also quite different, though he admits he was simply giving "in effect . . . her royall Speech." Here too, however, he refers to her describing her "Kingly faith." Aske described how Elizabeth called her "Seriant Maior" and "did will him do this message from her mouth."[58] Here is a woman's speech, calling herself a king, read aloud in a male voice, further complicating the response to the issue of gender and power.

We might see this scene as a parallel to other public events. Early in her reign, Elizabeth's speeches to Parliament were read by the speaker. In 1566, after the speaker had read her prepared, formal speech, the queen herself stood up to speak as well—a speech by a woman in her own, rather than a male, voice. Whatever the speech, however people heard it, wherever she spoke, the very presence of Elizabeth was a powerful one. Leicester wrote to the Earl of Shrewsbury in a private letter a few days later that, "our gracious Majesty hath been here with me to see her camp and people, which so inflamed the hearts of her good subjects, as I think the weakest person amongst them is able to match the proudest Spaniard that dares land in England."[59]

The issue of womanliness and peace and kingship and war continued to be one Elizabeth explored in the rhetoric at the end of her reign. In her 1593 speech before Parliament, while she seemed to denigrate "her womanhood and weakness," in fact she was proud of these female traits.

> It may be thought simplicity in me that all this time of my reign I have not sought to advance my territories and enlarge my dominions, for opportunity hath served me to do it. I acknowledge my womanhood and weakness in that respect. But it hath not been the hardness to obtain, or doubt how to keep the things so obtained, that only hath withheld me from these attempts. My mind was never to invade my neighbors, or to usurp over any. I am contented to reign over mine own and to rule as a just prince.

She went on, however, to sound more warlike and traditionally "kingly" when she responded to the potential renewed threat of Philip of Spain. "I fear not all his threatenings; his great preparations and mighty forces do not stir me. . . . I doubt not but (God assisting me, upon Whom I always trust), I shall be able to defeat him and overthrow him, for my case is just."[60]

Elizabeth was not the only female member of the royalty in the Renaissance to describe herself in male terms as being more worthy. Marguerite d'Angoulême wrote to her brother Francis I, "All my life I have wanted to serve you not as a sister but as a brother." For all her success at this means of presenting herself, one still senses Elizabeth's recognition of gender limitations, particularly at the end of her reign. In February 1603 she reproved the Venetian envoy because Venice had not sent a resident ambassador. She was convinced this was because England was ruled by a woman instead of a king. This was wrong indeed, since "my sex cannot diminish my prestige," she told the envoy.[61]

William Camden praised Elizabeth's actions throughout her reign in terms that were both positive and masculine. Discussing Elizabeth at the beginning of her reign, he wrote: "Queen Elizabeth, being a Virgin of a manly Courage, professed that she was an absolute free Princess to manage her actions by her self or her Ministers." Camden believed that she demonstrated this same courage four decades later. When the Lopez conspiracy was exposed in 1594, there was great concern over the possibility of a plot to have the queen poisoned; Elizabeth, however, "remained undaunted, with a manly spirit." Another interesting example from the end of the reign that demonstrates how the English people regarded Elizabeth is an anonymous commonplace book which contains some scenes from the play *Henry IV* written down from memory. The writer of the book, however, changed king to "queene." Perhaps this was an unconscious mistake, since to an Elizabethan, monarch had come to mean queen.[62]

In one of her last public speeches, her golden speech to Parliament in November 1601, Elizabeth deftly combined traditional male and female characteristics to provide a view of monarchy that extends gender definitions.

> To be a King and wear a crown is a thing more glorious to them that see it, than it is pleasant to them that bear it. For myself, I was never so enticed with the glorious name of a King or royal authority of a Queen, as delighted that God hath made me His instrument to maintain His truth and glory, and to defend this Kingdom (as I said) from peril, dishonour, and tyranny and oppression. . . .

Elizabeth ended her speech with a statement that sounds overwhelmingly female in gender expectation, presenting herself as one whose great strength came in the love she had, almost suggesting an all-loving mother, and implying that this was the key to her successful reign. "And though you have had, and may have, many mightier and wiser princes in this seat, yet you never had, nor shall have any, that will love you better."[63]

Yet for all of the use of male as well as female images, for all the doubling that occurred, Elizabeth existed in a female body. She presented herself to her Court and her country grandly and sumptuously as a queen. But sometimes people also spied her not so prepared, less the perfect queen, and more the imperfect—and real—woman. These glimpses may also have been calculated, and demonstrated not only her power but the ambivalence at the very heart of her monarchy. At eight in the morning on the first of May 1578 (May Day has a variety of connotations of its own) Gilbert Talbot was walking in the Tiltyard beneath the gallery where Elizabeth would stand at the window and watch her courtiers running at tilt. Though no performance was going on, Elizabeth was then standing at the window and Talbot looked up and saw "where by chance she was, and, looking out the window, my eye was full towards her, she shewed to me greatly ashamed thereof, for she was unready, and in her nightstuff." Elizabeth, in her nightgown, not ruffed and curled, was ashamed, as she told Talbot later. But she was also still his queen, whether presented in that fashion or not, and the one who had something to lose over the incident was not Elizabeth but Talbot. That evening, Talbot reported, "it pleased her to speak to me very graciously. . . . when she she saw me after dinner, as she went to walk, she gave me a great fillip on the forehead, and told my Lord Chamberlain, who was next to her, how I had seen her that morning, and how much ashamed thereof she was."[64] We might consider that Elizabeth would know that she could be observed from the Tiltyard when she stood at the window in her nightclothes, and yet she stood there anyway. Even without her queenly trappings, she was the one who held power. Yet there is also something vulnerable perhaps about this woman, in her private dress, standing looking down. Elizabeth might incorporate both male and female in her sovereignty, but her body was a very human female one and, hence to both Elizabeth herself and to her people, an imperfect one. Her people might regard her body politic as both pure and virginal, and the incarnation of the sacred principle of male monarchy, but the rumors and seditious words so carefully gathered suggest a perception of her body natural as potentially corrupt in a manifestly female way.

Robert Cecil said after Elizabeth's death, in what was certainly not entirely a compliment, that Elizabeth was "more than a man, and in truth, less than a woman." Perhaps he should have said instead that she was more than a man and more than a woman too. Shakespeare's magnificent heroines, powerful articulate women characters, spoke on the Elizabethan stage in male voices, and, in Rosalind's case at least, appeared in the epilogue in her female dress, the character referring to herself as the male actor and making it explicit to the audience that though he represented a female character, in the end it *was* a male actor. "If I were a woman I would kiss as many of you as had beards that pleas'd me, complexions that lik'd me, and breaths that I defied not" (*As You Like It*, Epilogue, 18–20).[65] The appearance of the actor in female garb serves as an echo to Elizabeth's multi-layered self-presentation. And Elizabeth, though she might have "the heart and stomach of a king," *had* a woman's body. Yet Elizabeth as queen and king, as both powerful and female, blurred the definitions of gender and role expectation in her particular position as ruler of Renaissance England.

7. Dreaming the Queen

On March 20, 1601 John Garnons, who had previously been a justice of the peace, wrote to Sir Robert Cecil in concern over some dreams that John Notte, "a gentleman well affected in religion," reported that his wife Joan had shared with him.[1] Notte assured Garnons he was "importunately moved by my wife" to deliver these notes to Garnons. Joan Notte was Garnons's godchild, which may be why they decided to use him as their intermediary. The Nottes had recorded not only Joan's dreams but also conversations, mostly about Robert Devereux, the Earl of Essex, she had overheard over the last few years that seemed to them at this time to possibly be treasonous. The dreams, which Joan Notte had on two successive Saturdays in early 1601, were "warnings against assassination to be addressed to the Queen and to Sir Robert Cecil."[2] Of course the early spring of 1601 was such a chaotic, dangerous time that one can imagine anyone having nightmares: only the month before Essex had marched armed with his followers through the streets of London, a rebel against his queen.[3] We know today that worries during the day are often reflected in dreams at night, a phenomenon of which some Elizabethans were aware as well. In *Terrors of the Night* Thomas Nash claimed, "A Dreame is nothing else but the Echo of our conceipts in the day. . . . In the day time wee torment our thoughts and imaginations with sundry cares and devices; all the night time they quake and tremble after the terror of their late suffering, and still continue thinking of the perplexities they have endured."[4] Joan Notte's dreams, like her memories she described at the same time, are filled with fear over the role the Earl of Essex was determined to play and what danger this posed for Elizabeth.

*   *   *

In 1601 the Essex rebellion shattered a dream about Elizabeth as sacred and glorious monarch as well as questioning her success at dealing with the issues of gender and power. Joan Notte's dreams, as well as some others to be discussed, lead us to a discussion of ways people felt about the queen at the end of her reign, how she responded, and how her image was used after her death. The concerns of the reign—the queen's sexuality, her ability to rule, the problems of the succession—are reflected in the dreams at the end of the reign, and in some of the pamphlets written both before and after her death. That Notte's dreams, among the few recorded dreams about Elizabeth, also include Essex, demonstrates his significance in reshaping attitudes toward Elizabeth, and the confluence between waking fears of danger and unconscious concerns and desires. We can see Essex as a touchstone for the problems and fears over Elizabeth's reign as it was nearing its close. Though Essex is not a character in all the recorded dreams we have, his concerns, the pressures he placed on Elizabeth to be the queen he desired her to be, and his actual presence in some of the dreams demonstrate the tensions and conflicts of Elizabeth's reign from the mid-1580s when he first appeared at court. A discussion of Essex will bring us back to the dreams in which he eventually appears.

Robert Devereux, second Earl of Essex, had first come to the court as a young man in 1584, protégé of his stepfather, Elizabeth's favorite, Robert, Earl of Leicester and son of her hated rival, Lettice Knollys Devereux. Both Essex and Sir Philip Sidney fought in the Low Countries; when Sidney was dying from his wounds after the battle of Zutphen in the fall of 1586, he left his sword to Essex. As McCoy points out, "Essex took on this chivalric legacy with reckless ardor."[5] For much of the populace as well, Essex took Sidney's place as the representative of honor and chivalry. In 1590 at the age of twenty-three Essex even secretly married Sidney's widow, Frances Walsingham. Elizabeth forgave Essex this marriage. That year she had already helped the financial burden that came in part, but only in part, from his reckless extravagance. Elizabeth gave him the "Farm of Sweet Wine" for a ten-year period. Essex had the right to levy all duties on sweet wines from the Mediterranean, which provided him with a considerable income. On Michaelmas Day 1600 this monopoly would revert back to the Crown. In 1590 ten years must have seemed an unimaginable amount of time to the twenty-three-year-old Essex; in 1600 Elizabeth's refusal to renew the monopoly was unmitigated financial disaster and the breaking point that led Essex to rebellion.

In the 1590s Elizabeth was also concerned over Essex's propensity for foreign adventures that were spectacular failures. While in Dieppe in 1591

Figure 11. Robert Devereux, second Early of Essex, from the studio of Marcus Gheeraerts the younger (by permission of the National Gallery of Art, Washington DC)

Essex promised Elizabeth once he returned to stay at court and not become involved in more foreign adventures.

> The two windows of your privy chambers shall be the poles of my sphere. . . .
> When your Majesty thinks that heaven too good for me, I will not fall like a
> star, but be consumed like a vapour by the same sun that drew me up to such

a height. While your Majesty gives me leave to say I love you, my fortune is as my affection, unmatchable. . . . It is not in your power, as great a Queen as you are, to make me love you less.[6]

But Essex was not to stay within this sphere, nor would he stay constant, and his love was as artificial as the language in which he expressed it.[7] Essex charmed Elizabeth, but he also alarmed her. He was wildly extravagant, he had outbursts of temper if he he did not get his way and his followers were not promoted to his satisfaction, and the martial exploits in which he delighted were too often highly costly. They yielded little, making Essex a glamorous hero to the populace but providing nothing practical for Elizabeth. Both at Rouen in 1591 and after the capture of Cadiz in 1596 Essex dispensed knighthoods with the abandon that would later characterize his behavior in Ireland.[8] Essex's letters to Elizabeth flattered her as if she were his lover, and put the problems between them within the context of a lovers' quarrel instead of the disagreements of a sovereign with a courtier. Essex wrote Elizabeth in 1597: "Since I was first so happy as to know what love meant, I was never one day, nor one hour, free from hope and jealousy . . . they are the inseparable companions of my life. If your Maj. do in the sweetness of your own heart nourish the one, and in the justness of love free me from the tyranny of the other, you shall ever make me happy. . . . I humbly kiss your fair hands. Your servant in love and duty before all men."[9]

But Essex was also scornful of Elizabeth as monarch. Essex confided in the French Ambassador André Hurault de Maisse that Elizabeth's "delay and inconstancy proceeded chiefly from the sex of the Queen."[10] Mervyn James argues that Essex's "relationship to the queen . . . became progressively charged with a tension which contained the seeds of violence. The tension, rooted in political failure and exclusion, was related to his view of their respective sexual roles, and the language in which this was expressed . . . the terminology of honour." The relationship between Essex and the queen finally exploded at a Council meeting in 1598 over whom to send to Ireland as Lord Deputy. The need was urgent, but the situation was so difficult no one was eager for the dubious honor. Essex's candidate was Sir George Carew. Few were impressed by Essex's panegyric of Carew, since it was well known that Carew was a friend to Robert Cecil and an enemy of Essex, and this was an all-too-transparent ploy to get one of Cecil's supporters away from Court and into a difficult situation. Elizabeth, well aware of the intensification of factionalism at her Court in the 1590s, dismissed Essex's suggestion. Losing his temper altogether, Essex "uncivily turned his Back upon her as it were in Contempt, and gave her a scornfull Look."[11] Furious at the insult, Elizabeth stood, too, and boxed Essex on the ear, bidding him go and be hanged. Essex's response horrified the already riveted Privy Councilors. He put his hand on his sword, an act that could be construed as treason. Charles Howard, Lord Admiral, had to step between the queen and Essex. Rather than realizing the gravity of what he had done, Essex declared he would not put up with so great an indignity; he would not have taken such an affront even from the hands of Henry VIII himself. He then stormed out and withdrew from Court. Though Henry VIII had died twenty years before Essex was born, the image of the king was extremely powerful, and Elizabeth herself frequently liked to invoke and to invite comparison with it. Yet the chance that Henry would have tolerated any such behavior as Essex performed was remote; despite his contempt the earl was fortunate indeed to be dealing with the daughter instead of the father, even if he did not realize it. Essex's letter to Elizabeth after this incident was hardly an apology; indeed, it seemed to demand one from her.

> Madam,—When I think how I have preferred your beauty above all things, and received no pleasure in life but by the increase of your favour towards me, I wonder at myself what cause there could be to make me absent myself one day from you. But when I remember that your Maj. hath, by the intolerable wrong you have done both me and your yourself, not only broken all laws of affection, but done against the honor of your sex, I think all places better than that where I am, and all dangers well undertaken, so I might retire myself from the memory of my false, inconstant, and beguiling pleasures. . . . I was never proud, till your Maj. sought to make me too base. And now since my destiny is no better, my despair shall be as my love was, without repentance.[12]

Mervyn James suggests that "The so-called 'great quarrel' of July 1598, the point of no return in relations between Essex and the queen, generated so much bitterness precisely because of the earl's assessment of their respective sexual roles in terms of honour."[13]

Despite the provocation, the queen and Essex patched up the quarrel, though the old intimacy was replaced by wariness. Elizabeth had other worries. To her great grief, in August of 1598 Lord Burghley died. His final advice to his son Robert was to "serve God by serving the Queen, for all other service is indede bondage to the devill." And the situation in Ireland was becoming more and more critical. In September Essex returned to the Council. At a council meeting Elizabeth suggested that if Essex knew what was best for Ireland he should go there. If he were finding fault with all the candidates for Lord Deputy, he should have the post himself. Being Essex, he could not refuse. "I am tied to my own reputation," he wrote, though "I am not ignorant what are the disadvantages of absence."[14]

Elizabeth told him he must stay in Ireland, since leaving it leaderless in such a time of crisis could be very dangerous. "We do charge you (as you tender our pleasure) that you adventure not to come out of that kingdom." Essex's command in Ireland was disastrous. He did not engage Tyrone. Rather, against explicit instructions and for little cause but courting his own popularity, he was again lavish with knighthoods; fifty-nine gentlemen were dubbed. His command in Ireland was such a failure he himself was aware of it, though he blamed the queen and Council, not himself. Though prohibited by the queen's orders, in September 1599 he returned to London. As soon as he and his small band landed in England, he made for London with great haste. He had to see the queen before she heard of his coming. Essex moved so swiftly that he burst into the court at Nonesuch, went straight through the presence chamber and the privy chamber, and into the queen's bedroom. The queen had had no idea that Essex was even in England when he strode into her bedchamber to find an Elizabeth who had just awakened, "with her hair about her face," no wig, unadorned, no formal dress that was part of the artifice of monarchy.[15] She did not know if he had come alone or had an army behind him. Faced with the chaos of this potentially dangerous intrusion, Elizabeth soothed Essex as he incoherently explained his presence. She suggested he return to her when they had both had time to prepare properly for such a meeting, and Essex emerged to say, that however stormy it had been abroad, there was sweet calm at home. But Elizabeth, once she had a greater grasp of the situation, was extremely distressed.[16] Essex was sent from Court and committed to Lord Keeper Egerton's charge at York House. After some months he was allowed to move to Essex House and by August 1600, after a commission had investigated the charges against him, and he had made his submission, Elizabeth agreed to his liberty with the proviso that he not come back to Court. But for Essex to retire to the country for a private life had other problems. He was deeply in debt; if Elizabeth did not renew the "Farm of Sweet Wines" he would be ruined. Essex sent Elizabeth letter after despairing letter begging to be allowed to return to Court and for the renewal of the monopoly. October 30 Elizabeth announced the grant would not be renewed. For Essex this meant ruin.

By the beginning of 1601, Essex House was the center of deep anti-Court feelings. In early February a group of conspirators met at the Earl of Southampton's lodging to discuss Essex's proposals for seizing the Court, the Tower, and the city and to force Elizabeth to change her advisors, particularly Robert Cecil in favor of Robert Devereux. The conspirators hoped they might do this without violence, but, as Sir Christopher Blount stated before his execution, "And although it be true, that . . . we never resolved of doing hurt to her Majesty's Person . . . yet, I know, and must confess, if we had failed of our ends, we should (rather than have been disappointed) even had drawn blood from herself." [17] At the same time Sir Gelly Meyrick went to the Globe theatre to ask the Lord Chamberlain's Men to stage a special performance of *Richard II* with the deposition scene included. On Saturday February 7, a group of Essex's followers attended the performance. [18] That same evening the Council summoned Essex to appear before them. Essex refused. Having thus lost his possibility of taking the Court by surprise, he fell back on his scheme to rouse the city of London in his favor with the claim that Elizabeth's government had planned to murder him and sold out England to Spain.

That evening and early Sunday morning (February 8) Essex and his followers hastily planned the rising. He and his followers, about two hundred young noblemen and gentlemen, made their way to the City with Essex shouting, "For the Queen! For the Queen! A plot is laid for my life!" Meanwhile, Robert Cecil had sent a warning to the Mayor and a herald who denounced Essex as a traitor in the streets of London. At the word traitor many of the earl's followers disappeared and none of the citizens joined him as he had expected. Essex's position was obviously desperate, and he decided to return to Essex House, which he managed to do by way of the river. The queen's men, under Lord Admiral Charles Howard, Earl of Nottingham, besieged the house. By the evening, after burning incriminating letters and documents, Essex surrendered. His rebellion had lasted twelve hours. Essex, the Earl of Southampton, and the other followers were placed under arrest.

Four days after the failed uprising, on February 12, Captain Thomas Lee, an admirer of Essex's, complained of injustice to Essex. Lee suggested that a half dozen men could confront Elizabeth and force her to free Essex and Southampton. Guards arrested Lee that evening as he lurked outside the queen's apartment. He was charged with planning "to lay violent hands on her sacred person, and to take her prisoner; thinking by that means to set at liberty the earls of Essex and Southampton, and other Traitors now in prison." Lee was found guilty and executed at Tyburn.

Elizabeth's Council, convinced the danger was not passed, had men stationed throughout the city for several weeks to keep the peace, fearing there might be an uprising of apprentices to free Essex from the Tower.[19]

On February 13 letters were sent to summon the peers of the realm who would sit in judgment of the two earls. The next day the government gave elaborate instructions to preachers throughout the country ordering them to present the government's point of view in their Sunday sermons. They should preach that Essex had plotted to overthrow Elizabeth and become king. Special prayers and thanksgivings were ordered to praise God for delivering England and its queen. On February 19, less than two weeks after the aborted rebellion, the Earl of Essex and the Earl of Southampton were brought from the Tower to Westminster to be tried for treason. The trial lasted only a day and the guilty verdict was a foregone conclusion. Most of Essex's fellow conspirators—including Southampton—turned against Essex in an attempt to escape some of the blame. Both earls were found guilty and condemned to death. On Ash Wednesday (February 25), 1601 Essex was beheaded in the confines of the Tower.[20] Lady Sandys had perhaps the most damning epitaph for him, in a letter to Robert Cecil: "Wild Essex's craft . . . hath been unlucky to many but never good to any. I would he had never been born."[21]

Curtis Breight has argued that labeling Copinger, Arthington, and Hacket as insane for their uprising of 1591 was political, and "no one judges Essex a madman for hoping that London would revolt against Elizabeth." But indeed Sir John Harington got exactly that impression after visiting Essex in 1600. Essex, Harington perceived, "shyftethe from sorrowe and repentaunce to rage and rebellion so suddenlie, as well provethe him devoide of goode reason or righte mynde . . . he uttered strange wordes borderinge on suche strange desygns, that made me hasten forthe and leave his presence."[22]

*   *   *

It is hardly surprising that news of the rebellion would invade people's dreams and cause them to bring warnings such as Joan Notte's to the authorities. One might speculate that people often dreamed about Elizabeth, though we have few recorded dreams of her. It may well have been too dangerous a topic to discuss.[23] Sixteenth-century English people were fascinated by their dreams, and Notte's worry that these dreams might presage ill to the queen was a common view of dreams as foretelling.[24] People in early modern Europe treated night-time visions with real seriousness, as Richard Kagan and Charles Carlton have demonstrated. Many people in the Renaissance, such as Francis Bacon and William Laud, recorded their dreams, and some were convinced that dreams were the way God spoke.[25]

Thomas Hill's *The moste pleasaunte arte of the interpretacion of dreames* (1576) was widely read. Much of Hill's book considers the issue of dreams as prophecy, and he distinguishes between "true dreams" and "vain" ones. Some people have

> vain dreames, no true signifiers of matters to come but rather shewers of present affections and desirers of the body. And yet dreames seene by grave & sober personnes, do signifie matters to come, and a spirite undoubtedlie shewinge to them, whiche by her nature is a Prophetesse. . . . Therefore this difference of true dreames from vayn ought diligently to be noted.

Hill reports many strange dreams, having to do with the universals of sex, death, and nourishment. Some of the interpretations are very specific to sixteenth-century issues; others are strangely modern. And some, like Notte's dream, also deal with royalty. Dreaming of kings or queens can mean a variety of things. Dreaming of a dead monarch would have a different meaning from dreaming of a live one. "The dream that hee seeth a Prince long a gone dead, with a mery countenaunce or lokynge merely, signifyeth a vaine hope to follow." But "to bee kissed of an Emperour or kynge, or to talke wyth him, signifyeth gayne with joy." Yet to dream of a queen "signifyeth deceite to follow." And the symbols in some dreams imply dangers to monarchs even if they are not in the dream. "To see the Sunne darkened, signifyeth the perill or danger of a king." Books like Hill's could provide a reading public with some pleasure if not an understanding of their dreams.[26]

Then as now, many people obviously dreamed, even if their dreams did not always have a political content. But the worry over the political nature of dreams, their prophetic ability, was much greater in the sixteenth century. If Hill's book worked as a guide to the meaning of dreams, James I disparaged dreams as prophecy to his son Henry in *Basilikon Doron*. "Take no heede to any of your dreames, for all prophecies, visions, and propheticke dreames are accomplished and ceased in Christ: And therefore take no heede to fret either in dreames, or any other things; for that errour proceededth of ignorance, and is unworthy of a Christian." This perspective would have been widely known in the early seventeenth century.

When James became king of England in 1603, thousands of copies of *Basilikon Doron* were printed and sold in the first few weeks of his reign.[27]

We do not know if Elizabeth agreed with her Scottish cousin that one could not foretell from one's dreams, nor do we even know about what the queen herself dreamed. The only hint that Elizabeth ever discussed her dreams is in a letter Christopher Hatton sent to Robert Dudley in June of 1578, and we cannot tell whether it was a real dream or a way for Elizabeth to speak indirectly. Hatton warned Leicester that

> Since your Lordship's departure the Queen is found in continual great melancholy. The cause thereof I can but guess at, notwithstanding that I bear and suffer the whole brunt for her mislike in generality. She dreameth of marriage that might seem injurious to her, making myself to be either the man or a pattern of him. I defend that no man can tie himself or be tied to such inconvenience as not to marry by law of God or man, except by mutual consents, as both parties, the man and woman, vow to marry each to other, which I know she hath not done to any man and therefore by any man's marriage she can receive no wrong.[28]

Hatton may have wondered what marriage was invading Elizabeth's dreams. And we might wonder if this was an actual dream at all. It was in the midst of the marriage negotiations with the Duke of Alençon, and given how problematic those negotiations turned out to be, Elizabeth might well have anxious dreams, whether she wanted to share them or not. There is some sense, however, that someone else's marriage is troubling the queen, since Hatton may be "either the man or a pattern of him." And the marriage that would most trouble Elizabeth, though theoretically she did not know of it, was Robert's secret marriage to Lettice Knollys, the widowed Lady Essex, in 1578.[29] Though this marriage was not brought out into the open until Simier told Elizabeth as a bargaining chip for allowing Alençon to come to England the next year, enough people knew for it to be quite possible that Elizabeth had some hint of it. Given her long relationship with Robert Dudley, it is certainly possible that dreams of his marriage might well be part of her unconscious.[30]

James warned against believing in dreams; in much the same fashion Thomas Nash gave a number of examples of princes' dreams that did not accurately presage the events accorded them. "To come to late dayes; Lewes the xi. dramt that he swam in blood on the toppe of the Alpes: which one Father Robert (a holy Hermit of his time) interpreted to present death in his next warres against Italy: though hee liv'd and prosperd in all his enterprises a longwhile after."[31] Nash also told of Cornelius

Agrippa misinterpreting Charles V's dream at the siege of Tunis and much the same happening to Alphonso of Naples. "These examples I alledge, to prove there is no certaintie in dreames; and that they are but according to our devisings and mediations in the day time."[32] But it is doubtful that either James or Nash would emphasize this point if many people did not believe in prophetic dreams, especially at times of political crisis. For example, in the latter end of August 1588 "one Brookes" sent Burghley three dreams he had he wanted to tell the government about "for I thought it was good for the Realm of England." Brookes's dreams, optimistic in a time of great fear of Spanish invasion, were filled with bright silver lights.[33] A dozen years later the level of anxiety in the country was even higher.

Early in February 1601 an anonymous letter to Elizabeth expressed the great fear her people had. "Your most obedient and loving subjects do with grievous sighs and tears behold the dangerous stay and standing both of your person and commonwealth. . . . A woeful and a dangerous time is this for us poor sheep to live in, when wolves and foxes shall thus prey upon our chiefest shepherds! . . . Thus praying for your majesty's long and prosperous reign, we conclude, most earnestly and most humbly entreating your Grace with speed mercifully to consider lest we all perish together. Your Majesty's poor distressed commonwealth full of bleeding hearts."[34] Risk to the queen meant risk to the people and the commonwealth. The sense of insecurity and anxiety was considerable. Equally, Notte was so impressed by his wife's dreams that he had recorded them and shared them with Garnons. Cecil, of course, was getting these dreams third hand—from Notte's wife to Notte, to Garnons, and now to Cecil (and hundreds of years later to us). The dreams, and the conversations that Joan Notte reported at the same time, greatly concerned Garnons. "Though some part of the said writings seems to be phantastical dreams, yet other part are to be tried out and the offenders punished. Had I been still in the commission of the peace, I would have searched out some of it myself. Had age and health permitted, I would have brought you the papers with my own hand."[35]

Joan Notte had two dreams she thought important enough to share with the government. In each of them a variety of beasts threaten both Elizabeth and Sir Robert Cecil. In one of the dreams Anne Boleyn is also a character. Joan Notte described how, although she had been dead for nearly seventy years "Queen Anne Boleyn . . . appeared warning Queen Elizabeth not to go further from London than St. James." Joan Notte would never have even seen Anne Boleyn, who died long before Notte was born.[36] We do not know whether she had ever seen Elizabeth either, though she might well have; Notte had been to London during the last few years, and Elizabeth did go on progress throughout the countryside. Of course, we can never know even with our own dreams why certain people and symbols appear, much less with the dream of a woman who lived hundreds of years earlier. Carlton cautions that "There are no forms of evidence more ephemeral than dreams. Trying to make head or tail of one's own dreams is difficult enough, without dealing with those of someone long dead." But, as Louis Montrose has also pointed out, a discussion of an Elizabethan dream can allow us "to emphasize the historical specificity of psychological processes" and allow "us to glimpse the cultural contours of an Elizabethan psyche."[37] So we might speculate as to why in Joan Notte's dream it is Elizabeth's mother rather than her father Henry VIII who comes back to deliver the warning. Perhaps Joan Notte as a woman imagined that a mother would be the one to care most, even more than a father, over what happened to their child, especially a daughter as opposed to a son. Or it may be that Anne Boleyn's own spectacular and horrific death was so much a matter of public memory that any worry over the fate of Elizabeth would coalesce with the image of that ritualized slaughter, the beheading, of the earlier queen. Joan Notte may have envisoned a connection between Anne Boleyn, a queen consort whose vulnerability was expressed by attacks on her sexual reputation and her inability to have a living son, and Elizabeth, queen regnant, who was called whore by some of her subjects and also had no heir of her body. Anne Boleyn was killed by her husband, the man who had so desired her, written her impassioned love letters, and waited almost seven years to make her his queen. Though over thirty years younger than the queen, Essex beseeched her favors by acting like a lover, and the rumors of sexual misconduct that had been circulating throughout the reign about Leicester and Hatton had their last appearance in whispers about Elizabeth and Essex. Henry the king had had his wife Anne executed. Essex might kill Elizabeth to become the king. And why does Anne Boleyn warn her daughter not to leave the city? The court near London was the center of power; for Elizabeth to leave, to abandon that power, would put her at terrible risk.

Joan Notte's second dream even more explicitly deals with the dangers of Essex and fears over the succession. Worries about Essex's role must have been in Notte's mind for a long time as we can see from the conversations she reported she heard about Essex and his claims over the previous few years. She described an actual trip she made to London, and how she was staying at an Inn near Charing Cross, while she sent one of her men to see if her lodgings at Paul's Wharf were ready. She was alone in her room near the window, and overheard in the courtyard below a serving man ask another: "Is great Robin out?" After some other speeches, which she could not completely understand since some strangers were coming in and out, one of them swore, "By God's wounds, the very city will set him up, for they have offered to pay all his debts for him." As the two men were leaving, one said to the other, "Thou shall see good sport among them before the end of the summer, if they walk abroad." Joan Notte was not sure whom they were discussing, "but by imagination since, and by hearing, which before she knew not, that the great man's name was Robert."[38]

The Nottes were concerned not only about the Earl of Essex himself but also about his supporters, one of whom they apparently knew personally. It is clear from the information John Notte presented Garnons that he and wife were acquainted with Sir Gelly Meyrick, a close confederate of Essex. Meyrick was the eldest son of the bishop of Bangor. His father had died when he was still a boy and from an early age Meyrick had made his fortune as a soldier, eventually serving with the young Earl of Essex in the Netherlands in the the mid-1580s. Essex made Meyrick the steward of his household, and Meyrick accompanied Essex on a number of his expeditions including Portugal, Normandy, Cadiz, and eventually the ill-fated Irish campaign. Meyrick, like so many others, received his knighthood from Essex, and was fanatically loyal to the earl. Joan Notte reported how at Christmas two years previously she had talked with Edward Reavell, "gentleman, a valiant soldier of the Low Country, that served under Sir Thomas Baskerville, and the son of Thomas Reavell, of Kilgarren in Pembrokeshire," and how he had told her about a conversation between two soldiers, one a follower of Meyrick and one of Mr. Roger Vaughan; both Meyrick and Vaughan were supporters of Essex. According to Reavell as reported by Notte, when the soldiers saw Essex, one said:

"There goeth," quod he (meaning by the Earl), "he that will be King of England one day." "Yea!" said the other, "and the old woman (meaning her Majesty) were dead." "Tush!" said the other, "dead or dead not, he will be king one day." "Then," said Mr. Vaughan's man, "My master, the great Vaughan is left at home to trust to guide the country, but if it so fall out, thy master" (meaning Meyrick) "will sure be a Duke and my master" (meaning the Vaughan), "will sure be an Earl at the least."[39]

Joan Notte also reported how at "another time" (she does not say when or how recent this conversation was) she had mentioned Meyrick to a Mrs. Powell, who also knew him. Mrs. Powell replied that Meyrick "the priest's son [showing she knew something of his background] hopeth for that day that I trust he never shall see." Joan asked her what was the day to which she was referring. "Mary!" said Mrs. Powell, "he hopeth to see his master king of England one day." Joan Notte expressed herself amazed. "What doth the two legged ass mean? For there is no colour nor likelihood thereof. I would I might hear one of the best of them dare to speak it." Mrs. Powell admitted that "they will keep their speeches secret enough, but sure I am this is their hope." This conversation translated itself into a dream about Meyrick. "Another dream was that a gentleman walking with Sir Gelly Meyrick, asked who after her Majesty should carry the crown. 'Who,' quoth he, 'but my Lord of Essex.'" This dream also apparently contained Elizabeth threatened by beasts. "In the dreams various beasts seemed to offer hurt to the Queen and to Sir Robert Cecil."[40]

The dreams and the statements John Notte gave Garnons were quite incendiary. His purpose, however, was not to cause trouble. Notte assured Garnons that "I speak this only of my fervent love to her Majesty." Given that by March 20, when Garnons is writing to Cecil, the rebellion is not only over but both Essex and Meyrick as well as some other followers are dead, Joan Notte's dreams are perhaps all too timely. Essex had been executed February 25 and Meyrick March 13.[41]

Though few people joined Essex in his march through the streets of London, he was an ever popular symbol and his rebellion and execution demonstrated all too clearly the fissures at the end of the reign over the policies of and responses to the queen. The concept of a major political event awakening the nation from a dream would have been familiar to Elizabethans. Robert Greene used this metaphor far more positively when writing about why God allowed Philip to send the Armada. God "brought in these Spaniardes to waken us out of our dreames, to teache the brave men of this realm that after peace comes warres." And in the 1590s this was exactly Essex's point; peace brought luxury and corruption, while warfare encouraged bravery and virtue. Essex's battles with Elizabeth over this issue broke the dream of her reign apart. The dreams of dread and warning Joan Notte had about Elizabeth reflect a sense that for Elizabethans in some sense their dream of Elizabeth as Gloriana is also ending. Joel Hurstfield argues perceptively, "Essex crashed through the gossamer fabric of her pride. There was nothing left, for he cruelly described the frailties of her body stripped of her trappings of her royal glory. The cult hero or heroine is also the cult victim. The god who is worshipped is also the god who is sacrificed."[42]

We do have several other examples of dreams others had about the queen. Interestingly enough, like Notte's dream, they occur at the end of the reign, and some are not even English, suggesting how far the impact of Elizabeth had spread. In 1590 a twenty-one-year old woman, Lucrecia de León, daughter of a legal clerk in Madrid, was arrested on the order of Philip II himself and brought before the Spanish Inquisition because of the widespread publicity her dreams had gotten. Lucrecia's dreams were highly critical of Philip and prophesied disasters for Spain because of the king's shortcomings and misguided policies. Critics of the king encouraged Lucrecia to tell her dreams and record them. Kagan suggests that, "The real importance of these dreams lies in their social and political criticism of Philip's Spain . . . as glosses on historical events."[43]

Lucrecia's dreams reflected the political concerns and worries of many people as Spain was preparing for war with England. Lucrecia watched helplessly in her dream as a Spanish nobleman, "a traitor to his king," wrote to Elizabeth about the true state of affairs in Spain. In some of her dreams Lucrecia visited foreign countries. In one such dream she saw Elizabeth, aided by her Protestant allies, preparing for the invasion of Spain. Her most vivid and horrifying dream of Elizabeth occurred on December 18, 1587, when she dreamed that she and a guide visited a palace in London. The queen, a fifty-year-old woman, was seated on a long bench. In the queen's lap "is a dead lamb whose stomach is cut open, its guts and entrails exposed. The Queen is busily shoving her hands into the stomach cavity and scooping up the animal's blood. Next to her sits a woman dressed in widow's weeds. When the Queen asks the woman to drink some of the lamb's blood, the woman refuses. Suddenly, in anger the Queen draws her sword and in a single stroke cuts off the woman's head."[44] The imagery here is powerful and horrific indeed. Lucrecia's dream guide does not explain the symbolism of this grisly scene, but the lamb, a particularly potent religious image that often represented Christ himself, might well suggest persecuted Catholics, and Kagan's identification of the widow as Mary Stuart, executed ten months earlier, is convincing.

The image of blood was even more central in the sixteenth century than our own. "God's blood!" or even just "Blood!" was used as an oath.[45] This is a powerful, masculinized queen, not afraid of blood or slaughter, who actually offers blood to drink, and expertly wields her sword against those who refuse her commands. We might question if the queen is offering blood as a parodic inversion of the mass itself. In the dream the ritual, with sword as well as blood, expresses not redemption but death. Lucrecia's contemporaries also found the dream powerful and disturbing, demonstrating Elizabeth's ruthlessness as an enemy of Spain. Lucrecia had met Doctor Alonso de Mendoza, a canon attached to the cathedral of Toledo, three months earlier. "It was after studying this particular dream that Mendoza avowed that Lucrecia's dreams 'do not proceed from an evil spirit, nor do they appear to be fictions composed by either human or diabolical invention; rather, they are truths advising us about the rigorous justice from heaven that we deserve for our sins.' "[46]

The preparations for the Armada caused great concern among the Spanish during the summer of 1588; the defeat of the Armada brought these feelings of vulnerability to the surface. Belief in Lucrecia's power grew ever stronger when her well-publicized dreams came true. "Her various dreams of Queen Elizabeth conspiring with Spain's enemies bespoke the fear then on every Spainiard's mind." In the fall of 1589 Lucrecia had another dream about the English queen. She dreamed of Spain's losses to an English fleet in the Indies that picked off treasure ships, and of Elizabeth gloating over the silver her ships had captured. Lucrecia's dreams suggest the power of Elizabeth's image in Spain; while Joan Notte was English, and may well have actually seen Elizabeth, Lucrecia de León in Spain had certainly not. Yet this did not stop her from dreaming of her and visualizing her in a particularly powerful, almost demonic fashion.[47]

Another person to dream about Elizabeth at the end of her reign—and to record his dreams—was the astrologer and physician Simon Forman.[48] He recorded in his diary on January 23, 1597 that he

> dreamt that I was with the Queen, and that she was a little elderly woman in a coarse white petticoat all unready. She and I walked up and down through lanes and closes, talking and reasoning. At last we came over a great close where were many people, and there were two men at hard words. One of them was a weaver, a tall man with a reddish beard, distract of his wits. She talked to him and he spoke very merrily unto her, and at last did take her and kiss her. So I took her by the arm and did put her away; and told her the fellow was frantic. So we went from him and I led her by the arm still, and then we went through a dirty lane. She had a long white smock very clean

and fair, and it trailed in the dirt and her coat behind. I took her coat and did carry it up a good way, and then it hung too low before. I told her she should do me a favour to let me wait on her, and she said I should. Then said I, "I mean to wait upon you and not under you, that I might make this belly a little bigger to carry up this smock and coat out of the dirt." And so we talked merrily; then she began to lean upon me, when we were past the dirt and to be very familiar with me, and methought she began to love me. When we were alone, out of sight, methought she would have kissed me.[49]

In what is all too often the ways of dreams, at that most interesting of moments Forman awoke. Montrose analyzes the dream in terms of Forman's unconscious linking of Elizabeth, mother of her country, and his own mother. As Montrose points out, the depiction of Elizabeth in the dream uncannily echoes actual descriptions of Elizabeth's appearance in 1597 and her impact on those who saw her. Forman's dream, with its sexual overtone, suggests the contradictory domination of queen over subject yet male over female. The woman in the dream is both queen and lover, both subordinate and in power. Though there is an obvious sexual component to the dream, in particular the white smock trailing in the dirt, the queen is not presented as a traditionally appealing sex-object. Forman did not dream of Elizabeth in the idealized form in which she preferred to be described, a "Venus" in Raleigh's words. Instead, Forman's dreamer's eye created a realistic portrait of an aging woman. Her attraction comes from her powerful position, the desire for sexual intimacy a desire for the power that intimacy with the sovereign confers. Montrose suggests that, "The aged Queen's body exerts a power upon the mind of Doctor Forman; and, in his dream, he exerts a reciprocal power upon the body of the Queen. . . . In the context of the cross-cutting relationships between subject and prince, man and woman, the dreamer insinuates into a gesture of homage, a will to power." Montrose delights in the connection of the weaver in Forman's dream and Shakespeare's *A Midsummer Night's Dream*. "It is strange and admirable that the dreamer's rival for the Queen should be a weaver—as if Nick Bottom had wandered out of Shakespeare's *Dream* and into Forman's." But Rowse finds more compelling Forman's description of the weaver as "a tall man with a reddish beard," since this could well be a description of Essex. If Rowse is right, how intriguing that yet another dream of Elizabeth is also a dream about Essex. In the dream the weaver "spoke very merrily unto her, and at last did take her and kiss her," a parallel Rowse may be right in making given the erotic element to the exchanges between the elderly queen and her young courtier. But what may be most interesting about the description, and eerily prophetic, is that this weaver is "distract of his wits," as one might well describe Essex to be, particularly in the last few years of his life.[50] By 1597 Forman and others in London may have already perceived the earl's dangerous and erratic mood swings.

A month later Forman had another dream about Elizabeth, this time "coming to him all in black, with a French hood." In the first dream Elizabeth wore white; in the second she was completely in black. White and black together were the Renaissance colors representing virginity and purity, and Elizabeth often wore them. Much earlier in her reign she referred to them as "my colors."[51] But if her white dress might well suggest Elizabeth's virginity, as well as the concerted attack on it by both the tall redheaded weaver and Forman himself, the later dream has a more somber tone. The queen all in black may suggest Forman's recognition that the reign is ending and that a dark time is coming for all of England, and he may perceive an Elizabeth who has not provided fully for her people. Oddly, given the Elizabethan view of dream as prophecy, at Elizabeth's funeral in 1603, John Clapham described how "first went two hundred and sixty poor women, four in a rank, appareled in black, with linen kerchiefs over their heads."[52] Elizabeth's headcovering, her French hood, is particularly interesting. Not only was this a head-dress women wore in the sixteenth and seventeenth centuries, but it could have a more specific meaning. There are cases in the late sixteenth century where women were forced to wear it during punishment for unchastity, again expressing at its deepest roots the discomfort with an unmarried queen, and the intersections of sexuality and power in considering Elizabeth.[53]

One reason for the intense insecurity and upset of the 1590s and the reactions to the Essex rebellion were the fears over the succession as Elizabeth became older and her death a more immediate possibility. Forman's second dream may suggest his fears over Elizabeth's death. Another image of her death appeared in Peter Wentworth's *A Pithie Exhortation to her Majestie for establishing her successor to the crowne*, a tract concerned with the succession. Written in 1587, it was in circulation in manuscript from 1589, though not published until 1598, in Edinburgh, two years after Wentworth's death. The tract was addressed to Elizabeth and urged her speedily to summon a Parliament that would then settle the succession on the rightful heir. Wentworth begged Elizabeth to name a successor; he recounted all the horrors of previous reigns if this were not done, and how such an act could secure the peace and safety of the country. If Elizabeth did not do so she courted the wrath of God and the enmity of her people after her death. Her very body would be scorned and mistreated.

> Wee beseeche your Majestie to consider, whither your noble person is like to come to that honorable burial, that your honourable progenitours have had. . . . Wee do assure ourselves that the breath shall be no sooner out of your body . . . but that all your nobility, counsellours, and whole people will be up in armes . . . and then it is to be feared, yea, undoubtedlie to be judged, that your noble person shall lye upon the earth unburied, as a dolefull spectacle to the worlde. . . . The shame and infamie hereof, wee beseeche your grace to be careful of . . . . Againe, we feare. . . . [that] you shall leave behind you such a name of infamie throughout the whole world.[54]

Wentworth's graphic imagery of what could happen to Elizabeth's body after her death works as parallel to her physicality in the dreams of her subjects as the reign was darkening.

Wentworth, after years in prison, was dead and not a member of the final Parliament of her reign in 1601. But despite her golden speech it was not an altogether happy occasion for Elizabeth. Few members saluted her with the customary "God save Your Majesty." John Neale describes Elizabeth leaving Parliament after its opening session: "As the Queen passed through the throng of Commons on her way out of the Upper Chamber she was silent and aloof, depressed there is reason to think, in health and spirit." Yet her love for her country came through in her closing speech of that Parliament, her last public speech to the realm. "This testimony I would have you carry hence for the world to know: that your Sovereign is more careful of your conservation than of herself, and will daily crave of God that they that wish you best may never wish in vain."[55]

London had refused to support Essex, even though he was the darling of the people. Eighteen months after his execution, however, a German visitor reported he heard only "Essex's Last Goodnight" sung in the streets of the city. And in the Court, people observed how much the queen had aged since the Essex Rebellion. One of James VI's confidants received a letter from someone at Elizabeth's court telling him that, "Our queen is troubled with a rheum in her arm, which vexeth her very much, besides the grief she hath conceived for my lord of Essex's death. She sleepeth not so much by day as she used, neither taketh rest by night. Her delight is to sit in the dark, and sometimes with shedding tears to bewail Essex."[56] John Manningham heard that six weeks before Elizabeth died she had to have the coronation ring cut from her finger; probably because her hands were swollen. "Dr. Parry told me the Countess Kildare assured him that the

Queene caused the ring where with shee was wedded to the crowne, to be cutt from hir finger some 6 weekes before hir death." Manningham adds in his diary entry, "but wore a ring which the Earl of Essex gave hir unto the day of hir death." Perhaps Elizabeth really did wear the earl's ring until the day of her death; perhaps it is yet another romantic, if contemporary, story that links together Elizabeth and Essex.[57]

By March of 1603 it was obvious to all that Elizabeth was deeply ill and would not recover. In March John Manningham recorded in his diary that he heard from Dr. Parry "that hir Majestie hath bin by fitts troubled with melancholy some three or four monethes, but for this fortnight extreame opressed with it, in soe much that shee refused to eate anie thing, to receive any phisike, or admit any rest in bedd, till within these two or three dayes. She hath bin in a manner speacheles for two dayes, verry pensive and silent." The French Ambassador wrote to Henry IV that the "Queen continued to grow worse and appeared already in a manner insensible, not speaking sometimes for two or three hours . . . holding her finger almost continually in her mouth, her eyes open and fix'd upon the ground." Robert Carey described how "the Queen grew worse and worse, because she would be so, none about her being able to persuade her to go to bed. . . . On Wednesday, the 23d of March, she grew speechless." On her deathbed Elizabeth never officially named James as her heir.[58] By then, however, she did not need to do so. Everyone assumed it, and men rushed from court to be the first to tell the Scottish king that Elizabeth was dead. The transition to James ran smoothly, and despite Wentworth's chilling prophecy James gave his predecessor a splendid funeral, in fact spending more money on hers than he would later on for those of his wife or his son, and building her a magnificent monument.[59] Yet most of the ceremonial that spring was welcoming James rather than mourning Elizabeth.

In March of 1603 for many of the English the return of the rule by a king was a welcome relief. For example, Stephen Smithe told Richard Wilder on March 24 when they were discussing the death of Elizabeth that, "our soveraigne lord of the Kinges Majestie that now is . . . Thankes be to god for him wee hope wee shall not now need to fear anie thinge."[60] The splendid dresses Elizabeth used to accentuate her special role as queen, which availed her of the aura of sacred monarchy, were reduced to being raided as costumes for Anne of Denmark's masques.[61] Yet within a few years this mood of thanksgiving was over. James's Scottishness, his favorites, his extravagances, his policies, especially peace with Spain, all led to dissatisfaction. Within two or three years of Elizabeth's death there began to be a nostalgia for "good Queen Bess" and the glories of her reign that swelled by the 1620s.[62] During the reign of James, William Camden wrote his "romantic and patriotic interpretation" of Elizabeth's reign. Simonds D'Ewes also considered writing "the history of the raigne of that most excellent princes, Queen Elizabeth." Her accession day, November 17, began to be celebrated again as it had been during her lifetime, "a perfectly safe way, of showing dislike of James's pro-Spanish foreign policy." David Cressy suggests that "as personal memory faded, the anniversary observances became further detached from the person of the queen, and promoted instead her mythic role as a Protestant deliverer." Ironically, however, much of what Elizabeth's reign was used to represent would have been values she herself deplored. Perhaps the best queen of all is a dead one; one who can be made to stand for whatever one wishes, one who can look down from heaven and advise on how things on earth ought to be different.[63]

Elizabeth is such a character in John Reynolds's 1624 pamphlet, *Vox Coeli, or News from heaven*. Publication of this pamphlet led to Reynolds's arrest.[64] With a sense of humor, Reynolds claimed his pamphlet was published in Elisium. The news from heaven was a conference held by Henry VIII, Edward VI, Mary, Elizabeth, Anne of Denmark, and Prince Henry to discuss contemporary issues in England, particularly the proposed match of the Spanish Infanta with Charles, and to vote on whether or not it should take place. "The newes of these projects," such as the proposed marriage, "having with as much fortunary as celeritie, passed the cloudes and pierced the vaults and windowes of heaven, it fast arrived there, to the understanding of that immortall mayden Queene Elizabeth, whose heart ever loved England as her soule did heaven." For our purposes the most interesting voice is that of Elizabeth, but the oddest person to be there is Mary. Despite her celestial home, she is characterized as vindictive and ill-tempered, just as Protestants would have viewed her on earth. Reynolds needed Mary as a foil, and he explained her presence in heaven by the prayers of forgiving Protestants. Mary speaks in favor the monk who assassinated Henry IV of France and proudly states of her marriage to Philip, "If we had any males, England had beene long since a province of Spaine." Elizabeth, with equal bluntness, responds: "God knew so much, and therfor prevented it; wherein I blesse his mercy and providence, as also your sterilitie."[65]

The Elizabeth of *News* knows God is on the side of her and Protestant England. Speaking of the Armada, she claims, "Yea, God was so gracious

Figure 12. Posthumous portrait of Elizabeth I by Francis Delaram after Nicholas Hilliard in T. Browne's translation of Camden's *Annales*, 1625 (by permission of the Folger Shakespeare Library)

to England, and so mercifull to mee, as not only my ships and people, but the windes and waves fought for my defence, and that of my countrey, against the pride and malice of Spane, who grew mad with anger and pale with griefe, to see this his great and warlike armado beaten, foyled, and confounded." She wants a strong and militaristic England and is horrified by the news that James had let the English fleet deteriorate. "What . . . my royall-navy lye rotting. . . . when I felt them, were capable to beate the power and pride of Spaine to shivers. O this grieves me!" This Elizabeth has forgotten the Essex rebellion of 1601 and admires the earl for his militaristic adventures, referring to him as "noble Essex" and "my Essex."[66]

Not only does being in heaven seem to have caused problems with Elizabeth's memory and reworked her values, it also seems to have changed Essex's view of his queen, or so it appears in a tract written by Thomas Scott and also published in 1624. Scott was a chaplain to James I, but in 1620 he published a tract, *Vox Populi*, against the proposed marriage of the Prince Charles and the Spanish Infanta. The pamphlet was suppressed and Scott fled the country. Though he returned briefly, he left permanently in 1623, and served as preacher to the English garrision at Utrecht. He continued to write pamphlets against Catholics, many of which were published in England. In a bizarre twist of fate, Scott was assassinated coming out church on June 18, 1626 by John Lambert, an English soldier subject to strange hallucinations. When ministers went to Lambert to help him prepare for his execution, "They found him as uncapable of instruction, and as full of his fond and imaginarie conceits as before." Lambert explained that his sovereign "daily and hourely appeared unto him as the spirit of the late Queene Elizabeth. . . . And from these vaine fantasies he could not bee brought neither by threatning of his temporall death, nor of his soules damnation hereafter."[67]

In Scott's tract, the ghost of Essex states, "You had a queene, in my time on earth, who was ever open handed to men of desert, yet never wastfull in her private expences; but maintayned armies and garrisons, not a few; a well-rigged navy; assisted and lent money to her neighbouring states."[68] The problems between Essex and his queen are ignored. Joan Notte's dream portrays the fears of what Essex might do to Elizabeth because she did not support him and his policies in the way he desired. Notte as dreamer had Elizabeth's mother as the one who tried to warn the queen. In the depiction of Elizabeth twenty years after her death, Elizabeth is in the presence of her father, sister, and brother. There is no mention of Anne Boleyn. It is odd to think of Elizabeth so surrounded by family; when one considers her reign, one is more often to agree with Francis Bacon on how isolated Elizabeth was from family: "Those that continue unmarried have their glory entire and proper to themselves. In her case was more especially so; inasmuch as she had no helps to lean upon in government, except such as she had herself provided; no own brother, no uncle, no kinsman of the royal family, to share her cares and support her authority."[69] Elizabeth, surrounded by family, has been transformed into the queen for whom Essex wished, martial, ready to spend money for militaristic displays, concerned with glory.

During her lifetime Elizabeth had been greatly loved, but in her reign as an unmarried woman who wielded power, refused to be the modest woman who listened to her advisors and preachers, and would not marry or name a successor, she had provoked deep anxieties and fears. By the end of the reign of her successor, the conflicts posed by her gender and use of power had been smoothed away to present a queen who finally could be made to support whatever was wanted. John Reynolds and

Thomas Scott portrayed such an Elizabeth in heaven, very different from the image of the woman in peril in Joan Notte's dream. Yet all these representations, these ways in which Elizabeth was dreamed and envisioned, never quite got to the heart of the queen. In the end Elizabeth was, as Sir Francis Bacon wrote, "ever her own mistress."[70]

Notes

Abbreviations used

APC	*Acts of the Privy Council of England*
CSP, Domestic	*Calendar of State Papers, Domestic Series*
CSP, Foreign	*Calendar of State Papers, Foreign Series*
CSP, Rome	*Calendar of State Papers, Relating to English Affairs Preserved Principally at Rome, Elizabeth, 1572–78*
CSP, Scotland	*Calendar of State Papers, Relating to Scotland and Mary, Queen of Scots, 1547–1603 Preserved in the Public Record Office, the British Museum, and Elsewhere in England*
CSP, Spain	*Calendar of the Letters and State Papers Relating to English Affairs Preserved in, or originally Belonging to, the Archives of Simancas*
CSP, Venice	*Calendar of State Papers and manuscripts relating to English affairs, existing in the archives and collections of Venice, and in other libraries of Northern Italy*
DNB	*Dictionary of National Biography.*
L&P	*Letters and Papers of the Reign of Henry VIII*
OED	*Oxford English Dictionary*
Salisbury Papers	Historical Manuscripts Commission. *Calendar of the Manuscripts of the Marquis of Salisbury Preserved at Hatfield House*
SP	*State Papers in the Public Records Office*

Chapter One: Introduction

1. Chapter six deals extensively with this and her other speeches; see note 43 there for a discussion of the evidence that these were her words.

2. Within the last few decades there have been many superb works on women's history that provide a complex theoretical structure to questions of historic gender roles, women's status, and avenues toward power for women. Works by such historians as Joan Kelly, Gerda Lerner, Joan Scott, and Natalie Davis have been instrumental in helping me form my own ideas about Elizabeth I and how to understand her within the context of larger issues about gender and history.

3. I am here following the lead of historian Jenny Wormald, who states unequivocally, "There can be no doubt of her failure as a ruler." *Mary Queen of Scots: A Study in Failure* (London: George Philip, 1988), 187.

4. Recently there have been a number of new biographies and studies of Elizabeth. Within the last few years we have seen the publication of Susan Bassnett, *Elizabeth I: A Feminist Perspective* (Oxford: Berg, 1988); Christopher Haigh, *Elizabeth I: Profile in Power* (London and New York: Longman, 1988); Anne Somerset, *Elizabeth I* (New York: Alfred A. Knopf, 1991); Christopher Hibbert, *The Virgin Queen: The Personal History of Eizabeth I* (Reading, MA: Addison-Wesley, 1991), Rosalind K. Marshall, *Elizabeth I* (Owings Mill, MD: Stemmer House, 1992), and Maria Perry, *The Word of A Prince: A Life of Elizabeth I from Contemporary Documents* (Woodbridge: Boydell Press, 1990). Bassnett's focus is interesting but the book is brief. Somerset's study is especially solid and accomplished; however, all these books except Haigh's are biographies. While Haigh's is also thematic, his approach is completely different from mine and examines Elizabeth in relationship to a variety of groups such as the nobility, the Council, the Court, and Parliament. My work complements but does not duplicate the work of such English Renaissance literary scholars as Louis Montrose, "Shaping Fantasies: Figurations of Gender and Power in Elizabethan Culture," *Representations* I, 2 (Spring, 1983), 61–94 and his "The Elizabethan Subject and the Spenserian Text," in *Literary Theory/Renaissance Texts*, ed. Patricia Parker and David Quint (Baltimore: Johns Hopkins University Press, 1986), 303–40; Leah Marcus, "Erasing the Stigma of Daughterhood: Mary I, Elizabeth I, and Henry VIII," in *Daughters and Fathers*, ed. Lynda E. Boose and Betty S. Flowers (Baltimore and London: Johns Hopkins University Press, 1989), 400–417; Marcus, "Shakespeare's Comic Heroines, Elizabeth I, and the Political Uses of Androgyny," in *Medieval and Renaissance Women: Literary and Historical Perspectives*, ed. Mary Beth Rose (Syracuse, NY: Syracuse University Press, 1986), 135–53; Marcus, *Puzzling Shakespeare: Local Reading and Its Discontents* (Berkeley and Los Angeles: University of California Press, 1988); John N. King, "Queen Elizabeth I: Representations of the Virgin Queen," *Renaissance Quarterly* 43 (Spring 1990), 30–74; King, *Tudor Royal Iconography: Literature and Art in an Age of Religious Crisis* (Princeton, NJ: Princeton University Press, 1989); King, *Spenser's Poetry and the Reformation Tradition* (Princeton, NJ: Princeton University Press, 1990); Philippa Berry, *Of Chastity and Power: Elizabethan Literature and the Unmarried Queen* (New York: Routledge, Chapman &

Hall, 1989); Susan Frye, *Elizabeth I: The Competition for Representation* (New York and Oxford: Oxford University Press, 1993). The work of Montrose, Marcus, and King has influenced my own thinking about Elizabeth, though I also disagree with some of their conclusions. As literary scholars they use their insights on Elizabeth to discuss the major writers of the time such as Shakespeare and Spenser and to place a study of Elizabeth within a framework of the impact of her reign on literary development. Berry's work, and even more Frye's, present interesting ways to see Elizabeth's impact, but their approaches are very different from mine. Berry's work explores the interrelationship between love discourses and the cult of Elizabeth; Frye is particularly concerned with pageant and ceremony. I am grateful to Professor Frye for sharing her manuscript with me prior to its publication. Allison Heisch has written important articles on Elizabeth's use of rhetoric and methods of power from a feminist perspective, though she is more critical of Elizabeth than I am, and, I would argue, places Elizabeth too much in a twentieth-century perspective. "Elizabeth I and the Persistence of Patriarchy," *Feminist Review* 4 (1980), 45–56; "Queen Elizabeth I: Parliamentary Rhetoric and the Exercise of Power," *Signs* I, 1 (Autumn, 1975), 31–55. As well as the new biographies of Elizabeth, John Neale's remains the standard. *Queen Elizabeth I* (1934; rpt. Garden City, NY: Anchor Books, 1957). Also insightful is the work of Elizabeth Jenkins: *Elizabeth the Great* (London: Victor Gollancz, 1958) and *Elizabeth and Leicester* (New York: Coward-McCann, 1962).

5. Jan Vansina, *Oral Tradition as History* (Madison: University of Wisconsin Press, 1985), 6. For a discussion of the cultural significance of gossip, see Max Gluckman, "Gossip and Scandal," 307–16, Robert Paine, "What is Gossip About? An Alternative Hypothesis," *Man* II, n.s. (1976), 278–85, and Gluckman's response to Paine, "Psychological, Sociological, and Anthropological Explanations of Witchcraft and Gossip: A Clarification," 20–34. Patricia Meyer Spacks provides an excellent treatment of gossip in literature in *Gossip* (Chicago: University of Chicago Press, 1985).

6. D. M. Loades, *The Tudor Court* (Totowa, NJ: Barnes and Noble, 1987), 169–70.

7. In 1503 Henry VII had applied to the pope for a dispensation for his son Henry to marry Catherine, since according to Leviticus it was against Biblical law for the two to marry. By the 1520s, though this may have simply been a ground that Henry used to dissolve his marriage, A. F. Pollard early argued "there is no reason to doubt Henry's assertion, that he had come to regard the death of his children as a Divine judgment, and that he was impelled to question his marriage by the dictates of conscience." *Henry VIII* (1902; new ed. London: Jonathan Cape, 1970), 143. J. J. Scarisbrick adds, "The miscarriages, and still-births, the denial of a son were clearly divine punishment for, and proof of, transgression of divine law." *Henry VIII* (Berkeley and Los Angeles: University of California Press, 1968), 152. Henry came to believe, when Pope Clement did not give him the annulment he sought, that even a pope could not dispense with this law and his marriage had never been valid. See Scarisbrick for a lengthy discussion of the legal and biblical ramifications of the divorce.

8. Retha Warnicke's provocative study of Anne Boleyn argues that the fetus

was deformed, thus convincing Henry the child was not his. *The Rise and Fall of Anne Boleyn* (Cambridge: Cambridge University Press, 1989).

9. See Marc Shell, *Elizabeth's Glass: With "the Glass of the Sinful Soul" (1544) by Elizabeth I, and "Epistle dedicatory" and "Conclusion" (1548) by John Bale* (Lincoln: University of Nebraska Press, 1993), 16 for a provocative discussion of views about incest and how this effected Elizabeth's relationship with Seymour.

10. G. B. Harrison, ed., *The Letters of Queen Elizabeth I* (London: Casell and Co., Ltd., 1935), 11, 13.

11. Somerset, *Elizabeth I*, 95; Alison Plowden, *Marriage with My Kingdom: The Courtships of Queen Elizabeth I* (New York: Stein and Day, 1977), 25.

12. His recognized illegitimate son, Henry Fitzroy, the Duke of Richmond, had died in 1536. Though John Perrot claimed to be Henry's son, the claim was not made in Henry's lifetime and he was never formally recognized as such.

13. *Cobbett's Complete Collection of State Trials and Proceedings for High Treason and Other Crimes and Misdemeanors from the Earliest Period to the Present Time*, ed. Thomas Bayly Howell (London: R. Bagshaw, 1809–26), I, 746, 747.

14. The one other attempt at having a woman rule had been disastrous. Henry I had attempted to force his barons to accept his daughter Matilda as his heir in the twelfth century. After Henry's death most of the barons abandoned Matilda for her cousin Stephen, leading to a civil war that was only resolved when Matilda's son became Henry II.

15. A number of historians have recently argued that in England in the early sixteenth century, most of the population were satisfied with Catholic forms of worship, and even after the break with Rome, there is little evidence, despite a few strongly committed men and women, of an early rapid move toward Protestantism. See especially Susan Doran and Christopher Durston, *Princes, Pastors and People: The Church and Religion in England, 1529–1689* (London and New York: Routlege, 1991); J. J. Scarisbrick, *The Reformation and the English People* (Oxford: Blackwell, 1984); Rosemary O'Day, *The Debate on the English Reformation* (London and New York: Methuen, 1986); Peter Lake and Maria Dowling, eds., *Protestantism and the National Church in Sixteenth Century England* (London: Croom Helm, 1987).

16. Harington to Mr. Robert Markham, 1606, John Harington, *Nugae Antiquae: Being a Miscellaneous Collection of Original Papers*, ed. Henry Harington and Thomas Park (London: Vernor and Hood, 1804), I, 360.

Chapter Two: Elizabeth as Sacred Monarch

1. John Knox, *Works*, ed. David Laing (Edinburgh: James Thin, 1895), IV, 366–67, 369, 375, 415, 380, 353; Patricia-Ann Lee, "A Bodye Politique to Governe: Aylmer, Knox and the Debate on Queenship," *The Historian* LII, 2 (1990), 248. Knox, despite the tone of his apology, was concerned about Elizabeth's reaction, as was Cecil. Protestants in Scotland looked to Elizabeth, and some of her Council hoped to see more active English support there.

2. John Aylmer, *An Harborrowe for Faithfull and Trewe Subiectes* (London: J. Daye, 1559). The original edition of the book is only occasionally paginated. The issue of "mixed monarchy," or what limits could be put on the ruler became critical in the seventeenth century. Certainly Aylmer's work suggests it was already being considered in the sixteenth as well, as Michael Mendle points out. "Aylmer's *An harborowe* . . . is a part of the shaky foundation for later mixed government, a part of the process by which Tudor Englishmen familiarized themselves with a strange and alluring vocabularity of politics; but it was . . . more wishful thinking and polemical exaggeration than a fair statement of fact." *Dangerous Positions: Mixed Government, the Estates of the Realm, and the Answer to the xix Propositions* (University: University of Alabama Press, 1985), 48. See also Corinne Comstock Weston and Janelle Renfrow Greenberg, *Subjects and Sovereigns: The Grand Controversy over Legal Sovereignty in Stuart England* (Cambridge: Cambridge University Press, 1981). My thanks to Gordon Schochet for these references.

3. Knox, *Works*, IV, 381.

4. "John Aylmer did eventually become bishop of London, but not until 1577. Elizabeth . . . may have disliked the condescending tone of his defence of the rule of women." William Haugaard, *Elizabeth and the English Reformation: The Struggle for a Stable Settlement of Religion* (Cambridge: Cambridge University Press, 1968), 49. The more traditional perspective was described in the nineteenth century by John Lingard. "His tract . . . made his fortune; the queen gave him preferment in the church, and in due time he was raised to the see of London." *The History of England from the First Invasion of the Romans to the Accession of William and Mary in 1688* (London: J. C. Nimmo and Bain, 1883), VI, 674. To put both Knox and Aylmer in context of other Renaissance writings, see Rebecca Bushnell, *Tragedies of Tyrants: Political Thought and Theater in the English Renaissance* (Ithaca, NY: Cornell University Press, 1990); Paula Louise Scalingi, "The Scepter or the Distaff: The Question of Female Sovereignty, 1516–1607," *The Historian* 41 (1978), 59–75; James E. Phillips, Jr., "The Background of Spenser's Attitude Toward Women Rulers," *Huntington Library Quarterly* 5 (1941), 5–32.

5. For a discussion of this issue in general, see Stephen Orgel, *The Illusion of Power: Political Theater in the English Renaissance* (Berkeley: University of California Press, 1975); Orgel, "Making Greatness Familiar," in *The Power of Forms in the English Renaissance*, ed. Stephen Greenblatt (Norman: University of Oklahoma Press, 1982), 41–47; Steven Mullaney, *The Place of the Stage: License, Play, and Power in Renaissance England* (Chicago and London: University of Chicago Press, 1988); Leonard Tennenhouse, *Power on Display: The Politics of Shakespeare's Genres* (London and New York: Methuen, 1986); Roy Strong, *Art and Power: Renaissance Festival, 1450–1650* (Bury St. Edmund's Suffolk: St. Edmundsbury Press, 1984). Roy Strong, *Splendour at Court: Renaissance Spectacle and the Theater of Power* (London: Weidenfeld and Nicolson, 1973).

6. As a counterpoint to the position of the homilies, however, is the acknowledgment in the Edwardian and Elizabethan prayer books that celibacy is a special gift.

7. "Of Excess of Apparel" is probably the work of Bishop Pilkington, and "On Marriage" is in part a translation from Velt Dietrich of Nuremberg. John

Griffiths, ed., *The Two Books of Homilies to be read in Churches* (Oxford: at the University Press, 1859), xxviii, xxxiii, xxvi–vii. *Sermons or Homilies Appointed to be Read in Church in the Time of Queen Elizabeth*, 4th ed. (Oxford: at the Clarendon Press, 1816), 259, 261–62.

8. *Sermons or Homilies*, 425, 427, 429; Haugaard, *Elizabeth and the English Reformation*, 275.

9. John Bruce, ed., *Correspondence of Matthew Parker* (Cambridge: at the University Press, 1853), 66. De Feria wrote to Philip that "The Queen has already declared in parliament that she will not be called head of the church, whereat the heretics are very dissatisfied." 11 April 1559, *CSP, Spain*, I, 52. But many Protestants were upset with the term. Haugaard, *Elizabeth and the English Reformation*, 105; Norman Jones, *Faith by Statute: Parliament and the Settlement of Religion, 1559* (Cambridge: Cambridge University Press, 1982), 131. How much influence Lever really had with Elizabeth is another matter. While reformers might take credit for the decision, Elizabeth balanced many issues and perspectives.

10. Jones, *Faith by Statute*, 130; John Strype, *Annals of the Reformation* (Oxford: at the Clarendon Press, 1821), I (ii), 406–7. Heath was soon after deprived of his see and briefly committed to the Tower. Elizabeth had not forgotten, however, that Heath had proclaimed her queen, and he was soon after set at liberty on condition that he agree not to publicly meddle with matters of religion, an undertaking he accepted. See *DNB*, IX, 345–46.

11. Hastings Robinson, ed. and trans., *The Zurich Letters* (Cambridge: University Press, 1846), I, 42.

12. Jones, *Faith by Statute*, 132. This was also recognized at the time. John Parkhurst wrote to Bullinger in May 1559: "The Queen is not willing to be called the head of the Church of England, although this title has been offered her; but she willingly accepts the title of governor, which amounts to the same thing." *Zurich Letters*, I, 38. Some Catholics also realized there was little distinction and still expressed horror over her title of supreme governor. Cardinal William Allen wrote in 1588, "As to her behaviour, she hath professed herself a heretic. She usurpeth, by Luciferian pride, the title of supreme ecclesiatical government, a thing in a woman unheard of, not tolerable to the masters of her own sect, and to all Catholics in the world most ridiculous, absurd, monstrous, detestable, and a very fable to the posterity." Lingard, *The History of England*, VI, 706. Of course, in calling Elizabeth "monstrous," Allen is echoing Protestant zealot Knox.

13. Haugaard, *Elizabeth and the English Reformation*, 129.

14. For example, over the question of the vestiarian campaign, "Parker felt that he was fighting a lone battle without support from the Privy Council or even from the queen who had ordered him to take action. . . . She also refused his request for a private royal letter to Grindal ordering him to execute the law. . . . Elizabeth probably did not think it her place to order one of Parker's suffragans to obey an unequivocal command that she had already relayed to the archbishop in proper form. . . . She would not subvert ecclesiastical order—even at the primate's own request. . . . Parker's position was difficult. Throughout the controversy the non-conformists publicly blamed him and his bishops as if they had foisted the campaign for uniformity on the queen." Haugaard, *Elizabeth and the English*

Reformation, 219, 220. Wallace MacCaffrey argues that "at the outset of her reign [Elizabeth refused] to give her bishops of the new order the kind of royal backing they desperately needed." *War and Politics, 1588–1603* (Princeton, NJ: Princeton University Press, 1992), 550.

15. Thomas Hill, *The moste pleasaunte arte of the interpretacion of dreames* (London: T. Marsh, 1576).

16. The king's evil was the disease scrofula, a tubercular inflammation of the lymph glands of the neck. Marc Bloch, *The Royal Touch: Sacred Monarchy and Scrofula in England and France*, trans. J. E. Anderson (London: Routledge and Kegan Paul, 1973), 130.

17. Quoted in Raymond Crawfurd, *The King's Evil* (Oxford: Clarendon Press, 1911), 45.

18. On Good Friday sovereigns went to the altar on their knees (known as creeping to the cross) and blessed metal in a dish by altar. This metal was then fashioned into rings that were said to be particularly effective in the treatment of epilepsy and cramp, and especially of use for pregnant women. For more on cramp rings, see Crawfurd, *The King's Evil*, 47; Bloch, *The Royal Touch*, 92–107; Keith Thomas, *Religion and the Decline of Magic* (New York: Charles Scribner's Sons, 1971), 198–99. Eric W. Ives discusses how valued cramp rings were in the reign of Henry VIII. *Anne Boleyn* (London: Basil Blackwell, 1986), 138. Many different amulets were used in this period to try to protect a pregnancy. See Audrey Eccles, *Obstretrics and Gynaecology in Tudor and Stuart England* (Kent, OH: Kent State University Press, 1982); M. J. Tucker, "The Child as Beginning and End: Fifteenth and Sixteenth Century English Childhood," in *The History of Childhood*, ed. Lloyd DeMause (New York: Psychohistory Press, 1974), 229–57, and Angus McLaren, *Reproductive Rituals: The Perception of Fertility in England from the Sixteenth to the Nineteenth Century* (London and New York: Routledge, Chapman, and Hall, Inc., 1984).

19. Max Weber, *On Charisma and Institution Building*, ed. S. N. Eisenstadt (Chicago and London: University of Chicago Press, 1968), 12. T. J. Scheff, *Catharsis in Healing, Ritual, and Drama* (Berkeley: University of California Press, 1979), 111.

20. For a rebuttal of this point see Haugaard, *Elizabeth and the English Reformation*, viii–ix, and passim, and Margaret Aston, *England's Iconoclasts, Vol. I: Laws Against Images* (Oxford: Clarendon Press, 1988), 294–342. Elizabeth Jenkins says of her, "Elizabeth held the unquestioning belief in the Christian faith which was universal in Europe, but her mind was incapable of religious fanaticism." *Elizabeth the Great*, 19. Lacey Baldwin Smith states "whatever Elizabeth may have felt about the doctinal forms of religion, she believed without reservation in the divinity of kings." *Elizabeth Tudor*, 160. Scarisbrick, *The Reformation and the English People*, 110.

21. *Zurich Letters*, I, 69.

22. Aston, *England's Iconoclasts*, 313. Haugaard, *Elizabeth and the English Reformation*, 198–99. Catholic Edward Rishton, writing in 1585, saw the cross and candlesticks in Elizabeth's chapel an the extreme of hypocrisy. "The queen is in the habit of boasting before strangers and the foreign ambassadors that the clergy of

her sect are held in honour, and are not mere starvelings like those of Geneva, and other Churches of the kind, not so well ordered as hers; and that she had not gone so far from the faith of other princes and of her own ancestors as many think. The better to keep up this fraud, she retained for some years on her table, which she had set up in the place of the altar, in her chapel, two wax candles, which were never lighted, with a silver crucifix between them. And then in order to please the Catholics, and to impose the more easily upon foreigners, she used to say from time to time that she was forced, not by her own convictions, but by the clamours of her subjects, to make a change of religion, but that she had practised great moderation in making it." Nicholas Sander, *Rise and Growth of the Anglican Schism. pub. A. D. 1585, with a Continuation of the History, by the Rev. Edward Rishton*, trans. and ed. David Lewis (London: Burns and Oates, 1877), 271–72.

23. *Zurich Letters*, I, 161; *CSP, Spain*, I, 682; *CSP, Spain*, I, 683 de Silva to Philip, 8 Nov, 1567; *CSP, Spain*, I, 690 de Silva to Philip 29 Dec. 1567.

24. *CSP, Spain*, I, de Feria to Philip 29 April 1559, 62; *CSP, Spain*, I, de Silva to Philip, 9 October 1564, 387.

25. Francis Bacon wrote in speaking of her leniency to Catholics, "Her majesty not liking to make windows into men's hearts and secret thoughts, except the abundance of them did overflow into overt express acts and affirmations, tempered her law so, as it restraineth only manifest disobedience in impugning and impeaching advisedly and ambitiously her majesty's supreme power." *Works*, ed. James Spedding (London: Longman and Co., 1858) V, 429. Of her own religious attitudes, he described her as "pious, moderate, constant, and an enemy to novelty." *Works*, III, 469.

26. Scarisbrick, *The Reformation and the English People*, 171.

27. For More's disdainful discussion of Uncumber, see *Complete Works*, ed. Thomas M. C. Lawler, Germain Marc'Hadour, and Richard C. Marius (New Haven, CT: Yale University Press, 1981), VI, 227, 323, 235. For more on Uncumber, see David Hugh Farmer, *The Oxford Dictionary of Saints*, 2nd ed. (New York: Oxford University Press, 1987), 437–38; Gillian Mary Edwards, *Uncumber and Pantaloon: Some Words with Stories* (New York: E. P. Dutton, 1969), 75–82; Agnes B. C. Dunbar, *A Dictionary of Saintly Women* (London: George Bell and Sons) II, 302–3; Lina Eckenstein, *Women Under Monasticism: Chapters on Saintlore and Convent Life Between A. D. 500 and A. D. 1500* (Cambridge: Cambridge University Press, 1896), 35–38; Katherine M. Briggs, *A Dictionary of British Folk-Tales in the English Language, Incorporating the F. J. Norton Collection* (Bloomington: Indiana University Press, 1971), II, 465–66.

28. For more on Frideswide, see John Blair, "Saint Frideswide Reconsidered" *Oxoniensia* LII (1987), 71–101; Blair, ed., *Saint Frideswide: Patron Saint of Oxford: the Earliest Texts* (Oxford: The Perpetua Press, 1988); Blair, ed. *Saint Frideswide's Monastery at Oxford: Archeological and Architectual Studies* (Gloucester: Sutton, 1990); Alban Butler, *Lives of the Saints*, ed. Herbert Thurston (London: Burnes, Oates and Washbourne, 1926–38), IV, 150–51; James Parker, *The Early History of Oxford, 727-1100* (Oxford: Clarendon Press, 1885), 95–101; C. Horstmann, *The Lives of Women Saints of Our Contrie of England* (London: Early English Text Society, 1886), 80–82; Richard Stanton, *A Menology of England and Wales*

(London: Burnes and Oates, Ltd; New York: Catholic Publication Society Co., 1887), 503–4; J. Charles Wall, *Shrines of British Saints* (London: Methuen and Co., 1905), 63–71; Dunbar, *A Dictionary of Saintly Women* I, 327–28; Christina Hole, *English Shrines and Sanctuaries* (London: Batsford, 1954), 48–49, 150–51.

29. Though H. H. Salter says of her, "When we examine the records about St. Frideswide we find that she certainly existed, which is more than can be said of some saints, for her bones were in one of the parish churches of Oxford, but we have nothing historical to show who she was, when she lived, or what she did. . . . In volumes containing lives of saints we have lives of St. Frideswide, which follow somewhat different patterns, but none of the manuscripts are earlier than the first half of the twelfth century." *Medieval Oxford* (Oxford: Clarendon Press, 1936), 4–5. F. M. Stenton concurs: "St. Frideswide is little more than a name. . . . unaccompanied by any genuine tradition of incident or personal relationships." "St. Frideswide and Her Times," *Oxoniensia* I (1936), 4. The stories that developed about her three or four centuries after her death are "an attempt to give some appearance of substance to one of the most nebulous of English monastic legends" (5). This does not mean, however, that it was not widely believed in in the sixteenth century.

30. Dunbar, *Dictionary of Saintly Women*, I, 328; James Parker, *The Early History of Oxford, 727-1100* (Oxford: Clarendon Press, 1885), 99–100; A. Leyland, "'Miller's Tale' [I(A) 3449]," *Notes and Queries* 219, 21 (April, 1974), 126; Thomas Duffus Hardy, *Descriptive Catalogue of Material Relating to the History of Great Britain and Ireland, to the end of the Reign of Henry VII* (1862; rpt. New York: Burt Franklin, n.d.), I, pt. 1, 462; Stanton, *Menology*, 504; H. M. Mayr-Harting, "Functions of a Twelfth-Century Shrine: the Miracles of St. Fridewide," in *Studies in Medieval History Presented to R. H. C. Davis*, ed. Henry Mayr-Harting and R. I. Moore (London: Hambledon Press, 1985), 193–206; "The Miller's Tale," *The Works of Geoffrey Chaucer*, ll. 3448–49. For more on Chaucer's use of Frideswide, see Ruth H. Cline, "Four Chaucer Saints," *Modern Language Notes* LX (1945), 480–82 and "Three Notes on The Miller's Tale," *Huntington Library Quarterly* XXVI (1962–63), 131–45.

31. *DNB*, XX, 253–55.

32. Blair, *Saint Frideswide*, 21. Apparently at first there was a suggestion to have Catherine Martyr's bones burned, but since she had neither taught nor written there was no enough evidence to justify burning her posthumously as a heretic. The papal legate then suggested that "as Catherine Cathie, of detestable memory, had called herself the wife of Peter Martyr, a heretic, although both he and she had before taken vows of religion; forasmuch as she had lived with him in Oxford in fornication, and after her death was buried near the sepulchre of the Holy Virgin St. Frideswide . . . the Dean of the Cathedral [should] cast out the carcase from holy ground, and deal with it according to his discretion." James Anthony Froude, *History of England from the Fall of Wolsey to the death of Queen Elizabeth*, 3rd ed. (London: Longmans, Green, and Co., 1867), VI, 468.

33. Blair, *Saint Frideswide*, 22; John Foxe, *Acts and Monuments*, ed. Stephen Reed Cattley (London: R. B. Seeley and W. Burnside, 1838), VIII, 297; John Strype, *The Life and Acts of Matthew Parker* (Oxford: at the Clarendon Press,

1821), I, 199; J. Charles Wall, *Shrines of British Saints*, 55–57. The story also appears in Anthony A. Wood, *Athenae Oxonienses*, ed. Philip Bliss (London, 1813. rpt. ed. Hildesheim: George Olms Verlagsbuchhandlung, 1969), I, 329 and was well enough known to appear in a contemporary French Catholic's work. Florimond de Rémond, *L'Histoire de la naissance, progrez et decadence de l'heresie de ce siecle* (Paris: Chez Charles Chastellain, 1610), 297. Rémond (c. 1540–1602), of course, was horrified that the revered saint's bones were treated in such a manner. My thanks to Alisa Plant for the Rémond reference.

34. For material on idea of the monarch as magical healer, see David Starkey, "Representation Through Intimacy: A Study in the Symbolism of Monarchy and Court Office in Early-Modern England," in *Symbols and Sentiments: Cross-Cultural Studies in Symbolism*, ed. Ioan Lewis (London, New York, and San Francisco: Academic Press, 1977), 187–224; Larner, *Witchcraft and Religion*, 148; Thomas, *Religion and the Decline of Magic*, 192–200; Crawfurd, *The King's Evil*; Bloch, *The Royal Touch*; Meller, "The King's Healing," 81–94; Percy Ernst Schramm, *A History of the English Coronation*, trans. Leopold G. Wickham Legg (Oxford: Clarendon, 1937), 125–26; W. Carew Hazlitt, *Faiths and Folklores of the British Isles, A Descriptive and Historical Dictionary* (1905; rpt. New York: B. Blom, 1965), II, 354–56.

35. Henry II cured a fourteen-year-old girl by touch. Thomas Duffus Hardy, *Descriptive Catalogue of Material Relating to the History of Great Britain and Ireland, to the end of the Reign of Henry VII* (1862, rpt. New York: Burt Franklin, n.d.), I, Pt. 1, 461.

36. In France in the fifteenth century the practice was very popular. Louis XI touched for the Evil once a week, always after first going to confession. Crawfurd, *The King's Evil*, 48.

37. Thomas, *Religion and the Decline of Magic*, 193; Crawfurd, *The King's Evil*, 51–52.

38. E. M. W. Tillyard, *Some Mythical Elements in English Literature* (London: Chatto and Windus, 1961), 46–52.

39. For more on the question of the political uses of these ceremonies, see Starkey, "Representation Through Intimacy."

40. Brian Robinson, *The Royal Maundy* (London: Kaye and Ward, 1977); Peter A. Wright, *The Pictorial History of the Royal Maundy* (London: Pitkin Pictorials, Ltd., 1981); Hazlitt, *Faiths and Folklores*, II, 395–96; Christina Hole, *British Folk Customs* (London: Hutchinson, 1976); Alexander Howard, *Endless Cavalcade: A Diary of British Festivals and Customs* (London: A Barker, 1964), 84–85 are useful on the topic of the monarchy's involvement in the Maundy. For a discussion of the Royal Maundy today, see Ilse Hayden, *Symbol and Privilege: The Ritual Context of British Royalty* (Tucson: University of Arizona Press, 1987), 18–20.

41. Quoted in Robinson, *The Royal Maundy*, 23–24.

42. See *The New Catholic Encyclopedia*, VII, 105–7; IX, 146; Hole, *British Folk Customs*, 169. See also Charlton, "Maundy Thursday Observances," 201–19.

43. Robinson, *The Royal Maundy*, 25; Bloch, *The Royal Touch*, 137–38.

44. Some others besides the king did it, including the Earl of Northumberland in 1511 and Cardinal Thomas Wolsey in 1530. Elizabeth of York and Catherine of Aragon both distributed money on Maundy Thursday; there is no evidence that

they actually washed the feet of the poor. See Robinson, *The Royal Maundy*, 26. Catherine of Aragon struggled over this issue after the Divorce, since Henry decreed she could only hold a Maundy as princess dowager, not as queen. This is discussed in a letter from Sir William Fitzwilliam, Treasurer of Henry VIII's Household to Thomas Cromwell. Henry Ellis, ed., *Original Letters, Illustrative of English History*, 2nd ed. (London: Harding, Triphook, and Lepard, 1825), II, 25–28.

45. Robinson, *The Royal Maundy*, 25–26.

46. Strong, *Splendour at Court*, 21–22. See also Strong, *Art and Power*, 19.

47. James II was probably the last monarch to perform the footwashing, though some historians claim that William III did a very modified version of the ritual. After the end of the seventeenth century monarchs did not distribute their own gifts of money, food, and clothing until George V restored the custom in 1932. Elizabeth II distributes to both men and women, each group numbering her age. The last monarch to touch for the king's evil was Queen Anne.

48. Crawfurd, *The King's Evil*, 64; Stephen Greenblatt, "Invisible Bullets: Renaissance Authority and Its Subversion, Henry IV and Henry V," in *Political Shakespeare: New Essays in Cultural Materialism*, ed. Jonathan Dollimore and Alan Sinfield (Ithaca: Cornell University Press, 1985), 44. For a discussion of Mary and Elizabeth as "Godly" queens, see King, *Tudor Royal Iconography*, 182–266.

49. Robinson, *The Royal Maundy*, 16; Henry John Feasey, *Ancient Holy Week Ceremonial* (London: T. Baker, 1897), 127.

50. Erna Auerbach, *Tudor Artists: A Study of Painters in the Royal Service and of Portraiture on Illuminated Documents from the Accession of Henry VIII to the Death of Elizabeth* (London: Athlone Press, 1954), 146; Thomas, *Religion and the Decline of Magic*, 199. I am indebted to Professor Dennis Moore for the reference to Fleetwood.

51. *CSP,Venice*, VI, 435.

52. *CSP,Venice*, VI, 436.

53. For useful discussions of the coronation and the pre-coronation pageants, see Richard C. McCoy, "'This Wonderfull Spectacle': The Civic Progress of Elizabeth I and the Troublesome Coronation," in *Coronations: Medieval and Early Modern Monarchic Ritual*, ed. Janos Bak (Berkeley: University of California Press, 1990), 217–27; King, *Tudor Royal Iconography*, 227–32; Grant McCracken, "The Pre-Coronation Passage of Elizabeth I: Political Theatre or the Rehearsal of Politics?" *Canadian Review of Sociology and Anthropoly* 21, 1 (1984), 47–61.

54. Particularly useful on this subject are Elkin Calhoun Wilson, *England's Eliza* (Cambridge, MA: Harvard University Press, 1939); Robin Headlam Wells, *Spenser's Faerie Queen and the Cult of Elizabeth* (Totowa, NJ: Barnes and Noble, 1983); Frances Yates, *Astraea: The Imperial Theme in the Sixteenth Century* (London: Routledge and Kegan Paul, 1975); Roy Strong, *Cult of Elizabeth: Elizabethan Portraiture and Pageantry* (Wallop, Hampshire: Thames and Hudson, 1977); Marcus, "Shakespeare's Comic Heroines, Elizabeth I, and the Political Uses of Androgyny," 135–54; King, "Queen Elizabeth I," 30–74. Eric Ives argues that in Anne Boleyn's coronation there was also an identification of the pregnant Virgin Mary with the pregnant Anne Boleyn. *Anne Boleyn*, 283–84.

55. Scarisbrick, *The Reformation and the English People*, 54–55, 171.

56. Yates, *Astraea*, 78; Wilson, *England's Eliza*, 206; John Buxton, *Elizabethan Taste* (London: Macmillan, 1963), 50.

57. Yates, *Astraea*, 78; Strong, *Art and Power*, 67; Strong, *Cult of Elizabeth*, 125; King, *Spenser's Poetry*, 111.

58. One can sense how much Cecil identified Elizabeth with his religion by the final letter he wrote his son Robert in 1598: "Serve God by serving the Quene, for all other Service is indede bondage to the devill." Thomas Wright, ed., *Queen Elizabeth and Her Times* (London: H. Colburn, 1838), II, 488.

59. See John Nichols, *The Progresses and Public Processions of Queen Elizabeth* (London: J. Nichols and Son, 1823; rpt. New York: Burt Franklin, n.d.); Strong, *Art and Power*, 77; Neale, *Queen Elizabeth I*, 210–17; Jean Wilson, *Entertainments for Elizabeth I* (Totowa, NJ: Rowman and Littlefield, 1980), 7.

60. Sir Robert Burton, *The Anatomy of Melancholy*, ed. Floyd Dell and Paul Jordan-Smith (New York: Tudor Publishing Co., 1938), 445; Andrew Belsey and Catherine Belsey, "Icons of Divinity: Portraits of Elizabeth I," in *Renaissance Bodies: The Human Figure in English Culture, c. 1540–1660*, ed. Lucy Gent and Nigel Llewellyn (London: Reaktion Books, Ltd., 1990), 35.

61. David Cressy, *Bonfires and Bells: National Memory and the Protestant Calendar in Elizabethan and Stuart England* (Berkeley: University of California Press, 1989), 50, 53.

62. William Keatinge Clay, ed., *Liturgies and Occasional Forms of Prayer set forth in the Reign of Queen Elizabeth* (Cambridge: at the University Press, 1847), 554–55.

63. Thomas Holland, *A Sermon Preached at Paul's in London to 17 of November 1599, the one and fortieth yeare of her Maiesties raigne, and augmented in those places wherein, for the shortnes of the time, it could not be then delivered* (Oxford: Joseph Barnes, 1601). Richard Brakinbury to Lord Talbot, 20 November, 1590, in Edmund Lodge, *Illustrations of British History* (London: John Chidley, 1838), II, 419.

64. Clay, *Liturgies*, 557n.

65. Wright, *Queen Elizabeth*, II, 309.

66. Sander, *Rise and Growth of the Anglican Schism*, 284–85.

67. Wells, *Spenser's Faerie Queen*, 19. When Elizabeth died an engraving was published with the inscription, "This Maiden Queen Elizabeth came into this world the Eve of the Nativity of the Blessed Virgin Mary; and died on the Eve of the Annunciation of the Virgin Mary." Buxton, *Elizabethan Taste*, 51.

68. Quoted in Wilson, *England's Eliza*, 382.

69. Quoted in Yates, *Astraea*, 79.

70. G. B. Harrison, ed., *A Second Jacobean Journal* (Ann Arbor: University of Michigan Press, 1958), 26.

71. McCoy, "'The Wonderfull Spectacle,'" 218; King, *Tudor Royal Iconography*, 229. Grant McCracken does warn, however, "that for all its illuminative power . . . the theatre metaphor has distorting powers of its own." "The Pre-coronation Passage," 47. For more on the importance and symbolism of royal entries, see R. M. Smuts, "Public Ceremony and Royal Charisma: The English Royal Entry in London, 1485–1642," in *The First Modern Society: Essays in Engish History in Honour of Lawrence Stone*, ed. A. L. Beier, David Cannadine, and James M. Rosenheim (Cambridge: Cambridge University Press, 1989), 65–93.

72. Reginald Scot, *The Discoverie of Witchcraft*, with an introduction by the Rev. Montague Summers (New York: Dover, 1972), 172.

73. Struma is another term for scrofula. Crawfurd, *The King's Evil*, 75. William Clowes, *A right frutefull treatise for the artificiall cure of struma* (London: E. Allde, 1602), 49–50.

74. *Robert Laneham's Letter: Describing a Part of the Entertainment unto Queen Elizabeth at the Castle of Kenilworth in 1575*, edited with an introduction by F. J. Furnivall (New York: Duffield and Co., 1907), 35.

75. *CSP Venice*, IX, 505.

76. Tooker described Elizabeth's behavior at Gloucester; see Crawfurd, *The King's Evil*, 75. A colleague, anthropologist Karin Andriolo, has suggested that Elizabeth may have refused to touch because she might have been menstruating. See also Janice Delaney, Mary Jane Lupton, and Emily Toth, *The Curse: A Cultural History of Menstruation* (revised expanded ed. Urbana and Chicago: University of Illinois Press, 1988), 40–42 and Eccles, *Obstetrics and Gynaecology in Tudor and Stuart England*, 49–51 for attitudes on menstruation in early modern England. For non-Western attitudes, see Mary Douglas, *Purity and Danger: An Analysis of Concepts of Pollution and Taboo* (New York: Praeger, 1966), 147, 151, 176–77.

77. John Neale, *Queen Elizabeth I and Her Parliaments, 1584–1601* (London: Jonathan Cape, 1957), 29; Charlton, "Maundy Thursday Observances," 205; Thomas, *Religion and the Decline of Magic*, 195; Crawfurd, *The King's Evil*, 70; Haigh, *Elizabeth I*, 152.

78. This description is taken from William Lambarde's eyewitness account of Elizabeth's 1572–73 Maundy. Nichols, *The Progresses and Public Processions of Queen Elizabeth*, II, 325–27.

79. John Calvin, *Institutes of the Christian Religion*, ed. John Baille, John T. McNeill, Henry P. Van Dusen, trans. Ford Lewis Battles (Philadelphia: Westminster Press, 1960), 1322.

80. March 23, 1564: "Proclamation remitting the distribution of the Maundy by the Queen in person, in the present time of contagious sickness, but alms will be given to the poor of Windsor and Eton." *CSP, Domestic*, I, 236.

81. *Salisbury Papers*, V, 171. Fletcher, once a favorite of Elizabeth's, had offended her by contracting a second marriage two years after his first wife's death, soon after he became bishop of London. He wrote piteously to Burghley asking for help in being restored to Elizabeth's favor.

82. *CSP, Spain*, I, 419, 425.

83. James had not touched while king of Scotland as the ceremony had never taken hold there. He may have performed a Maundy service, though it is doubtful since the Scots Presbyterians probably believed it too popish. His father Henry Stuart, Lord Darnley, did perform a Maundy during the brief time he was king of Scotland after his marriage to Mary Stuart. De Silva mentions it in a letter of 29 April 1566. *CSP, Spain*, I, 546.

84. Mullaney, *The Place of the Stage*, 105.

85. William Camden, *The History of the Most Renowned and Victorious Princess Elizabeth, late Queen of England containing all the most important and remarkable passages of state, both at home and abroad (so far as they were linked with English affairs) during her long and prosperous reign*, 4th ed. (London: M. Flesher, 1688), 17–18; the

Earl of Shrewsbury to Sir Francis Walsingham, 18 October 1582, Lodge, *Illustrations of British History*, II, 237.

86. Clowes, *A right frutefull treatise*, 50.

87. At the beginning of her reign such a prayer might well have been seen as blasphemous. Thomas Gargrave beseeched Elizabeth to marry since "we beg of God in our daily prayers. . . . [that] your most gratious Government may be perpetuated to the English Nation unto all eternity." But, said Gargrave, the only way this might happen would be "your Majesty should either reign for ever (which to hope for is not lawfull) or else by Mariage bring forth Children." Camden, *The History of the Most Renowned and Victorious Princess Elizabeth*, 4th ed., 25. By 1601 that prayer was obviously no longer of any use.

Chapter Three: The Official Courtships of the Queen

1. *CSP, Spain*, I, 367–68, 633; Dennis Kay, "'She was a Queen, and Therefore Beautiful': Sidney, His Mother, and Queen Elizabeth," *Review of English Studies* XLIII, 169 (1992), 29; Jenkins, *Elizabeth the Great*, 105; King, *Spenser's Poetry*, 127, 130; Strong, *Cult of Elizabeth*, 71, 74.

2. T. F. Hartley, ed., *Proceedings in the Parliaments of Elizabeth I, 1558–1581* (Leicester: University Press, 1981), 45. This speech was read in the queen's name by Mr. Mason, a member of the House of Commons, to some five hundred members of Parliament. This version is originally in Stow's *Annales of England*, 1615 ed., 635–63 republished in George P. Rice, Jr., ed., *The Public Speaking of Queen Elizabeth: Selections from Her Official Addresses* (New York: Columbia University Press, 1951), 114.

3. As King points out in "Queen Elizabeth I."

4. For works on the courtships, still of great value is Martin Hume, *The Courtships of Queen Elizabeth* (London: E. Nash and Grayson, 1926). Also of value is Plowden, *Marriage with My Kingdom*. For an excellent discussion of the negotiations around the Archduke Charles, see Susan Doran, "Religion and Politics at the Court of Eizabeth I: The Habsburg Marriage Negotiations, 1559–1567," *English Historical Review*, 104 (1989), 908–26; for a discussion of the negotiations with the French, see Wallace MacCaffrey, *Queen Elizabeth and the Making of Policy, 1572–1588* (Princeton, NJ: Princeton University Press, 1981) and *The Shaping of the Elizabethan Regime* (Princeton, NJ: Princeton University Press, 1968).

5. Loades, *The Tudor Court*, 192; Catherine Bates, "'Of Court it seemes': A Semantic Analysis of Courtship and to Court," *Journal of Medieval and Renaissance Studies* 20, 1 (spring, 1990), 39. Norbert Elias, *The History of Manners, Vol. I: The Civilizing Process*, trans. Edmund Jephcott (New York: Pantheon Books, 1978), 179. For more on the court, see David Starkey, ed., *The English Court: From the Wars of the Roses to the Civil War* (London, New York: Longman, 1987).

6. Camden, *The History of the Most Renowned and Victorious Princess Elizabeth*, 1635 ed., 16.

7. King, "Queen Elizabeth I," 30–74. Hartley lists it as "an independent

version from an unknown source," and presents a slightly different speech that is still very wary of the need to marry. *Proceedings in the Parliaments of Elizabeth I*, 44–45. I include a discussion of it because it is cited so heavily.

8. Charles Howard McIlwain, ed., *The Political Works of James I* (Cambridge, MA: Harvard University Press, 1918), 272; J. P. Kenyon, *The Stuart Constitution, 1603–1688: Documents and Commentary*, 2nd ed. (New York: Cambridge University Press, 1986), 43. Kevin Sharpe also sees the parallels in the speech of Elizabeth and that of James. *Politics and Ideas in Early Stuart England: Essays and Studies* (London and New York: Pinter Publishers, 1989), 60; Foxe, *Acts and Monuments*, VI, 414, 415. I discuss the concept of the queen's two bodies more in chapter six.

9. The Lansdowne copy republished in Hartley, *Proceedings in the Parliaments of Elizabeth*, 44–45.

10. Hartley, *Proceedings in the Parliaments of Elizabeth*, 146–47.

11. Wormald, *Mary, Queen of Scots*, 105. That also might certainly be said about Henry VIII, especially in some of his later marriages.

12. Philip Yorke Hardwicke, ed., *Miscellaneous State Papers: from 1501 to 1726* (London: W. Strahan and T. Cadell, 1778), I, 174; Wright, *Queen Elizabeth*, I, 80, 187–88, 225; Dudley Digges, *The Compleat Ambassador: or Two Treaties of the intended marriage of Qu. Elizabeth of Glorious Memory . . .* (London: Gabriel Bedell and Thomas Collins, 1655), 54.

13. Frederick Chamberlin, *The Sayings of Queen Elizabeth* (London: John Lane, 1923), 61, 68.

14. *CSP, Spain*, I, 75, 463, 468; Lewis Spence, *The Fairy Tradition in Britain* (New York: Rider and Co., 1948), 207; Ruth Bottigheimer, ed., *Fairy Tales and Society: Illusion, Allusion, and Paradigm* (Philadelphia: University of Pennsylvania Press, 1986), 8, 252; Bruno Bettelheim, *The Uses of Enchantment: The Meaning and Importance of Fairy Tales* (New York: Alfred A. Knopf, 1976), 336.

15. See Chapter four.

16. King argues of Dudley that "When members of Parliament and the privy council prodded the queen to marry during the 1560s, this royal favorite was her most eligible subject." *Spenser's Poetry*, 152. But the pressure against the Dudley match was intense, especially given the mystery surrounding Amy Robsart's death.

17. *CSP, Spain*, I, 112.

18. This is the theory of Ian Aird. "The Death of Amy Robsart: Accident, Suicide, or Murder—or Disease?" *English Historical Review* 71, 278 (1956), 69–79. Alan Kendall and Elizabeth Jenkins argue that Aird's theory is plausible. Kendall, *Robert Dudley, Earl of Leicester* (London: Cassell, 1980), 35; Jenkins, *Elizabeth and Leicester*, 65.

19. Robert Naunton, *Fragmenta Regalia: Being a History of Queen Elizabeth's Favourites* (Edinburgh: A. Constable and Co., 1808), 17. I would add, however, that Naunton composed *Fragmenta Regalia* probably about 1630, so this is not a truly contemporary story and should be accepted with that caution.

20. *CSP, Spain*, I, 141, 404.

21. Richard McCoy, *The Rites of Knighthood: The Literature and Politics of Elizabethan Chivalry* (Berkeley, Los Angeles, and London: University of California Press, 1989), 42. *CSP, Spain*, I, 518. MacCaffrey suggests that after 1564 Leicester

had no chance of marrying Elizabeth. Whether he was aware of this or not, however, is another whole issue. *Shaping*, 227, 468. John King argues that Spenser was still advancing Dudley's candidacy as a royal husband in the "October" eclogue of the *The Shepheardes Calendar*, published in December 1579 and dedicted to Sir Philip Sidney. King, *Spenser's Poetry*, 152.

22. Doran, "Religion and Politics at the Court of Eizabeth I," 913; MacCaffrey, *Shaping*, 237. It does appear after the Kenilworth entertainment of 1575 that it was clear to Robert that Elizabeth would never marry him, and in 1578 he secretly married his by then pregnant mistress, Lettice Knollys, widow of the Earl of Essex. The revelation of that marriage by Simier in 1579 had great emotional impact on Elizabeth.

23. Victor von Klarwill, ed., *Queen Elizabeth and Some Foreigners: Being a Series of Hitherto Unpublished Letters from the Archives of the Hapsburg Family*, trans T. H. Nash (London: John Lane, 1928), Queen Elizabeth to the Emperor Ferdinand, 5 June 1559, 76.

24. Bassnett, *Elizabeth I*, 107.

25. Wormald suggests that Mary's failures as queen in Scotland, especially her lack of will in dealing with Protestantism, made her an unattractive prospect for either France or Spain. *Mary Queen of Scots*, 129–47.

26. The Duchess of Parma had set a trade embargo, meant to bring the English to their knees because she considered England the fountainhead of the heretics and the patron of political discontent. Instead, the English were able to find other markets, and the embargo hurt Antwerp far more than English textile interests. When the duchess and her advisors attempted to mend their fences they found the English unwilling. Finally, de Silva, newly arrived as Ambassador in 1564, was able to bring about an agreement. Trade was reopened in late 1564; eventually a trade treaty was signed two years later. MacCaffrey, *Shaping*, 272; G. D. Ramsay, *The Queen's Merchants and the Revolt of the Netherlands* (Manchester: Manchester University Press, 1986), 12–15.

27. *CSP, Spain*, I, 409–10.

28. For an explicit statement to that effect at the very beginning of the negotiations in 1559, see *CSP, Spain*, I, 73.

29. *CSP, Spain*, I, 70, 72–73; Digges, *The Compleat Ambassador*, 335; Philip Barrow, *The Methode of Phisicke*, 3rd ed. (London: R. Field, 1596), 201. In 1560 King Erik of Sweden decided to come in person to woo Elizabeth; fierce winds forced him to turn around. Elizabeth immediately wrote to tell him not to make another attempt since "as yet she has had no desire to marry. She deems it strange that he should write that he had been informed by his brother and his envoys that she had determined not to marry an absent person. . . . It is very true that she had often said that she would never decide on an absent man for her husband . . . , but she never said that she deferred answering him until she had seen him. She told his envoys that she had no desire to marry, and much preferred a single life." *CSP, Foreign*, II, 401.

30. MacCaffrey, *Shaping*, 229–30; Doran, "Religion and Politics at the Court of Eizabeth I," 914.

31. 23 July 1565 de Silva to Philip, *CSP, Spain*, I, 453; Emperor Maximilian to

the Ambassador at the Spanish Court, Count Dietrichstein, 19 November 1565, von Klarwill, *Elizabeth I and Some Foreigners*, 255.

32. Doran, "Religion and Politics at the Court of Eizabeth I," 916, 917; *CSP, Spain*, I, 631.

33. Doran, "Religion and Politics at the Court of Eizabeth I," 922; MacCaffrey, *Shaping*, 228.

34. Von Klarwill, *Elizabeth I and Some Foreigners*, 225, 237; *CSP, Spain*, I, 465–66. Yet Elizabeth did seem at least to consider the possibility that Charles might come in disguise. In 1559 de Quadra reported that the German ambassador "says she plied him with a thousand silly stories. She said one thing, however, that I think was meant for a hint, although he did not understand it. It was that one of her fools told her that it was current in London that the gentleman who acted as the ambassador's chamberlain was really the archduke Charles who had come thus in order to see the Queen. In my opinion this only meant that the archduke might come in this fashion to see and be seen which she hinted to me last Sunday." *CSP, Spain*, I, 74.

35. Elizabeth did attempt to restart the negotiations with the archduke in 1570, but he refused to be brought into the dance again, and soon married Mary, daughter of Albert V, Duke of Bavaria. Lodge, *Illustrations of British History*, I, 446n.

36. Digges, *The Compleat Ambassador*, 47, 139.

37. *CSP, Spain*, II, 10. In the same letter de Silva also reveals the difficulty of being the Spanish Ambassador to Protestant England. He says of the Council: "All their efforts are directed to making [Elizabeth] shy of me, now more than ever, and neither suavity nor a show of simplicity and frankness, which I have hitherto adopted, suffices to disarm them. . . . They are lovers of change, although they do not show it, for they are false in everything. . . . This is a grave inconvenience for those of us who live here, on account of the danger to which it exposes our households, who are exposed for a long time to the consequences of so much freedom and bad conversation. This gives great and constant anxiety . . . because the failure to attend regularly at church and perform the sacred offices and duties, cools devotion and causes a greater fall still and, for this reason, the long continued residence of all ministers in this country is a matter to be deeply considered." *CSP, Spain*, II, 10 de Silva to Philip 16 February 1568. In September Philip finally rewarded de Silva's dedication with an embassy to Venice.

38. Ramsay, *The Queen's Merchants*, 89.

39. MacCaffrey, *Shaping*, 392; Neale, *Elizabeth I*, 227.

40. Digges, *The Compleat Ambassador*, 62–64.

41. *CSP, Domestic, Addenda, 1566–79*, 330.

42. Strype, *Annals*, II, Pt 1, 22. Strype says, "I have met among his papers with such a judgment made, written all with his own hand." Strype, *Annals*, II, Pt 1, 22. He also provides a transcript of the astrological chart in Latin in his appendix (II, Pt 2, 417–18). We must take Strype as a historian with some caution, however. For example, he incorrectly dates the letter Sidney sent Elizabeth against the Alençon marriage to 1572 (II, Pt 1, 218) rather than placing it within the debate of 1579 over her marriage.

43. Strype, *Annals*, II, Pt I, 23; see also II, Pt 2, 417–18 appendix.

44. Digges, *The Compleat Ambassador*, 67, 70, 196.

45. Digges, *The Compleat Ambassador*, 195–97.

46. Digges, *The Compleat Ambassador*, 139, 164.

47. Digges, *The Compleat Ambassador*, 120; *CSP, Spain*, II, 410.

48. For more on the background and significance of these negotiations, see Wallace MacCaffrey, "The Anjou Match and the making of Elizabethan foreign policy," in Peter Clark, Alan Smith, and Nicholas Tyacke, ed., *The English Commonwealth, 1547–1640: Essays in Politics and Society* (New York: Barnes and Noble, 1979), 59–75.

49. MacCaffrey, "The Anjou Match," 61. In *Elizabeth and the Making of Policy* MacCaffrey writes, "One cannot demonstrate with absolute certainty that the Queen did really intend marriage," but argues that the evidence supports such an interpretation (249–50). Christopher Haigh also argues that in 1579 "Elizabeth may have seriously considered marriage." *Elizabeth I*, 15.

50. Camden, *The History of the Most Renowned and Victorious Princess Elizabeth*, 1635 ed., 205.

51. A. G. Dickens suggests that "It was Elizabeth's misguided persistence on the Alençon match which gave the Massacre far more domestic significance than it could otherwise have acquired." *Reformation Studies* (London: Hambledon Press, 1982), 487.

52. John Stubbs, *Gaping Gulf*, ed. Lloyd E. Berry (Charlottesville: The Folger Shakespeare Library for the University Press of Virginia, 1968), 4, 11, 51.

53. MacCaffrey, *Making of Policy*, 256; Camden, *The History of the Most Renowned and Victorious Princess Elizabeth*, 1635 ed., 239.

54. Steuart A. Pears, trans., *The Correspondence of Sir Philip Sidney and Hubert Languet* (London: William Pickering, 1845), 187; Sir Philip Sidney, *Miscellaneous Prose*, ed. Katherine Duncan-Jones and Jan Van Dorsten (Oxford: Clarendon Press, 1973), 33, 48, 55. The original of the letter to the Count of Hanau, in Latin, June, 1575 appears in *The Works of Sir Philip Sidney*, ed. A. Feuillerat (Cambridge: at the University Press, 1912–26), III, 103. I use the translation in Duncan-Jones, 37.

55. McCoy, *The Rites of Knighthood*, 174 n14. Berry suggests that Sidney "found it to his advantage to absent himself from Court" (li). Duncan-Jones, however, argues that "there is in fact no contemporary evidence that the Queen in any sense banished Sidney. . . . One of the main functions of the courtier according to all theorists was to advise the monarch" (34, 35). Dennis Kay suggests that "Sidney's relationship with the Queen was decidedly complex and problematic. Its context . . . is the repeated reluctance of the monarch to set on Sidney's parents the value they felt their service warranted," "'She was a Queen, and Therefore Beautiful,'" 27. The Sidneys felt particularly ill-used because Mary Sidney was permanently scarred from smallpox from nursing Elizabeth through the disease.

56. *Salisbury Papers*, II, 272.

57. *CSP, Spain*, III, 226, 243, 348; Camden, *The History of the Most Renowned and Victorious Princess Elizabeth*, 1635 ed., 235; Perry, *The Word of a Prince*, 242, 243; MacCaffrey, *Making of Policy*, 279.

58. Elizabeth wrote to Catherine that her grief "cannot exceed mine; for, although you were his mother, yet there remain to you several other children. But for myself, I find no consolation if it be no death, which I hope will make us soon to meet." G. B. Harrison, ed., *The Letters of Queen Elizabeth*, 162.

59. Neale, *Queen Elizabeth I*, 155.

Chapter Four: Wanton and Whore

1. Francis Osborne, *Osborne's Works*, 8th ed. (London: Printed for R.D., 1682), 383–84. In the early seventeenth century Henry Clifford gives a slightly different version of this story. He writes, "The queen when she came to the crown was full twenty-five years of age, a gracious lady and gallant of aspect. Yet she would not be persuaded to marry, but would have it written on her tomb that she lived and die a virgin. King Henry the Fourth of France merrily said the world would never believe this, or would the many favourites she had." Henry Clifford, *The Life of Jane Dormer, Duchess of Feria*, ed. Joseph Stevenson (London: Burns and Oates, 1887), 96. Clifford, of course, is writing from a hostile Catholic perspective.

2. For discussions of these issues, see Chapter two and Chapter six.

3. As Jean Wilson puts it, "The most important fact about Elizabeth I was her sex." *Entertainments for Elizabeth I*, 3. Other particularly significant studies that consider the question of Elizabeth and gender are by Leah Marcus, Louis Montrose, Frances Yates, John King, and Allison Heisch, referred to in the introduction. Also interesting is Larissa J. Taylor-Smither, "Elizabeth I: A Psychological Profile," *Sixteenth Century Journal* XV, 1 (1984), 47–72, in looking at gender issues in terms of Elizabeth's psychological development and how that affected her rule.

4. Speaking of Elizabeth while a princess, Henry Clifford, writing early in the next century, says, "In King Edward's time what passed between the Lord Admiral, Sir Thomas Seymour, and her Dr. Latimer preached in a sermon, and was a chief cause that the Parliament condemned the Admiral. There was a bruit of a child born and miserably destroyed, but could not be discovered whose it was; only the report of the midwife, who was brought from her house blindfold thither, and so returned; saw nothing in the house while she was there, but candlelight; only she said, it was the child of a very fair young lady, who was then between fifteen and sixteen years of age. If it were so, it was the judgement of God unto the Admiral; and upon her, to make her ever after incapable of children." *The Life of Jane Dormer, Duchess of Feria*, 86–87.

5. G. W. Prothero, ed., *Select Statutes and Other Constitutional Documents Illustrative of the Reigns of Elizabeth and James I*, 4th ed. (Oxford: at the Clarendon Press, 1913), 109.

6. Haigh, *Elizabeth I*, 19; Marcus, "Erasing the Stigma of Daughterhood," 406.

7. Linda Woodbridge, *Women in the English Renaissance: Literature and the Nature of Womankind, 1540–1620* (Urbana and Chicago: University of Illinois Press, 1984), 53.

8. Digges, *The Compleat Ambassador*, 196.

9. Lacey Baldwin Smith, *Treason in Tudor England: Politics and Paranoia* (Princeton, NJ: Princeton University Press, 1986), 137; Prothero, *Select Statutes*, 23; Camden, *The History of the Most Renowned and Victorious Princess Elizabeth*, 1688 ed., 28; Haigh, *Elizabeth I*, 18; Joel Samaha, "Gleanings from Local Criminal-Court Records: Sedition Amongst the 'Inarticulate' in Elizabethan Essex," *Journal of Social History* 8 (Summer, 1975), 64–65.

10. *APC*, VII, 31, 71, 92, 94, 180, 299; Samaha, "Gleanings from Local Criminal-Court Records," 68; *Calendar of the Assize Records: Essex Indictments, Elizabeth I*, ed. J. S. Cockburn (London: Her Majesty's Stationery Office, 1978), 203. I am in no way suggesting that Elizabeth was unique in the seditious words said about her. Particularly at the time of the Divorce, the records are filled with seditous comments about Henry VIII.

11. 6 December 1559, William Murdin and Samuel Haynes, ed., *A Collection of State Papers Relating to Affairs in the Reign of Queen Elizabeth from 1542 to 1596 left by William Cecil, Lord Burghley* (London: William Bowyer, 1740–1759), I, 212; Camden, *The History of the Most Renowned and Victorious Princess Elizabeth*, 1688 ed., 129; *CSP, Spain*, I, 368.

12. Jonathan Goldberg, *Endlesse Worke: Spenser and the Structures of Discourse* (Baltimore and London: Johns Hopkins University Press, 1981), 152.

13. Useful modern studies of Robert Dudley include Alan Haynes, *White Bear: Robert Dudley, the Elizabethan Earl of Leicester* (London: Peter Owen, 1987); Kendall, *Robert Dudley, Earl of Leicester*; Eleanor Rosenberg, *Leicester, Patron of Letters* (New York: Columbia University Press, 1958); Derek Wilson, *Sweet Robin: A Biography of Robert Dudley, Earl of Leicester* (London: Hamilton, 1981). On the relationship between Elizabeth and Robert Dudley see Milton Waldman, *Elizabeth and Leicester* (London: Collins, 1944) and Jenkins, *Elizabeth and Leicester*.

14. *CSP, Spain*, I, 57–58.

15. 4 May 1559, *CSP, Venice*, 81.

16. Murdin and Haynes, *Collection of State Papers*, I, 362; 22 January 1561, *CSP, Spain*, I, 179; Hardwicke, *Miscellaneous State Papers*, I, 121–23, 163; *CSP, Foreign, 1560–1561*, 348, 377.

17. Of course her statement of the relationship in 1562 does not cover what went on between Dudley and Elizabeth after the smallpox scare. *CSP, Spain*, I, 178; *Miscellaneous State Papers*, I, 167; John Nichols, *The Progresses and Public Processions of Queen Elizabeth* (London: J. Nichols and Son, 1823; rpt. New York: Burt Franklin, n.d.), I, xxxiii, II, 617; *CSP, Spain*, I, 263.

18. John Dee, *The Comendious Rehearsall*, ed. James Crossley, Remains Historical and Literary, 24 (Manchester: The Chetham Society, 1851), 21; *CSP, Venice*, VII, 105, 301–2; *CSP, Spain*, I, 214.

19. *CSP, Spain*, I, 274; Digges, *The Compleat Ambassador*, 146; Lodge, *Illustrations of British History*, I, 550–51, II, 25, 41, 94, 174.

20. I would, however, disagree with Elizabeth Jenkins, in her otherwise excellent and intuitive study of Elizabeth and Robert Dudley, when she suggests that one way we know they were not lovers is that Elizabeth was never emotionally yielding to Robert in the way a woman would be after she had slept with her lover.

This point seems to suggest more about Jenkins' 1950s values than a real historical analysis.

21. See Warnicke, *The Rise and Fall of Anne Boleyn* for a full discussion of this issue.

22. *CSP, Domestic Eliz.*, XIII, 157; Jenkins, *Elizabeth the Great*, 96; F. G. Emmison, *Elizabethan Life: Vol. 1, Disorder* (Chelmsford: Essex County Council, 1971), 41; *CSP, Dom. Addenda, Eliz.*, XI, 534; Spacks, *Gossip*, 32; Lawrence Stone, *Family, Sex, and Marriage* (New York: Harper and Row, 1977), 503–4. For a very useful discussion of women's honor and sexuality, particularly as it affected Elizabeth's mother, Anne Boleyn, see Warnicke, *The Rise and Fall of Anne Boleyn*. For a discussion of the impact of Protestantism on the concept of honor, see also Mervyn James, *English Politics and the Conception of Honour, 1485–1642* (Cambridge: Cambridge University Press, 1986). It is also useful to look at proverbs about women in the Renaissance to see the linking of sexual misconduct and generally dishonorable behavior. Morris Palmer Tilley, *A Dictionary of the Proverbs in England in the Sixteenth and Seventeenth Centuries* (Ann Arbor: University of Michigan Press, 1950), 741–49.

23. J. A. Sharpe, *Defamation and Sexual Slander in Early Modern England: The Church Courts at York* (York: Borthwick Institute of Historical Research, 1980).

24. *CSP, Scotland*, I, 646; Wormald, *Mary Queen of Scots*, 145; *CSP, Foreign, 1566–68*, 256; Patrick Collinson, *The English Captivity of Mary Queen of Scots* (Sheffield: Sheffield History Pamphlets, 1987), 5. After the Ridofi Plot of 1572, and even more in the 1580s, Protestants in Parliament did all they could to encourage the image of Mary Stuart as an adulterous murderer as a justification for having her killed to safeguard Elizabeth. Collinson, *The English Captivity of Mary Queen of Scots*, 7–8. Elizabeth, of course, refused to listen to this argument for the nearly nineteen years of Mary's presence in England.

25. *CSP, Spain*, I, 387.

26. *CSP, Spain*, I, 592; Wright, ed., *Queen Elizabeth and Her Times*, I, 225.

27. *CSP, Spain*, I, 381.

28. *CSP, Spain*, I, 520–21.

29. Murdin and Haynes, *Collection of State Papers*, II, 203, 204, 208.

30. Wright, ed., *Queen Elizabeth and her Times*, I, 374, 440–41; Strype, *Annals of the Reformation*, II, Part 2, 503. I am indebted to Dennis Moore for the reference to Blosse in Strype. Robert Blosse also spread rumors that Edward VI was still alive, and fifteen years later actually claimed to be Edward VI. See Chapter five.

31. MacCaffrey, *War and Politics, 1588–1603*, 457.

32. Nicholas Harris Nicholas, *Memoirs of the Life and Times of Sir Christopher Hatton* (London: R. Bentlye, 1847), 26, 155.

33. *CSP, Spain*, I, 362, II, 491; *CSP, Rome, 1572–78*, 238, 250.

34. Lingard, *The History of England*, VI, 706–8. These stories were current in such works as *Leicester's Commonwealth*, published 1584. That work, however, saw Elizabeth as his victim, rather than as evil in her own right. During the time of the Divorce there were some rumors that Henry had years earlier had an affair

with Anne Boleyn's mother. He denied it but admitted her sister Mary had previously been his mistress.

35. For more on this story, see Ettwell A. B. Barnard, *Evesham and a Reputed Son of Queen Elizabeth* (Evesham: published by the author, 1926).

36. *CSP, Spain*, IV, 101–12. Martin Hume suggests, "The poor foolish young man [was] apparently under the impression that King Philip was an amiable altruist, who would help him to a crown for the sake of his *beaux yeux*." *Courtships*, 341.

37. Hume, *Courtships*, 345; Jenkins, *Elizabeth and Leicester*, 334.

38. Stubbs, *Gaping Gulf*, 51. John Stanhope wrote to Lord Talbot in December 1589, "The Queen is so well as I assure you." The next year he wrote again, "The Queen for health is wondrous well." At the end of the year Stanhope wrote "God be thanked she is in better health this winter than I have seen her before." In September of 1602 Fulke Greville wrote to the Countess of Shrewsbury, "The best news I can yet write your Ladyship is of the Queen's health and disposition of body, which I assure you is excellent good, and I have not seen her every way better disposed these many years." Lodge, *Illustrations of British History*, II, 386, 422, 433, 582.

39. Samaha, "Gleanings from Local Criminal-Court Records," 68–69.

40. Montrose, "The Elizabethan Subject and the Spenserian Text," 311; Emmison, *Elizabethan Life*, 42–43; *Calendar of Assize Records: Essex*, 195; *CSP, Domestic Eliz.*, CXLVIII, 12; Samaha, "Gleanings from Local Criminal-Court Records," 69.

41. Emmison, *Elizabethan Life*, 42; Samaha, "Gleanings from Local Criminal-Court Records," 69.

42. *CSP, Domestic Eliz.*, CCLXIX, #22, 136–37; G. B. Harrison, ed., *The Elizabethan Journals* (New York: Macmillan Co., 1939), II, 51.

43. *CSP, Domestic Eliz.*, CCLXXIX, #48, 24.

44. Katherine Park and Lorraine J. Daston, "Unnatural Conceptions: The Study of Monsters in Sixteenth- and Seventeeth-Century France and England," *Past and Present* 92 (1981), 20–54; Joseph Lilly, ed., *A Collection of Seventy-Nine Black-Letter Ballads and Broadsides, printed in the reign of Queen Elizabeth between the year 1559 and 1597* (London: Joseph Lilly, 1867), xvi. A further bizarre account that reflects some gender confusion occurred in 1583. The Spanish Ambassador de Mendoza reported in a letter: "I cannot help mentioning a very strange thing that has happened in this country, as I am assured by very trustworthy persons. In a place called Beaumaris, in the province of Chester, there is a hermaphrodite, who has hitherto chosen to dress as a man, and as such, was married and had children. A few months ago, however, he changed his functions and is now pregnant. It seems contrary to nature that he should both conceive and engender as well." *CSP, Spain*, III, 475. John Neale also notes the monstrous births of 1562, but argues they were perceived as Protestant omens against a proposed meeting between Elizabeth and Mary Stuart. *Queen Elizabeth I*, 115–16.

45. Harrison, *A Second Jacobean Journal*, 143–44.

46. Francis Osborne, *Historical Memoires on the Reigns of Queen Elizabeth and King James* (London: Francis Grismond, 1658), 384. The belief that Elizabeth had children continued in the centuries after her death. In 1850 a correspondent to

Notes and Queries stated "there s a current belief in Ireland that the family of Mapother, in Roscommon, is descended from Queen Elizabeth." II, 60 (December 21, 1850), 500.

47. Jenkins, *Elizabeth the Great*, 77; *CSP, Spain*, I, 63; *CSP, Venice*, I, 105; *CSP, Rome*, II, 363; Camden, *The History of the Most Renowned and Victorious Princess Elizabeth*, 1688 ed., 83, 269; *DNB*, X, 192–93.

48. Quoted in Stefan Zweig, *Mary Queen of Scots and the Isles* (New York: Viking Press, 1935), 299. The original letter appears in French in Murdin and Haynes, ed., *A Collection of State Papers*, 558–59. I have used Zweig's translation. David Laing, ed., *Notes of Ben Jonson's Conversations with William Drummond* (London: Printed for the Shakespeare Society, 1842), 23; *CSP, Spain*, I, 569.

49. Elizabeth is not the only one to put it in those terms. De Feria wrote to Philip II at the very beginning of her reign that Elizabeth "is very much wedded to the people." *CSP, Spain*, I, 4. In analyzing Elizabeth's parliamentary rhetoric, Heisch points out that, throughout her reign, Elizabeth "pictures and presents herself as a loving and yet virginal mother." "Queen Elizabeth I," 32.

50. Montrose, "Shaping Fantasies," 78.

51. Camden, *The History of the Most Renowned and Victorious Princess Elizabeth*, 1688 ed., 27. In 1563 she told her Parliament, "I assure you all, that thoughe, after my death, you may have many stepdames yet shall you never [have] a more naturall mother than I meane to be unto you all." Harington, *Nugae Antiquae*, I, 83.

52. Norman Egbert McClure, ed., *The Letters and Epigrams of Sir John Harington* (Philadelphia: University of Pennsylvania Press, 1930), 96; John Ayre, *The Works of John Jewel* (Cambridge: Cambridge University Press, 1845–50), III, 118; Nichols, *The Progresses and Public Processions of Queen Elizabeth*, II, 146, 165; Camden, *The History of the Most Renowned and Victorious Princess Elizabeth*, 1688 ed., 84–85. The image of Elizabeth as nurse is a common one. See, for example, a speech in her honor at Cambridge, 1578. She was thanked for what she did "particularly to the two Universities, which were kept by her as by a Nurse in quietness to be nourished in piety, and all other learning." Nichols, *Progresses*, II, 110. In 1588 Anthony Marten, keeper of the royal library at Westminster, described Elizabeth as "sent from above, to nurse and protect the true Christian commonwealth." "An Exhortation to stirre the Minds of all Her Majesty's faithfull Subjects, to defend their Countrey, in this dangerous Time, from the Invasion of Enemies" (London: John Windet, 1588) in *The Harleian Miscellany*, ed. William Oldys and Thomas Park (London: John White and John Murray, 1808), I, 174. In his ground-breaking article on gender and power in Elizabethan England, Louis Montrose argues that "by fashioning herself into a singular combination of Maiden, Matron, and Mother, the queen transformed the normal domestic life-cycle of an Elizabethan female into what was at once a social paradox and a religious mystery." "Shaping Fantasies," 80.

53. *Salisbury Papers*, X, 172–73. One can see how much of a psychological pull a female monarch has even to this day. The incident with Edwards is eerily reminiscent of the case of Michael Fagin, who broke into the second Elizabeth's

bedchamber, also professing love. Fagin was also perceived as having "serious personal problems and . . . suicidal tendencies." *Time*, August 2, 1982; Osborne, *Works*, 54.

54. *CSP, Spain*, I, 368.

55. George Lyman Kittredge, *Witchcraft in Old and New England* (Cambridge, MA: Harvard University Press, 1929), 129; Jasper Ridley, *Henry VIII: The Politics of Tyranny* (New York: Fromm International, 1986), 306–7; Carolly Erickson, *Great Harry* (New York: Summit Books, 1980), 266.

56. Lodge, *Illustrations of British History*, II, 413.

57. *CSP, Venice*, VII, 557; Stowe cited in Wright, *Queen Elizabeth and Her Times*, II, 381.

58. John Strype, *Memorials of the Reverend Father in God, Thomas Cranmer*, (Oxford: Oxford University Press, 1840), 456. In the seventeenth century, Lady Eleanor Davies was convinced that her second husband, Sir Archibald Douglas, was the true oldest son of James I. *The New Jerusalem at Hand* (London, 1649), 11; *The Lady Eleanor Douglas, Dowager, Her Jubiles Pleas or Appeal* (London, 1650), 2–3. I am indebted to Esther Cope for this reference.

59. Camden, *The History of the Most Renowned and Victorious Princess Elizabeth*, 1688 ed., 26; Montrose, "Shaping Fantasies," 80; *Miscellaneous State Papers*, I, 174.

Chapter Five: The Return of the King

1. Bruce, ed., *Correspondence of Matthew Parker*, 469–70; Strype, *The Life and Acts of Matthew Parker*, 391–92; Andrew Forest Scott Pearson, *Thomas Cartwright and Elizabethan Puritanism* (Cambridge: at the University Press, 1925), 393, 483.

2. For a discussion of the mock king idea, see Sandra Billington, *The Mock King* (New York: Oxford University Press, 1991).

3. A number of modern studies have considered the belief in Edward VI's survival at least briefly. Very useful is the early article by Margaret Cornfield, "A Legend Concerning King Edward VI, "*English Historical Review* 23 (1908), 286–90. Thomas, *Religion and the Decline of Magic*, 420 and Emmison, *Elizabethan Life: Disorder*, 41 treat the issue of impostors at least briefly in much larger books. Cynthia Chermely's essay is provocative but errors and omissions mar it. "'Nawghtye Mallenchollye': Some Faces of Madness in Tudor England," *The Historian* 49, 3 (1987), 309–29.

4. Norman Cohn, *The Pursuit of the Millennium* (1963; rev. expanded ed., London: T. Smith, 1970), 79.

5. For more on these cases, see Harold Hutchison, *Edward II: The Pliant King* (London: Eyre and Spotiswoode, 1971), 144; Harold Hutchinson, *The Hollow Crown* (London: Eyre and Spottiswoode, 1961), 235–36; Caroline Bingham, *The Life and Times of Edward II* (London: Weidenfeld and Nicolson, 1973), 212–17. There are of course many parallels in Russian history as well: the false Dimitri of

the Time of Troubles, Pugachev calling himself Peter III during the rebellion of 1773 against Catherine II, and the rumors of the survival of the last czar's daughter Anastasia after 1917. I think, however, that these may well be part of a rather different tradition, and I am not sure how fruitful a comparison can be made with the medieval/early modern English examples.

6. For more on Simnel see Michael J. Bennett, *Lambert Simnel and the Battle of Stoke* (New York: St. Martin's Press, 1987) and Michael Van Cleave Alexander, *The First of the Tudors: A Study of Henry VII and His Reign* (Totowa, NJ: Rowman and Littlefield, 1980), 53–57. For more information on Warbeck see James Gairdner, *The History of the Life and Reign of Richard the Third, to which is added the story of Perkin Warbeck* (revised ed., Cambridge: Cambridge University Press, 1898; rpt., New York: Kraus Reprint, 1968), 263–335.

7. J. J. Scarisbrick suggests that "English experience of the queen regnant was remote and unhappy, and Henry's conventional mind, which no doubt accorded with his subjects', demanded a son as a political necessity." *Henry VIII*, 150.

8. His illegitimate son Henry Fitzroy had died a decade previously. While John Perrot claimed to be Henry VIII's son, he was never so acknowledged by Henry.

9. *L&P*, VI, 1193. See also, Erickson, *Bloody Mary*, 106.

10. For a discussion of the case, see Natalie Davis, *The Return of Martin Guerre* (Cambridge MA: Harvard University Press, 1983), who argues that the imposture lasted for the length of time that it did because Martin's wife Bertrande de Rols collaborated with the impostor. Stephen Greenblatt's essay, "Psychoanalysis and History," discusses the case in connection with drama and identity issues of the time. *Literary Theory/Renaissance Texts*, ed. Parker and Quint, 210–24.

11. Very useful on this subject is Jackson Cope, who discusses the metaphor of the world as dream in Renaissance drama. *The Theater and the Dream: from Metaphor to Form in Renaissance Drama* (Baltimore: Johns Hopkins University Press, 1973), 211–44.

12. However, in *Edward VI: The Threshold of Power* (Cambridge, MA: Harvard University Press, 1970), 515, W. K. Jordan does suggest that it was Edward himself who thought of excluding his sisters, and presented it to Northumberland. In a thoughtful essay, Dale Hoak has written, "Contrary to what has been thought, the scheme to alter the succession originated in Northumberland's camp and not in King Edward's brain." Furthermore Hoak asserts, "Edward VI's 'speeches' and papers really present the somewhat pathetic figure of an articulate puppet far removed from the realities of government." "Rehabilitating the Duke of Northumberland: Politics and Political Control," in *The Mid-Tudor Polity, c. 1540–1560*, ed. Robert Tittler and Jennifer Loach (Totowa, NJ: Rowman and Littlefield, 1980), 43, 48.

13. Susan Brigden, *London and the Reformation* (Oxford: Oxford University Press, 1991), 523.

14. Cornfield, "A Legend Concerning King Edward VI," 286–90; John G. Dubois, ed. *Chronicle of the Grey Friars of London* (Camden Soc., Old Series LIII, 1852), 78; John Clapham, *Elizabeth of England*, ed. Evelyn Plummer Read and Conyers Read (Philadelphia: University of Pennsylvania Press, 1951), 54. There were

also rumors early in Mary's reign that Edward had received a popish burial, even though Mary had been persuaded against burying her brother with full Roman obsequies. Brigden, *London and the Reformation*, 528.

15. *APC*, IV, 363, 364, 367, 390, 391–92.

16. *APC*, IV, 383–84; Cornfield, "A Legend Concerning King Edward VI," 287.

17. D. M. Loades, *Politics and the Nation, 1450–1660* (London: Oxford University Press, 1974), 235, 235n. Also, many scholars believe Protestantism did not really become deeply entrenched until the 1560s.

18. Carolley Erickson, *Bloody Mary* (Garden City, NY: Doubleday, 1978), 415.

19. *CSP, Venice*, VI, 85; *Holinshed's Chronicles*, IV, 75; D. M. Loades, *Two Tudor Conspiracies* (Cambridge: at the University Press, 1965), 148; John Stow, *Annals of England faithfully collected out of the most authenticall authors, records, and other monuments of antiquitie, from the first inhabitation until this present yeare 1592* (London: R. Newbery, 1592), 1062.

20. John Gough Nichols, ed., *The Diary of Henry Machyn* (London: Camden Society, 1848), ix; *CSP, Venice*, VI, 85.

21. Charles Wriothesley, *A Chronicle of England During the Reigns of the Tudors, from 1485 to 1559*, ed. William Douglas Hamilton (Westminster: Camden Society, 1875–1877), II, 129; Stow, *Annals of England*, 1592 ed., 1062.

22. *APC*, V, 221, 228.

23. *CSP, Venice*, VI, 324.

24. Stow, *Annals of England*, 1592 ed., 1064–65; *CSP, Venice*, VI, 339.

25. Howard Dobin, *Merlin's Disciples: Prophecy, Poetry, and Power in Renaissance England* (Stanford, CA: Stanford University Press, 1990), 123.

26. John Harvey, *A Discoursive Probleme concerning Prophesies* (London: J. Jackson, 1588), 61.

27. *OED*, IX, 337; *SP, Domestic*, 12/186; Cornfield, "A Legend Concerning Edward VI," 289.

28. *SP, Domestic*, 12/186.

29. Strype, *Annals*, II, Part 2, 503–5; *Lansdowne Manuscripts*, vol. 16, #8, reel 7.

30. The dating of when Mantell made this claim is a bit obscure. According to the *Acts of the Privy Council* it was about 1578 and Mantell was finally executed in 1581. The *Calendar of State Papers, Domestic*, however, give the examinations of those who supported Mantell as having been taken in 1585.

31. *Calendar of the Assize Records: Essex*, 175.

32. *Calendar of the Assize Records: Essex*, 191; *APC*, 11, 194, 214.

33. Chermely, "'Nawghtye Mallenchollye,'" 322. Chermely's discussion of Mantell is interesting, but her description of the events is also quite problematic. It is hard to sort through. Keith Thomas admits "I have not been able to resolve all the difficulties of fact and interpretation which the evidence for this case presents." *Religion and the Decline of Magic*, 420n3. I too have difficulty with the Mantell case.

34. *SP, Domestic*, 12/186; *Calendar of the Assize Records: Essex*, 209, 215; *APC*, 13, 80; *CSP, Domestic, 1581–90*, II, 315.

35. *Calendar of Assize Records: Essex,* 214, 294; Emmison, *Elizabethan Life: Disorder,* 41; Thomas, *Religion and the Decline of Magic,* 420; *CSP, Domestic, 1581–90,* II, 469–70; Cornfield, "A Legend Concerning Edward VI," 289.

36. People in the sixteenth century did have some concept of mental illness. For example, Thomas Elyot published *Castel of Helth* in 1539 (revised 1541). After 1580 there were many reported cases of melancholy. For more on sixteenth-century ideas of madness, see Michael MacDonald, *Mystical Bedlam: Madness, Anxiety, and Healing in Seventeenth-Century England* (Cambridge: Cambridge University Press, 1981); Winfried Schliener, *Melancholy, Genius, and Utopia in the Renaissance* (Wiesbaden: Otto Harrassowitz, 1991); Vieda Skultans, *English Madness: Ideas of Insanity, 1580–1890* (London and Boston: Routledge and Kegan Paul, 1979).

37. Ellis, *Original Letters,* 3rd Ser., IV, 60–63; *Lansdowne Manuscripts,* vol. 99, #6.

38. *Calendar of the Assize Records: Essex,* 287.

39. Mark Eccles, *Christopher Marlowe in London* (Cambridge, MA: Harvard University Press, 1934), 154; Charles Nicholl, *The Reckoning: The Murder of Christopher Marlowe* (London: Picador, in association with Jonathan Cape, 1993), 185–88; Chermely, "'Nawghtye Mallenchollye,'" 325. That year Drake destroyed some of the Spanish fleet at Cadiz. He then heard that ships rich in cargo were somewhere near the Azores and could possibly be taken. The *San Felipe* was reputedly among the greatest in the fleet and was the greatest prize Drake and the English had taken in eight years. Its cargo included great quantities of spices and other goods such as ebony, silk, jewels, china, gold, and silver. "The capture of the *San Felipe* had 'made' the 1587 voyage. The attack at Cadiz . . . may have disrupted Spanish preparations for the Armada, but in the eyes of most English contemporaries the dazzling fortune brought home in the carrack was the perfect consummation of the adventure." John Sugden, *Sir Francis Drake* (London: Barrie and Jenkins, 1990), 216. The departure to the Azores also helped slow the preparations for the Armada since Philip sent his fleet after Drake to try to protect the treasure ships returning from the East.

40. F. A. Inderwick, ed., *A Calendar of the Inner Temple Records* (London: Published by order of the Masters of the Bench and Sold by Henry Sotheran and Co.; Stevens and Haynes; Stevens and Sons, Ltd., 1896), 473; P. W. Hasler, *The History of Parliament: The House of Commons, 1558–1603* (London: HMSO, 1981), II, 8–9; *The Records of the Honourable Society of Lincoln's Inn: The Black Books. I, 1422–1586* (Lincoln's Inn, 1897), 408; Stow, *Annals of England,* 1615 ed., 728.

41. *Lansdowne Manuscript,* vol. 53, # 79.

42. Nicholl, *The Reckoning,* 188.

43. "Writers of the [Elizabethan] period distinguish so many subcategories of melancholy that it almost seems as though Renaissance psychopathology regards all mental abnormality as a species of melancholy. Roughly speaking, our term madness is synonymous with the Elizabethan term melancholy." Skultans, *English Madness,* 18.

44. Reginald R. Sharpe, *London and the Kingdom* (London: Longmans, Green, and Co., 1894), I, 552.

45. *Index of Wills Proved in the Prerogative Court of Canterbury, Vol. IV,*

1584–1604, and Now Preserved in the Principal Probate Registry, Somerset House, London, compiled by S. A. Smith, M.D., ed. Edward Alexander Fry (London: The British Record Society, 1902), PROB 11/75. The Edward Burnell who died in 1587 appears to be Anne's husband. It was certainly not the Edward Burnell who died ten years later. This Anne Burnell is also a different person from the Anne Burnell mentioned in the Inquisition after the death of Elizabeth Kennett. *Inquisitions Post Mortem of the Tudor Period for the City of London, Part III, Elizabeth, 1577–1603*, ed. Edward Alexander Fry (London: The British Record Society, 1908), 130–31. My thanks to Carol Brobeck, Bill Spellman, and especially Geoffrey Hood for their aid in obtaining this information.

46. *APC*, 23, 331.

47. *APC*, 23, 366–67.

48. Hyder E. Rollins, *An Analytical Index to the Ballad-Entries in the Registers of the Company of Stationers of London* (orig. pub. 1924 by the University of North Carolina; Hatboro, PA.: Tradition Press, 1967), 209–10; Stow, *Annals of England*, 1615 ed., 764.

49. For more on Hacket, see Curtis Charles Breight, "Duelling Ceremonies: The Strange Case of William Hacket, Elizabethan Messiah," *Journal of Medieval and Renaissance Studies* 19, 1 (Spring, 1989), 35–67; John Booty, "Tumult in Cheapside: The Hacket Conspiracy," *Historical Magazine of the Protestant Episcopal Church* 42 (1973), 293–317; Thomas, *Religion and the Decline of Magic*, 133–35; Richard Bauckham, *Tudor Apocalypse* (Oxford: Sutton Coutenay Press, 1979), 191–207; Patrick Collinson, *The Elizabethan Puritan Movement* (London: Jonathan Cape, 1967), 405–31.

50. Thomas, *Religion and the Decline of Magic*, 134.

51. Richard Cosin, *Conspiracie for Pretended Reformation* (London: Christopher Barker, 1592), 5; Breight, "Duelling Ceremonies," 41, 45, 48; Camden, *The History of the Most Renowned and Victorious Princess Elizabeth*, 1635 ed., 400.

52. Cosin, *Conspiracie for Pretended Reformation*, 35, 36; Stow, *Annals of England*, 1592 ed., 1100.

53. Cosin, *Conspiracie for Pretended Reformation*, 55; Stow, *Annals of England*, 1615 ed., 1288.

54. Cosin, *Conspiracie for Pretended Reformation*, 55.

55. Breight, "Duelling Ceremonies," 52.

56. Cosin, *Conspiracie for Pretended Reformation*, 56–57.

57. Cosin, *Conspiracie for Pretended Reformation*, 58; Stow, *Annals of England*, 1615 ed., 1288.

58. Cosin, *Conspiracie for Pretended Reformation*, 60, 62–63; *CSP, Domestic, 1591–94*, III, 75; Stow, *Annals of England*, 1615 ed., 1288; Camden, *The History of the Most Renowned and Victorious Princess Elizabeth*, 1635 ed., 401; Breight, "Duelling Ceremonies," 55, 57.

59. *CSP, Spain*, II, 611; Barbara Rosen, ed., *Witchcraft* (New York: Taplinger, 1972), 83. There was also an attempt at image magic very early in the reign, for which John Dee was called in to help. See previous chapter. Nor was Elizabeth alone in being the target of attacks through witchcraft. Mabel Brigge attempted

a spell on Henry VIII (see previous chapter). In the reign of the first Tudor monarch, conspirators obtained a magic ointment to spread on a doorway, so that when Henry VII walked through it, he would be murdered by "those who loved him best." This spell also failed, perhaps because Henry VII had few who loved him. Erickson, *Bloody Mary*, 20–21.

60. Cosin, *Conspiracie for Pretended Reformation*, 22; Camden, *The History of the Most Renowned and Victorious Princess Elizabeth*, 1635 ed., 407.

61. Cosin, *Conspiracie for Pretended Reformation*, 65, 71–72, 76, 78.

62. Sandra Clark, *The Elizabethan Pamphleteers* (London: Athlone Press, 1983), 88. In 1597 Arthington wrote *Provision for the Poor now in Penry* in which he attempted to systematically analyze the causes of poverty and makes some proposals. His need to effect reform had taken a rather different, and much more sober turn. A. G. Dickens, *Reformation Studies* (London: Hambledon Press, 1982), 231.

63. Collinson, *The Elizabethan Puritan Movement*, 424–25.

64. *CSP, Domestic, 1591–94*, III, 76; Bacon, *Works*, ed. Basil Montagu, V (London: William Pickering, 1825–34) 412; Thomas, *Religion and the Decline of Magic*, 133; Breight, "Duelling Ceremonies," 61–3; Cosin, *Conspiracie for Pretended Reformation*, 62–63; *OED*, II, 518; Loades, *Mary Tudor*, 335. It is possible that Thomas Deloney also wrote about the Hacket case as there is a lost pamphlet written prior to 1596 called "Repent, England, Repent." Deloney, *Works*, ed. Francis Oscar Mann (Oxford: Clarendon Press, 1912), 495–96.

65. In 1568 Bartholomew Taylor was imprisoned for saying "We shall never have a merye world so longe as we have a woman govener and as the quene lyved." *Calendar of the Assize Records: Kent*, 77.

66. *Calendar of the Assize Records: Kent*, 246. The scatalogical motif was echoed a decade and a half later. In 1599 Mary Bunton was whipped and placed in the stocks after she said, "I care not a Turde for the Queene nor hir precepts." *Calendar of the Assize Records: Kent*, 445.

67. *Calendar of the Assize Records: Surrey*, 282, 345.

68. *Calendar of the Assize Records: Essex*, 373; *Calendar of the Assize Records: Kent*, 402, 431, 440; *CSP, Domestic*, III, 282, V, 136–37. Fraunces made these comments after he had failed to seduce Elizabeth Baylie. His "line" to Baylie was that, since the queen had lovers and even three illegitimate children, why did she refuse him. For more on this case see previous chapter.

69. *Salisbury Papers*, X, 201, 202; XI, 574; Emmison, *Elizabethan Life: Disorder*, 65.

70. *Salisbury Papers*, IX, 167–68, 173. A Puritan minister named Gervase Smith did, however, talk in 1606 of prophecies that included the eventual restoration of the true faith by someone named Edward, possibly Edward VI, "who was either dead or living 'in Africa' and would be miraculously raised again." Smith was known in his neighborhood for his obsessive interest in prophecy. By this time, Keith Thomas suggests, Edward VI had taken on something of the character of the sleeping emperor who would come back when his people needed him most. As late as 1652 a published collection of prophecies declared, "Up Edward the Sixth . . . the time is come." Thomas, *Religion and the Decline of Magic*, 421–22.

71. See previous chapter for more on this issue.

72. Catherine Belsey, *The Subject of Tragedy: Identity and Difference in Renaissance Drama* (London and New York: Methuen, 1985), 190–91.

73. Christopher Hill, *The World Turned Upside Down: Radical Ideas During the English Revolution* (Middlesex: Penguin, 1972), 16.

Chapter Six: Elizabeth as King and Queen

1. Critical to my thinking in this chapter is the work of Constance Jordan and Leah Marcus. Even though in a number of ways I disagree with their interpretations, their ideas have helped me deeply to think through this material. Also valuable is Theodora A. Jankowski, "'As I am Egypt's Queen': Cleopatra, Elizabeth I, and the Female Body Politic," *Assays: Critical Approaches to Medieval and Renaissance Texts* V (1989), 91–110. Conversations with Richard Horwich, Lena Orlin, and Jo Carney were also very helpful.

2. Strype, *Annals of the Reformation*, I (ii), 399, 406. For more on Heath, see chapter two.

3. J. R. Tanner, *Tudor Constitutional Documents, A.D. 1485–1603, with an Historical Commentary* (Cambridge: at the University Press, 1948), 123, 124; Constance Jordan, "Representing Political Androgyny: More on the Siena Portrait of Queen Elizabeth I," in *The Renaissance Englishwoman in Print: Counterbalancing the Canon*, ed. Anne M. Haselkorn and Betty S. Travitsky (Amherst: University of Massachusetts Press, 1990), 158.

4. Marie Axton, *The Queen's Two Bodies: Drama and the Elizabethan Succession* (London: Royal Historical Society, 1977), x, 12; Joel Hurstfield, *The Illusion of Power in Tudor Politics* (London: Athlone Press, 1979), 24; Bushnell, *Tragedies of Tyrants*, 67–69.

5. Starkey, "Representation Through Intimacy," 189; Digges, *Compleat Ambassador*, 364. In the reign of Mary as well there was the suggestion of the two bodies of the queen—one her own, the other, the nation. The Earl of Arundel wrote to the Earl of Shrewsbury during the Wyatt rebellion: "God be thanked, the Queen's Highness is in good health of her body, but sick in certain naughty members of her commonwealth, as the Carews, in the west parts, and Wyat . . . in Kent; of which disease I trust Almighty God shall shortly deliver her freely." 28 January 1553/4, Lodge, *Illustrations of British History*, I, 231.

6. Lodge, *Illustrations of British History*, II, 36, 57; Walter Bourchier Devereux, *Lives and Letters of the Devereux, Earls of Essex, in the Reigns of Elizabeth, James I, and Charles I: 1540–1646* (London: John Murray, 1853), I, 246–47. Essex will be further discussed in the next chapter.

7. Anne (Righter) Barton, *Shakespeare and the Idea of the Play* (London: Chatto and Windus, 1962), 113.

8. James Melville, *Memoirs*, ed. A. Francis Steuart (New York: E. P. Dutton, 1930), 97–98.

9. Many scholars have approached this issue from a variety of perspectives.

For example, Peter Erickson argues that "the presence of strong women in Shakespeare's work from the Elizabethan period can be read as oblique glances at the cultural presence of Queen Elizabeth I." *Rewriting Shakespeare, Rewriting Ourselves* (Berkeley and Los Angeles: University of California Press, 1991), 24.

10. Sam Schoenbaum, *Shakespeare and Others* (London: Scolar Press, 1985), 70; Arthur Gould Lee, *The Son of Leicester* (London: Victor Gollancz, Ltd., 1964), 116; R. Mark Benbow, cited in Jean E. Howard, "Crossdresssing, the Theatre, and Gender Struggle in Early Modern England," *Shakespeare Quarterly* 39 (1988), 420; Howard, "Crossdressing," 421; Philip Stubbes, *Anatomy of Abuses* (1583), ed. William B. D. D. Turnbull (London: W. Pickering, 1836), 68; William Averell, *A mervailous combat of contrarieties* (London: Thomas Hacket, 1588). For more on this controversy, see Woodbridge, *Women in the English Renaissance*, 139–51.

11. Both Frances Teague and Allison Heisch have done important work on the variant texts of Elizabeth's speeches. Teague, "Queen Elizabeth in Her Speeches," in *Gloriana's Face: Women, Public and Private in the English Renaissance*, ed. S. P. Cerasano and Marion Wynne-Davies (Detroit: Wayne State University Press, 1992), 63–78. I am grateful to Professor Teague for sharing her work with me in manuscript.

12. R. W. Heinze, *The Proclamations of the Tudor Kings* (Cambridge: Cambridge University Press, 1976), 22.

13. Haigh, *Elizabeth I*, 120.

14. Marcus, "Shakespeare's Comic Heroines," 137.

15. Mullaney, *The Place of the Stage*, 105; Barton (as Righter), *Shakespeare and the Idea of the Play*, 114.

16. Orgel, *The Illusion of Power*, 9; Neale, *Elizabeth I and Her Parliaments, 1584–1601*, 119; *Holinshed's Chronicles*, IV, 933–35; McIlwain, *The Political Works of James I*, 43.

17. Letter to John Chamberlain July 4, 1603. Maurice Lee, Jr., ed., *Dudley Carleton to John Chamberlain, 1603–1624: Jacobean Letters* (New Brunswick, NJ: Rutgers University Press, 1972), 35–36.

18. Jerzy Limon, "The Masque of Stuart Culture," in *The Mental World of the Jacobean Court*, ed. Linda Levy Peck (Cambridge: Cambridge University Press, 1991), 214.

19. Marcus, *Puzzling Shakespeare*, 238n86; Ben Jonson, *Works*, ed. C. H. Herford and Percy and Evelyn Simpson. 11 vols. (Oxford: Clarendon Press, 1925–52), I, 373–74.

20. For a discussion of Elizabeth as a character, see Frederick Boas, "Queen Elizabeth in Elizabethan and Later Drama" in Boas, *Queen Elizabeth in Drama and Related Studies* (London: George Allen & Unwin, 1950), 9–35.

21. Stephen Greenblatt, *Renaissance Self-Fashioning: From More to Shakespeare* (Chicago: University of Chicago Press, 1980); Lacey Baldwin Smith, *Treason in Tudor England: Politics and Paranoia* (Princeton, NJ: Princeton University Press, 1986), 88–89.

22. Patricia Fumerton, "'Secret' Arts: Elizabethan Miniatures and Sonnets," in *Representing the English Renaissance*, ed. Stephen Greenblatt (Los Angeles and Berkeley: University of California Press, 1988), 94; Beryl Hughes, "Success in a

Man's World: The Reign of Elizabeth I of England," *Women's Studies Journal* I (April, 1985), 39. Another example in Shakespeare is Antonio in *The Merchant of Venice*: "I hold the world but as as the world . . . /A stage, where every man must play a part" (I.i.).

23. Howard, "Crossdresssing," 435; Bassnett, *Elizabeth I*, 127.

24. James Osborn, *The Quenes Maiesties Passage through the Citie of London to Westminster the Day before her Coronation*, ed. J. E. Neale (New Haven, CT: Published for the Elizabethan Club by Yale University Press, 1960), 11, 28; *Holinshed's Chronicle*, IV, 176; Aylmer, *Harborrowe*.

25. Melville, *Memoirs*, 94; Marcus, "Shakespeare's Comic Heroines," 140; Goldberg, *Endlesse Worke*, 150; Neale, *Elizabeth I and Her Parliaments, 1559–1581*, 160; Neale, *Elizabeth I and Her Parliaments, 1584–1601*, 385.

26. Wright, *Queen Elizabeth and Her Times*, I, 58.

27. *CSP, Spain*, I, 364. Constance Jordan argues that Elizabeth's comment suggests the male body of the body politic, "Representing Political Androgyny," 160. I believe, however, that Elizabeth was well aware that her people saw her as female despite any philosophy of two bodies.

28. See Elizabeth's comment on marriage in plays given at the beginning of chapter three.

29. Eric Mercer, "Minatures," in *English Art, 1553–1625*, ed. Eric Mercer (Oxford: Clarendon Press, 1962), 196; Fumerton, "'Secret' Arts," 96; Haigh, *Elizabeth I*, 148; Heisch, "Patriarchy," 46.

30. Richard Brathwait, *The English Gentlewoman Drawne Out to the Full Body: Expressing What Habilliments Do Best Attire Her* (London: B. Alsop and T. Fawcet, 1631), 88. For further analysis of Brathwait and other Renaissance conduct book authors, see Ann Rosalind Jones, "Nets and Bridles: Early Modern Conduct Books as Sixteenth Century Women's Lyrics," in *The Ideology of Conduct: Essays on Literature and the History of Sexuality*, ed. Nancy Armstrong and Leonard Tennenhouse (New York and London: Methuen, 1987).

31. André Hurault de Maisse, *A Journal of all that was Accomplished by Monsieur de Maisse, Ambassador, in England from Henry IV to Queen Elizabeth, 1597*, translated from the French and edited with introduction by G. B. Harrison and R. A. Jones (Bloomsbury: Nonesuch Press, 1931), 110.

32. In the same way that we think about some of the portraits of Elizabeth at the end of the reign which show a young, beautiful idealized image. See Elizabeth Pomeroy, *Reading the Portraits of Queen Elizabeth I* (Hampden, CT: Archon Books, 1989), 76. For more on Raleigh, see Marion Campbell, "Inscribing Imperfection: Sir Walter Ralegh and the Elizabethan Court," *English Literary Renaissance* 20, 2 (Spring, 1990), 233–53.

33. Devereux, *Lives and Letters of the Devereux*, I, 493; II, 131.

34. Marcus, "Shakespeare's Comic Heroines," 146; Stephen Greenblatt, "Fiction and Friction," in Greenblatt, *Shakespearean Negotiations* (Berkeley: University of California Press, 1988), 69; Howard, "Crossdresssing," 431, 432.

35. Susan C. Shapiro, "Feminists in Elizabethan England," *History Today* XXVII, 11 (November, 1977), 703–11; *CSP Spain*, I, 467.

36. Winfried Schleiner, "*Divina virago*: Queen Elizabeth as an Amazon," *Studies in Philology* LXXV (1987), 179; Aylmer, *Harborrowe*, H2.

37. In *Puzzling Shakespeare*, Leah Marcus argues that the character Joan in *1 Henry VI* is a fractured mirror of Elizabeth. Since Joan helped to win back French lands from the English, Elizabethans would attribute her skills as coming from the devil.

38. Bassnett, *Elizabeth I*, 123. By the time Essex left Ireland September 24, 1599 he had knighted 81 of his followers. Smith, *Treason*, 312n46. This was not the first time Essex had been over-liberal in bestowing this honor. In 1591 in Rouen he had given out twenty-four knighthoods and was equally openhanded with the honor in 1595 after Cadiz. Robert Lacey, *Robert Earl of Essex: An Elizabethan Icarus* (London: Weidenfeld and Nicolson, 1971), 121, 161.

39. Denis Hay, trans. and ed., *The Anglica Historia, A.D. 1485–1537 by Polydore Vergil*, Camden Society, 3rd ser., vol. 74 (London: Royal Historical Society, 1950), 197.

40. Starkey, "Representation Through Intimacy," 198; Erickson, *Bloody Mary*, 302.

41. *Shakespeare's Europe: A Survey of the Condition of Europe at the end of the 16th Century: Being the unpublished chapters of Fynes Moryson's Itinerary (1617)*, ed. Charles Hughes (first published London, 1913; second edn. New York: Benjamin Blom, 1967), 245.

42. *CSP, Spain*, IV, 17–18.

43. *CSP, Spain*, IV, 131; Camden, *The History of the Most Renowned and Victorious Princess Elizabeth*, 1688 ed., 142.

44. Stubbs, *Gaping Gulf*, 11. For more on Stubbs, see chapter three.

45. Augustus Jessopp describes Topcliffe as a "monster," whose "cruelties would fill a volume." *One Generation of a Norfolk House* (London: Burns and Oates, 1879), 70. Neale describes him as "that curious, sadistic gentleman, Richard Topcliffe, a man of birth, education, and religious zeal, who revelled in his official task of torturing Catholics." *Elizabeth I and Her Parliaments, 1584–1601*, 153. Charles Nicholl says of Topcliffe, "We would call Topcliffe a sadist. . . . You will find Master Topcliffe, many times over, in the files of Amnesty International." *The Reckoning*, 111, 112. For an alternative view, see A. L. Rowse, "The Truth About Topcliffe," in *Court and Country: Studies in Tudor Social History* (Brighton, Sussex: Harvester, 1987), 181–210. Rowse is far more sympathetic to Topcliffe than I am.

46. Nichols, *Progresses*, II, 217; Jessopp, *One Generation of a Norfolk House*, 70–71; *DNB*, XIX, 79–80. For an example of Topcliffe's dedication to hunting Catholics, see his letter to the Earl of Shrewsbury of August 30, 1578 in Nichols, *Progresses*, II, 215–19.

47. Birch, *Memoirs of Queen Elizabeth*, I, 160; Nichols, *Progresses*, II, 219; Richard Challoner, *Memoirs of Missionary Priests*, ed. John Hungerford Pollen, new ed. (New York: P. J. Kenedy and Sons, 1924), 186.

48. Anthony G. Petti, ed., *The Letters and Despatches of Richard Verstegan* (London: Catholic Record Society, 1959), 97; John Hungerford Pollen, ed., *Unpublished Documents Relating to the English Martyrs, 1584–1603* (London: Catholic Record Society, 1908), 209; Harrison, *First Elizabethan Journal*, 104; Nicholl, *The Reckoning*, 112.

49. Petti, *The Letters and Despatches of Richard Verstegan*, 98; Pollen, *Unpublished Documents Relating to the English Martyrs*, 209.

50. For a discussion of the differences in presentations of Henry and Elizabeth in portraiture and their implications for questions of gender and power, see Belsey and Belsey, "Icons of Divinity: Portraits of Elizabeth I." Several scholars (Marcus, *Puzzling Shakespeare*, 55; Johnson, *Elizabeth I*, 79) have stated that Elizabeth liked to stand beside the portrait as a visual expression of her connection with the royalty of her father. While it seems quite a probable thing for Elizabeth to have done, I have seen no contemporary account of it.

51. Carel van Mander in Ian Dunlop, *Palaces & Progresses of Elizabeth I* (London: Jonathan Cape, 1962), 67. My thanks to Lena Orlin for the point about why Elizabeth wore wigs.

52. There is, however, no hard and fast evidence that this is how she dressed. Winfried Schleiner states "I cannot determine what Elizabeth wore that August day. . . . Curiously enough, the writers' descriptions became more and more precise as the Tilbury event receded into the past." *"Divina virago,"* 174, 175.

53. James Aske, *Elizabetha Triumphans: Conteyning the Damned Practizes, that the Diuelish Popes of Rome Have Used Ever Sithence Her Highnesse First Comming to the Crowne, by Mouing her Wicked and Traiterous Subiects to Rebellion and Conspiracies, Thereby to Bereaue Her Maiestie Both of her Lawfull Seate, and Happy life* (London: Printed by Thomas Orwin for Thomas Gubbin, and Thomas Newman, 1588), 19.

54. Camden, *The History of the Most Renowned and Victorious Princess Elizabeth*, 1688 ed., 416.

55. Thomas Deloney, *Works*, ed. Francis Oscar Mann (Oxford: Clarendon Press, 1912), 478.

56. Of course, there is some dispute about the actual words of Elizabeth's speech at Tilbury. What is generally accepted as her speech was not so accepted until the seventeenth century. It originally comes from Leonel Sharp's letter to the Duke of Buckingham written sometime before 1631. *Cabala, Mysteries of State and Government: in Letters of Illustrious Persons and Great Ministers of State* (London: G. Beddell and T. Collins, 1663), 372–74. His report of her speech is on p. 373. Felix Barker, "If Parma Had Landed," *History Today* 38 (May, 1988), 38. Frances Teague suggests "a tentative acceptance of the speech is warranted" "Queen Elizabeth in Her Speeches," 77 n14. John Neale argues "I see no serious reason for rejecting the speech," *Essays in Elizabethan History* (London: Jonathan Cape, 1958), 105, and gives the background to the publication of the speech in a letter from Sharp that was published in *Cabala*.

57. Susan Frye, "The Myth of Elizabeth at Tilbury," *Sixteenth Century Journal* XXIII, 1 (1992), 101; William Leigh, *Queene Elizabeth, Paraleld in Her Princely Vertues, with David, Iosua, and Hezekia* (London: Printed by T. C. for Arthur Johnson, 1612), 94.

58. Barker, "If Parma Had Landed," 38; Aske, *Elizabetha Triumphans*, 25, 26. Thomas Deloney reports Elizabeth's speech as:

And then bespake our noble Queene,
my loving friends and countriemen:
I hope this day the worst is seen,

that in our wars ye shall sustain.
But if our enimies do assaile you,
never let your stomackes faile you.
For in the midst of all your troupe,
we our selves will be in place:
to be your joy, your guide and comfort,
even before your enimies face.

(*Works*, 478)

59. Lodge, *Illustrations of British History*, II, 345.

60. George P. Rice, Jr., *The Public Speaking of Queen Elizabeth: Selections from Her Official Addresses* (New York: Columbia University Press, 1951), 101.

61. Quoted in Nancy Lyman Roelker, *Queen of Navarre: Jeanne d'Albret* (Cambridge, MA: Belknap Press of Harvard University Press, 1968), 36–37; Neale, *Elizabeth I*, 395.

62. Camden, *The History of the Most Renowned and Victorious Princess Elizabeth*, 1688 ed., 23; Wright, *Queen Elizabeth and Her Times*, II, 435. The commonplace book is recorded in the Sotheby Catalogue, *English Literature and History: Comprising Printed Books, Autography Letters and Manuscripts*, also known as the "Hotspur" catalogue (1986). I am indebted to Dr. Peter Beal of Sotheby's for this reference.

63. The speech is quoted in full in Neale, *Elizabeth I and Her Parliaments, 1584–1601*, 388–91. See Teague for a discussion of the different versions of this speech and how they reflect different audiences—whether to Parliament or later printed for all the people. "Queen Elizabeth in Her Speeches," 75.

64. Gilbert Talbot to the Earl of Shrewsbury, 3 May 1578, Lodge, *Illustrations of British History*, 97–98. For more on the Talbots, see Alasdair Hawkyard, "Guardians of Claimants to the throne: the Talbots," in *Rivals in Power: Lives and Letters of the Great Tudor Dynasties*, ed. David Starkey (London: Macmillan, 1990), 230–49.

65. Harington, *Nugae Antiquae*, I, 345. Though Robert Kimbrough takes a rather different stand; see "Androgyny Seen Through Shakespeare's Disguise," *Shakespeare Quarterly* 33 (Spring, 1982), 17. And Catherine Belsey sees it as equally "a male actor and a female character speaking." "Disrupting Sexual Difference," in *Alternative Shakespeare*, ed. John Drakakis (London: Methuen, 1985), 181. Especially useful is the discussion by Marcus, *Puzzling Shakespeare*, 100–101. See also Howard, "Crossdressing," 435. Steve Brown points out that in *Antony and Cleopatra* the character Cleopatra makes a similar sort of statement in the last act when she says, " . . . and I shall see / Some squeaking Cleopatra boy my greatness," (V.ii.19–20) Thus at the the most dramatic moment of the play there is a reminder to the audience that this is really a boy acting. Brown adds, however, "Of course, metadramatic comment also works to intensify theatrical illusion: '*this* boy doesn't squeak, *this* boy doesn't posture, so *this* boy can't be a boy but is Cleopatra herself.'" "The Boyhood of Shakespeare's Heroines: Notes on Gender Ambiguity in the Sixteenth Century," *Studies in English Literature* 30, 2 (Spring, 1990), 244. See also Michael Shapiro, "Lady Mary Wroth Describes a Boy Actress," *Medieval &*

Renaissance Drama in England IV (1989), 187–94 for a discussion of audience response to a boy actor playing a woman and Stephen Orgel, "Nobody's Perfect: Or Why Did the English Stage Take Boys for Women?" *South Atlantic Quarterly* 88,1 (Winter, 1989), 7–29.

Chapter Seven: Dreaming the Queen

1. For more on attitudes toward dreams in the Renaissance, see Susan Parman, *Dream and Culture: An Anthropological Study of the Western Intellectual Tradition* (New York: Praeger, 1991), 71–90; Manfred Weidhorn, *Dreams in Seventeenth-Century English Literature* (The Hague and Paris: Mouton, 1970), 13–43; Nancy Armstrong and Leonard Tennenhouse, *The Imaginary Puritan: Literature, Intellectual Labor, and the Origins of Personal Life* (Berkeley, Los Angeles, and Oxford: University of California Press, 1992), 175–77, 182–85, 190–91; Peter Burke, "L'histoire social des reves,' " *Annales* 28, 2 (March/April, 1973), 329–42; Thomas, *Religion and the Decline of Magic*, 128–30.

2. *Salisbury Papers*, XI, 135.

3. For more on Essex, see Lacey, *Robert Earl of Essex*; G. B. Harrison, *The Life and Death of Robert Devereux* (New York: Henry Holt, 1937); Mervyn James, *Society, Politics and Culture: Studies in Early Modern England* (Cambridge: Cambridge University Press, 1986); Devereux, *Lives and Letters of the Devereux*; and Richard C. McCoy, "'A Dangerous Image': The Earl of Essex and Elizabethan Chivalry," *Journal of Medieval and Renaissance Studies* 13, 2 (1983), 313–29; MacCaffrey, *War and Politics*. For the trial of Essex and the other conspirators, see *Cobbett's Complete Collection of State Trials* I, 1333–60, 1409–52. Peter Erickson approaches the connections between Essex and Shakespeare's plays, *All's Well That Ends Well* and *Hamlet*, in his *Rewriting Shakespeare, Rewriting Ourselves*.

4. Thomas Nash, *The Terrors of the Night Or, A Discourse of Apparitions* (London: William Jones, 1594), C3v.

5. McCoy, "A Dangerous Image," 315.

6. 18 October 1591, Devereux, *Lives and Letters of the Devereux*, I, 250.

7. Mervyn James suggests that "many of these letters, in spite of their 'amorous' and high-flown phraseology, were in fact the work of Essex's secretaries." *Society, Politics and Culture*, 444n98.

8. By the end of his career Essex had dubbed 170 knights, over a quarter of the total in the whole of England. Lacey, *Robert Earl of Essex*, 238.

9. Devereux, *Lives and Letters of the Devereux*, I, 465.

10. André Hurault de Maisse already had a negative view of Elizabeth describing her as "haughty" and "very avaricious." De Maisse, *A Journal of all that was Accomplished by Monsieur de Maisse*, 3, 115.

11. James, *Society, Politics and Culture*, 443. Camden, *The History of the Most Renowned and Victorious Princess Elizabeth*, 1688 ed., 556. Joel Hurstfield suggests of the 1590s: "A new restless generation was emerging, and it had little sympathy for her traditional ways. Faction in her privy council she had never been able wholly

to restrain but it had been kept within bounds. Now it was dangerous and publicly visible as the young Earl of Essex began to claim a dominance over the council and the queen. Their relationship, whatever its meaning and content, had now become turbulent." *Illusion of Power*, 22. For more on factions in Elizabeth's court, particularly in the 1590s, see Alison Wall, "'Points of Contact': Court Favourites and County Faction in Elizabethan England," *Parergon* 6 (1988), 215–26; Simon Adams, "Faction, Clientage and Party English Politics, 1550–1603," *History Today* 32 (1982), 33–39; MacCaffrey, *War and Politics*, 13.

12. Devereux, *Lives and Letters of the Devereux*, I, 493, 501.

13. James, *Society, Politics and Culture*, 445.

14. Wright, *Queen Elizabeth and Her Times*, II, 488; 4 January 1598/9 Essex to Lord Willoughby, *Salisbury Papers*, IX, 10. See also, MacCaffrey, *War and Politics*, 414.

15. Harrison, *Life of Devereux*, 236; Lacey, *Robert Earl of Essex*, 239; Rowland White to Sir Robert Sidney, Devereux, *Lives and Letters of the Devereux*, II, 78.

16. This is my reading of what happened. We of course do not know what Elizabeth was thinking when Essex burst in on her, and it is possible that she simply changed her mind during the day.

17. *Cobbett's State Trials*, I, 1415.

18. See Leeds Barroll's article for a discussion of the staging of *Richard II* prior to the Essex rebellion and the significance of the Richard II theme in Elizabethan politics. "A New History for Shakespeare and His Time," *Shakespeare Quarterly* 39 (1988), 441–64. Barroll points out that we need to take care of how much we relate the staging of the play to the rebellion. Eleven conspirators were known to have attended the performance, including Meyrick and Christopher Blount, but Henry Cuffe, Sir Charles Danvers, the Earls of Southampton, Rutland, and Bedford, and Essex himself did not attend. Captain Thomas Lee also attended the performance. He did not join the uprising but staged his own attack on Elizabeth February 12. *Richard II* may have been quite a popular play with those involved with the Court. In 1597 Raleigh wrote to Robert Cecil about having been to see it. *CSP, Dom., 1595–97*, IV, 451. Robert Cecil himself may have seen it in December 1597, as is implied in a letter to him from Sir Edward Hoby. *Salisbury Papers*, V, 487.

19. *Cobbett's State Trials*, I, 1403; *Salisbury Papers*, XI, 77–78.

20. Southampton, however, survived in the Tower to be freed upon the accession of James I. On March 5, 1601 Sir Christopher Blount, Sir Gelli Meyrick, Henry Cuffe, Sir John Davies, and Sir Charles Danvers all stood trial for high treason and were found guilty. Davies was reprieved but the other four were executed. There were no widescale executions, however; the other members of the conspiracy were let off with fines that were for the most part never paid in full.

21. *Salisbury Papers*, XIV, 193.

22. Breight, "Duelling Ceremonies," 53; Harington, *Nugae Antiquae*, I, 178–79. Many historians today question Essex's mental balance. For example, Alan Haynes talks of his "psychotic fears that his enemies controlled the Queen." *Robert Cecil, Earl of Salisbury, 1563–1612: Servant of Two Sovereigns* (London: Peter Owen, 1989), 62.

23. CBS news reported in February 1992 that 40 percent of the surveyed British public report that they dream about Elizabeth II. In the early seventeenth century Archbishop Laud recorded thirty-two dreams in his diary, in some of which both James I and the Duke of Buckingham appeared. Charles Carlton, "The Dream Life of Archbishop Laud," *History Today* 36 (December, 1986), 9–14.

24. This was a belief in all levels of society. For example, Sir Francis Bacon wrote that "I myself remember, that being in Paris, and my father dying in London, I had a dream (which I told to divers English gentlemen) that my father's house in the country was plaistered all over with black mortar." Quoted in Brian Hill, *Gates of Horn and Ivory: An Anthology of Dreams* (New York: Taplinger, 1967), 13.

25. Richard Kagan, *Lucrecia's Dream: Politics and Prophecy in Sixteenth-Century Spain* (Berkeley: University of California Press, 1990), 3; Charles Carlton, *Archbishop William Laud* (London and New York: Routledge and Kegan Paul, 1987), 144–45.

26. Hill, *The moste pleasaunte arte of the interpretacion of dreames.*

27. *The Political Works of James I*, 45; Peck, *Mental World*, 4. See also Jenny Wormald, "James VI and I, *Basilikon Doron* and *The Trew Law of Free Monarchies*: The Scottish Context and the English Translation," in *Mental World*, ed. Peck, 36–54.

28. 18 June, 1578, Derek Wilson, *Sweet Robin: A biography of Robert Dudley, Earl of Leicester* (London: Hamilton, 1981), 229–30; E. M. Tenison, *Elizabethan England, Vol.III: 1575–1580* (Royal Leamington Spa, Warwick: issued by the author, 1933), III, 148.

29. Robert married Lettice secretly in the spring of 1578 when she found she was pregnant. This did not satisfy Lettice, however, which is understandable given that he had clandestinely married Douglas Sheffield five years earlier and later disavowed it. He convinced Douglas to renounce her claim to a marriage and helped her to marry Edward Stafford. Lettice and her father Sir Francis Knollys insisted on a second secret marriage ceremony on September 21, with Knollys himself, Ambrose Dudley, and the Earl of Pembroke as witnesses.

30. Interestingly enough, Robert described his feelings after the mysterious death of his first wife Amy as if being in a dream. He wrote to Cecil in September 1560: "I thank you much for your being hear: And the great Frendshipp you have shewyd towardes me, I shall not forgett. . . . I pray you lett me hear from you, what you think best for me to doe. . . . I am sorry so sodden a Chaunce shald breede me so great a chandge, for methinks I am hear all this while, as it wear in a Dreame, and to farr, to farr, from the Place I am bound to be. . . . I pray you help him, that sues to be at liberty, owt of so great Bondage. Forgett me not, though you se me not, and I will remember you, and fayll ye not." Murdin and Haynes, *A Collection of State Papers*, I, 361–62.

31. Nash, *The Terrors of the Night*, Fv.

32. Nash, *The Terrors of the Night*, F2.

33. *Lansdowne Manuscripts*, Vol. 99, item 34.

34. *Salisbury Papers*, XI, 91. This kind of message was not ususual. In June 1601 John Richardson sent an even more panicked and bizarre message to

Elizabeth, claiming he had a message or errand from the God Almighty, "sent by the revelation of the Holy Ghost, to none but the Queen." The letter is endorsed "A frantic man." *Salisbury Papers*, XI, 219.

35. *Salisbury Papers*, XI, 132.

36. I am assuming this since Joan Notte's godfather is still alive and she is healthy enough to have traveled to London within the last two years. This does not sound like a woman in her seventies, which she would have had to be to have even a child's consciousness in the mid-1530s.

37. Carlton, *Archbishop William Laud*, 144; Montrose, "Shaping Fantasies," 63.

38. *Salisbury Papers*, XI, 134–5.

39. *Salisbury Papers*, XI, 134. One is reminded of Pistol bringing the news of Henry IV's death to Falstaff with the words, "Sweet knight, thou art now one of the greatest men in this realm." *2 Henry IV* (V.iii.90).

40. *Salisbury Papers*, XI, 133.

41. *Salisbury Papers*, XI, 133. In further irony and coincidence, the linking of Anne Boleyn and Essex in Joan Notte's dream is echoed in Essex's final resting place—near where Anne Boleyn is also buried. Harrison, *Life of Robert Devereux*, 350.

42. Robert Greene, *The Spanish Masquerado* (London: Roger Ward, 1589), B4; Hurstfield, *Illusion of Power*, 22–23.

43. Kagan, *Lucrecia's Dream*, 2. After five years of deliberations, the Inquisition finally condemned Lucrecia as guilty of blasphemy, falsehood, sacrilege, and sedition. Another of her crimes was relating her dreams to others and allowing them to be transcribed. Her punishment, however, was relatively light; she was to receive one hundred lashes and be banished from Madrid. Kagan brilliantly analyzes Lucrecia's dreams and their significance.

44. Kagan, *Lucrecia's Dream*, 70.

45. *OED*, II, 302. One might be reminded as well of the Salem witch trials a century later, when at her execution Sarah Good said to the minister Nicholas Noyes who had called on her to repent: "I am no more a witch than you are a wizard! If you take away my life, God will give you blood to drink." Marion L. Starkey, *The Devil in Massachusetts: A Modern Inquiry into the Salem Witch Trials* (New York: Alfred A. Knopf, 1950), 176.

46. Kagan, *Lucrecia's Dream*, 71.

47. Kagan, *Lucrecia's Dream*, 124, 125.

48. Louis Montrose has already brilliantly analyzed one of these dreams ("Shaping Fantasies"), as has A. L. Rowse, *Simon Forman: Sex and Society in Shakespeare's Age* (London: Weidenfeld and Nicolson, 1974). I draw on both Montrose and Rowse's interpretations. John Dee also recorded his dreams but does not mention any about Elizabeth. He did, however, have a very disturbing one about Burghley where Dee himself was dead and disembowelled while Burghley came to his house to burn his books. Basil Clarke, *Mental Disorder in Earlier Britain: Exploratory Studies* (Cardiff: University of Wales Press, 1975), 250.

49. Rowse, *Simon Forman*, 20.

50. Montrose, "Shaping Fantasies," 65; Rowse, *Simon Forman*, 20. Lacey

suggests of Essex by 1600: "His behaviour had been growing more and more erratic in the course of the last years." *Robert Earl of Essex*, 261.

51. Rowse, *Simon Forman*, 20. See beginning of chapter three of this study for this reference.

52. Clapham, *Elizabeth of England*, 111. See also Henry Chettle, "The Order and Proceedings of the Funerall of the Right High and mightie Princesse Elizabeth," in *Somers Tracts*, I, ed. Walter Scott (London: T. Cadell and W. Davies, 1809), 248–50.

53. *OED*, VI, 176.

54. Peter Wentworth, *A Pithie Exhortation to her Majestie for establishing her successor to the crowne* (Edinburgh: R. Waldegrave, 1598), 101–3.

55. Lacey, *Robert Earl of Essex*, 319; Neale, *Elizabeth I and Her Parliaments, 1584–1601*, 375, 431.

56. Lacey, *Robert Earl of Essex*, 317–18; Birch, *Memoirs of Queen Elizabeth*, II, 506; Johnson, *Elizabeth I*, 434.

57. 3 April 1603, John Manningham, *Diary*, ed. John Bruce (Westminster: J. B. Nichols and Sons, 1868), 159. A further story that has no contemporary basis suggests that Elizabeth gave Essex a ring which he could return to her if she were ever angry with him. In the Tower before his death, Essex entrusted the ring to a page to take to Lady Scrope to give to the queen. Alas, the boy gave the ring instead to her sister Lady Nottingham, whose husband was a sworn foe of Essex. Lady Nottingham kept the ring and Elizabeth waited in vain for this token from Essex that would have saved his life. When Lady Nottingham as she was dying told Elizabeth about the ring, it caused the queen such grief that she too pined and died. As Robert Lacey points out, "It is a fine story, but definitely not of contemporary origin." Lacey, *Robert Earl of Essex*, 315.

58. March 23, 1603, Manningham, *Diary*, 146; Birch, *Memoirs of Queen Elizabeth*, II, 507; Robert Cary, *Memoirs*, ed. John, Earl of Corke (Edinburgh: A. Constable and Co., 1808), 119–20. Cary claimed that Elizabeth put her hand to her head as a sign of agreement when asked if James was to be the next king, but it is not clear that this was what she meant. Rather, it was a useful story with which to begin the next reign.

59. Nigel Llewellyn, "The Royal Body: Monuments to the Dead, For the Living," in *Renaissance Bodies: The Human Figure in English Culture, c. 1540–1660*, ed. Lucy Gent and Nigel Llewellyn (London: Reaktion Books, Ltd., 1990), 225.

60. *Sir Henry Whithed's Letter Book, Vol. I, 1601–1614*, prepared by members of the staff of the Hampshire Record Office (Hampshire County Council, 1976), I, 15–16.

61. On December 18, 1603 Lady Arabella Stuart wrote to her uncle, the Earl of Shrewsbury that "the queen intendeth to make a mask this Christmas, to which end my Lady of Suffolk and my Lady of Walsingham have warrants to take of the late queen's best apparel out of the Tower at their discretion." The apparel they found was grand indeed. Dudley Carleton wrote to John Chamberlain that this masque "was the best presentation I have at any time seen. Their attire was alike, loose mantles and petticoats, but of different colors, the stuffs embroidered satins and cloth of gold and silver, for which they were beholden to Queen Elizabeth's

wardrobe." E. T. Bradley, *Life of the Lady Arabella Stuart* (London: Richard Bentley and Son, 1889), II, 195; Lee, *Dudley Carleton to John Chamberlain*, 55.

62. For more on the view of Elizabeth in the seventeenth century, see Sharpe, *Politics and Ideas*; Cressy, *Bonfires and Bells*; Anne Barton, "Harking Back to Elizabeth: Ben Jonson and Caroline Nostalgia," *ELH* 48 (1981), 706–31; Simon Shepherd, *Amazons and Warrior Women: Varieties of Feminism in Seventeenth-Century Drama* (Brighton, Sussex: Harvester, 1981); Jerzy Limon, *Dangerous Matter: English Drama and Politics, 1623/24* (Cambridge: Cambridge University Press, 1986); D. R. Woolf, "Two Elizabeths? James I and the Late Queen's Famous Memory," *Canadian Journal of History* XX, 2 (1985), 167–91.

63. John McGurk, "William Camden: Civil Historian or Gloriana's Propagandist?" *History Today* 38 (April, 1988), 47; Simonds D'Ewes, *Diary*, ed. Elisabeth Bourcier (Paris: Didier, n.d.), April 3, 1622, 72; Maurice Lee, *Great Britain's Solomon: James VI and I in His Three Kingdoms* (Urbana and Chicago: University of Illinois Press, 1990), 311; Cressy, *Bonfires and Bells*, 136; Sharpe, *Politics and Ideas in Early Stuart England*, 35.

64. John Reynolds, "*Vox Coeli*, or News From Heaven," *Somers Tracts*, II, ed. Walter Scott. (London: T. Cadell and W. Davies, 1809), II, 555–96. This pamphlet has frequently been identified as by Thomas Scott, who wrote similar pamphlets (see below), and whose work may well have been a model for Reynolds. The Folger Shakespeare Library identifies the author of *Vox Coeli* as Reynolds. Reynolds, a merchant of Exeter, wrote a number of original works as well as translations during the 1620s and 1630s. For more on his life, see *DNB*, XVI, 933. David Norbrook and Annabel Patterson both discuss *Vox Coeli* in the context of other early 1620s tracts critical of James I. Norbrook, *Poetry and Politics in the English Renaissance* (London and Boston: Routledge and Kegan Paul, 1984), 219–20; Patterson, *Censorship and Interpretation: The Conditions of Writing and Reading in Early Modern England* (Madison: University of Wisconsin Press, 1984), 77.

65. Reynolds, *Vox Coeli*, 561, 580, 581.

66. Reynolds, *Vox Coeli*, 565, 581, 582.

67. *DNB*, XVII, 1006–08; *A briefe and true relation of the murther of Mr. Thomas Scott preacher of Gods word and batchelor of divinitie. Committed by John Lambert souldier of the garrison of Utricke, the 18. of June, 1626* (London, 1628), Biv.

68. Thomas Scott, "Robert Earl of Essex his Ghost," *Somers Tracts*, II, 602.

69. Bacon, *Works*, ed. Spedding, III, 310.

70. Bacon, *Works*, ed. Spedding, VI, 310. This has also been translated as "She herself remained in all things an absolute princess." Bacon, *Works*, ed. Montagu, III, 466.

Works Cited

Manuscripts: The State Papers, Domestic in the Public Record Office and the Lansdowne Manuscripts in the British Library were both used on microfilm at the Folger Shakespeare Library.

Acts of the Privy Council of England, ed. John Roche Dasent. New Series. London: HMSO, 1890–1943.

Adams, Simon. "Faction, Clientage and Party English Politics, 1550–1603." *History Today* 32 (1982), 33–39.

Aird, Ian. "The Death of Amy Robsart: Accident, Suicide, or Murder—or Disease?" *English Historical Review* 71, 278 (1956), 69–79.

Alexander, Michael Van Cleave. *The First of the Tudors: A Study of Henry VII and His Reign*. Totowa, NJ: Rowman and Littlefield, 1980.

Armstrong, Nancy and Leonard Tennenhouse. *The Imaginary Puritan: Literature, Intellectual Labor, and the Origins of Personal Life*. Berkeley, Los Angeles, and Oxford: University of California Press, 1992.

Aske, James. *Elizabetha Triumphans: Conteyning the Damned practizes, that the diuelish Popes of Rome have used ever sithence her Highnesse first comming to the Crowne, by mouing her wicked and traiterous subiects to Rebellion and conspiracies, thereby to bereaue her Maiestie both of her lawfull seate, and happy life*. London: Printed by Thomas Orwin for Thomas Gubbin, and Thomas Newman, 1588.

Aston, Margaret. *England's Iconoclasts,* Vol. I: *Laws Against Images*. Oxford: Clarendon Press, 1988.

Auerbach, Erna. *Tudor Artists: A Study of Painters in the Royal Service and of Portraiture on Illuminated Documents from the Accession of Henry VIII to the Death of Elizabeth*. London: Athlone Press, 1954.

Averell, William. *A mervailous combat of contrarieties*. London: Thomas Hacket, 1588.

Axton, Marie. *The Queen's Two Bodies: Drama and the Elizabethan Succession*. London: Royal Historical Society, 1977.

Aylmer, John. *An Harborrowe for Faithfull and Trewe Subiectes*. London: J. Daye, 1559.

Ayre, John, ed. *The Works of John Jewel*. 4 vols. Cambridge: Cambridge University Press, 1845–50.

Bacon, Francis. *The History of the Reign of King Henry the Seventh*, ed. Roger Lockyer. London: The Folio Society, 1971.

———. *Works*. Ed. Basil Montagu. 16 vols. London: William Pickering, 1825–34.

———. *Works*. Ed. James Spedding. 14 vols. London: Longman and Co., 1858.

Barker, Felix. "If Parma Had Landed." *History Today* 38 (May, 1988), 34–41.

Barnard, Etwell A. B. *Evesham and a Reputed Son of Queen Elizabeth*. Evesham: published by the author, 1926.

Barroll, Leeds. "A New History for Shakespeare and His Time." *Shakespeare Quarterly* 39 (1988), 441–64.

Barrow, Philip. *The methode of Phisicke*. 3rd edn. London: R. Field, 1596.

Barton, Anne. "Harking Back to Elizabeth: Ben Jonson and Caroline Nostalgia." *ELH* 48 (1981), 706–31.

Barton (Righter), Anne. *Shakespeare and the Idea of the Play*. London: Chatto and Windus, 1962.

Bassnett, Susan. *Elizabeth I: A Feminist Perspective*. Oxford: Berg, 1988.

Bates, Catherine. "'Of Court it seemes': A Semantic Analysis of Courtship and to Court." *Journal of Medieval and Renaissance Studies* 20, 1 (Spring, 1990), 21–57.

Bauckham, Richard. *Tudor Apocalypse*. Oxford: Sutton Courtenay Press, 1979.

Belsey, Andrew and Catherine Belsey. "Icons of Divinity: Portraits of Elizabeth I." In *Renaissance Bodies: The Human Figure in English Culture, c. 1540–1660*. Ed. Lucy Gent and Nigel Llewellyn. London: Reaktion Books, 1990, 11–35.

Belsey, Catherine. "Disrupting Sexual Difference." In *Alternative Shakespeare*. Ed. John Drakakis. London: Methuen, 1985, 166–90.

———. *The Subject of Tragedy: Identity and Difference in Renaissance Drama*. London and New York: Methuen, 1985.

Bennett, Michael J. *Lambert Simnel and the Battle of Stoke*. New York: St. Martin's Press, 1987.

Berry, Philippa. *Of Chastity and Power: Elizabethan Literature and the Unmarried Queen*. New York: Routledge, Chapman and Hall, 1989.

Bettelheim, Bruno. *The Uses of Enchantment: The Meaning and Importance of Fairy Tales*. New York: Alfred A. Knopf, 1976.

Billington, Sandra. *The Mock King*. New York: Oxford University Press, 1991.

Bingham, Caroline. *The Life and Times of Edward II*. London: Weidenfeld and Nicolson, 1973.

Birch, Thomas. *Memoirs of Queen Elizabeth*. 2 vols. London: A. Millar, 1754.

Blair, John. "Saint Frideswide Reconsidered." *Oxoniensia* LII (1987), 71–101.

———, ed. *Saint Frideswide: Patron of Oxford: The Earliest Texts*. Oxford: Perpetua Press, 1988.

———, ed. *Saint Frideswide's Monastery at Oxford: Archeological and Architectual Studies*. Gloucester: Sutton, 1990.

Bloch, Marc. *The Royal Touch: Sacred Monarchy and Scrofula in England and France*. Trans. J. E. Anderson. London: Routledge and Kegan Paul, 1973.

Boas, Frederick S. "Queen Elizabeth in Elizabethan and Later Drama." In Boas, *Queen Elizabeth in Drama and Related Studies*. London: Allen and Unwin, 1950, 9–35.

Booty, John. "Tumult in Cheapside: The Hacket Conspiracy." *Historical Magazine of the Protestant Episcopal Church* 42 (1973), 293–317.

Bottigheimer, Ruth, ed. *Fairy Tales and Society: Illusion, Allusion, and Paradigm*. Philadelphia: University of Pennsylvania Press, 1986.

Bradley, E. T. *Life of the Lady Arabella Stuart*. 2 vols. London: Richard Bentley and Son, 1889.

Brathwait, Richard. *The English Gentlewoman Drawne Out to the Full Body: Expressing What Habilliments Do Best Attire Her.* London: B. Alsop and T. Fawcet, 1631.

Breight, Curtis Charles. "Duelling Ceremonies: The Strange Case of William Hacket, Elizabethan Messiah." *Journal of Medieval and Renaissance Studies* 19, 1 (Spring, 1989), 35–67.

A briefe and true relation of the murther of Mr. Thomas Scott preacher of Gods word and batchelor of divinitie. Committed by John Lambert souldier of the garrison of Utricke, the 18. of June. 1626. London: N. Butter, 1628.

Brigden, Susan. *London and the Reformation.* Oxford: Oxford University Press, 1991.

Briggs, Katherine M. *A Dictionary of British Folk-Tales in the English Language, Incorporating the F. J. Norton Collection.* 4 vols. Bloomington: Indiana University Press, 1971.

Brown, Steve. "The Boyhood of Shakespeare's Heroines: Notes on Gender Ambiguity in the Sixteenth Century." *Studies in English Literature* 30, 2 (Spring, 1990), 243–64.

Bruce, John, ed. *Correspondence of Matthew Parker.* Cambridge: at the University Press, 1853.

Burke, Peter. "L'histoire sociale des reves." *Annales* 28, 2 (March/April, 1973), 329–42.

Burton, Robert. *The Anatomy of Melancholy.* Ed. Floyd Dell and Paul Jordan-Smith. New York: Tudor Publishing Co., 1938.

Bushnell, Rebecca. *Tragedies of Tyrants: Political Thought and Theater in the English Renaissance.* Ithaca, NY: Cornell University Press, 1990.

Butler, Alban. *Lives of the Saints.* Ed. Herbert Thurston. 12 vols. London: Burnes, Oates and Washbourne, 1926–38.

Buxton, John. *Elizabethan Taste.* London: Macmillan and Co., 1963.

Cabala, Mysteries of State and Government: in Letters of Illustrious Persons and Great Ministers of State. London: G. Beddell and T. Collins, 1663.

Calendar of the Assize Records: Essex Indictments, Elizabeth I. Ed. J. S. Cockburn. London: HMSO, 1978.

Calendar of the Assize Records: Kent Indictments, Elizabeth I. Ed. J. S. Cockburn. London: HMSO, 1979.

Calendar of the Assize Records: Hertfordshire Indictments, Elizabeth I. Ed. J. S. Cockburn. London: HMSO, 1975.

Calendar of the Assize Records: Surrey Indictments, Elizabeth I. Ed. J. S. Cockburn. London: HMSO, 1980.

Calendar of the Assize Records: Sussex Indictments, Elizabeth I. Ed. J. S. Cockburn. London: HMSO, 1975.

Calendar of State Papers and manuscripts relating to English affairs, existing in the archives and collections of Venice, and in other libraries of Northern Italy. Ed. Rawden Brown. 7 vols. London: Longman, HMSO, 1864.

Calendar of State Papers, Domestic Series, of the reigns of Edward VI, Mary, Elizabeth, 1547–1625. Ed. Robert Lemon and Mary Anne Everett Green. 12 vols. London: Longman, Brown, Green, Longmans, and Roberts, 1856–72.

Calendar of State Papers, Foreign Series, of the reign of Elizabeth, 1558–1588. Ed. Joseph Stevenson. 25 vols. Nendeln, Liechtenstein: Kraus Reprint, Ltd., 1966.

Calendar of State Papers, Relating to Scotland and Mary, Queen of Scots, 1547–1603 Preserved in the Public Record Office, the British Museum, and Elsewhere in England. Ed. Joseph Bain, William K. Boyd, and J. D. Mackie. 13 vols. Edinburgh: H. M. General Register House, 1898–1969.

Calendar of State Papers, Relating to English Affairs Preserved Principally at Rome, Elizabeth, 1572–78. Ed. J. M. Rigg. 2 vols. London: HMSO, 1916–26.

Calendar of the Letters and State Papers Relating to English Affairs Preserved in, originally Belonging to, the Archives of Simancas. Ed. Martin Hume. 4 vols. London: HMSO, 1892–99.

Calvin, John. *Institutes of the Christian Religion*. Ed. John Baille, John T. McNeill, Henry P. Van Dusen; trans. Ford Lewis Battles. Philadelphia: Westminster Press, 1960.

Camden, William. *The History of the Most Renowned and Victorious Princess Elizabeth, late Queen of England containing all the most important and remarkable passages of state, both at home and abroad (so far as they were linked with English affairs) during her long and prosperous reign*. 3rd ed. London: B. Fisher, 1635; 4th ed. London: M. Flesher, 1688.

Campbell, Marion. "Inscribing Imperfection: Sir Walter Ralegh and the Elizabethan Court." *English Literary Renaissance* 20, 2 (Spring, 1990), 233–53.

Carlton, Charles. *Archbishop William Laud*. London and New York: Routledge and Kegan Paul, 1987.

———. "The Dream Life of Archbishop Laud." *History Today* 36 (December, 1986), 9–14.

Cary, Robert. *Memoirs*. Ed. John, Earl of Corke. Edinburgh: A. Constable and Co., 1808.

A Catalogue of the Lansdowne Manuscripts in the British Museum. London: Printed by command of the king, 1819.

Cerasano, S. P. and Marion Wynne-Davies, eds. *Gloriana's Face: Women, Public and Private in the English Renaissance*. Detroit: Wayne State University Press, 1992.

Challoner, Richard. *Memoirs of Missionary Priests*. Ed. John Hungerford Pollen. new ed. New York: P. J. Kenedy and Sons, 1924.

Chamberlin, Frederick. *The Sayings of Queen Elizabeth*. London: John Lane, 1923.

Charlton, William. "Maundy Thursday Observances: The Royal Maundy Money." *Transactions of the Lancashire and Cheshire Antiquarian Society* (1916), 201–19.

Chermely, Cynthia. "'Nawghtye Mallenchollye': Some Faces of Madness in Tudor England." *The Historian* 49, 3 (1987), 309–29.

Chettle, Henry. "The Order and Proceedings of the Funerall of the Right High and Mightie Princesse Elizabeth." In *Somers Tracts*. Ed. Walter Scott. London: T. Cadell and W. Davies, 1809, I, 248–50.

Clapham, John. *Elizabeth of England*. Ed. Evelyn Plummer Read and Conyers Read. Philadelphia: University of Pennsylvania Press, 1951.

Clark, Peter. *The English Alehouse: A Social History, 1200–1830*. London and New York: Longman, 1983.

Clark, Sandra. *The Elizabethan Pamphleteers*. London: Athlone Press, 1983.

Clarke, Basil. *Mental Disorder in Earlier Britain: Exploratory Studies*. Cardiff: University of Wales Press, 1975.

Clay, William Keatinge, ed. *Liturgies and Occasional Forms of Prayer set forth in the Reign of Queen Elizabeth*. Cambridge: at the University Press, 1847.

Clifford, Henry. *The Life of Jane Dormer, Duchess of Feria*. Ed. Joseph Stevenson. London: Burns and Oates, 1887.

Cline, Ruth H. "Four Chaucer Saints." *Modern Language Notes* LX (1945), 480–82.

————. "Three Notes on the Miller's Tale." *Huntington Library Quarterly* XXVI (1962–63), 131–45.

Clowes, William. *A right frutefull treatise for the artificiall cure of struma*. London: E. Allde, 1602.

Cobbett's Complete Collection of State Trials and Proceedings for High Treason and Other Crimes and Misdemeanors from the Earliest Period to the Present Time. Ed. Thomas Bayly Howell. 33 vols. London: R. Bagshaw, 1809–26.

Cohn, Norman. *The Pursuit of the Millennium*. 1963; rev. expanded ed. London: T. Smith, 1970.

Collinson, Patrick. *The Elizabethan Puritan Movement*. London: Jonathan Cape, 1967.

————. *The English Captivity of Mary Queen of Scots*. Sheffield: Sheffield History Pamphlets, 1987.

Cope, Jackson. *The Theater and the Dream: From Metaphor to Form in Renaissance Drama*. Baltimore: Johns Hopkins University Press, 1973.

Cornfield, Margaret. "A Legend Concerning King Edward VI." *English Historical Review* 23 (1908), 286–90.

Cosin, Richard. *Conspiracie for Pretended Reformation*. London: Christopher Barker, 1592.

Crawfurd, Raymond. *The King's Evil*. Oxford: Clarendon Press, 1911.

Cressy, David. *Bonfires and Bells: National Memory and the Protestant Calendar in Elizabethan and Stuart England*. Berkeley: University of California Press, 1989.

Davies, Lady Eleanor. *The Lady Eleanor Douglas, Dowager, Her Jubiles Pleas or Appeal*. London, 1650.

————. *The New Jerusalem at Hand*. London, 1649.

Davis, Natalie. *The Return of Martin Guerre*. Cambridge, MA: Harvard University Press, 1983.

————. *Society and Culture in Early Modern France*. Stanford, CA: Stanford University Press, 1975.

Dee, John. *The Comendious Rehearsall*. Ed. James Crossley. *Remains Historical and Literary*, Vol 24, Manchester: Chetham Society, 1851.

Delaney, Janice, Mary Jane Lupton, and Emily Toth. *The Curse: A Cultural History of Menstruation*. Revised expanded ed. Urbana and Chicago: University of Illinois Press, 1988.

Deloney, Thomas. *Works*. Ed. Francis Oscar Mann. Oxford: Clarendon Press, 1912.

De Maisse, André Hurault. *A Journal of all that was Accomplished by Monsieur deMaisse, Ambassador, in England from Henry IV to Queen Elizabeth, 1597.* Trans. and ed. with introduction by G. B. Harrison and R. A. Jones. Bloomsbury: Nonesuch Press, 1931.

Devereux, Walter Bourchier. *Lives and Letters of the Devereux, Earls of Essex, in the Reigns of Elizabeth, James I, and Charles I: 1540–1646.* 2 vols. London: John Murray, 1853.

D'Ewes, Sir Simonds. *Diary.* Ed. Elisabeth Bourcier. Paris: Didier, n.d.

Dictionary of National Biography. Ed. Leslie Stephen and Sidney Lee. 66 vols. London: Smith, Elder, Co., 1885–1901.

Dickens, A. G. *Reformation Studies.* London: Hambledon Press, 1982.

Digges, Dudley. *The Compleat Ambassador: or Two Treaties of the intended marriage of Qu. Elizabeth of Glorious Memory: Comprised in Letters of Negotiations of Sir Francis Walsingham, Her Resident in France Together with the Answers of the Lord Burleigh, the Earl of Leicester, Sir Thos. Smith, and others Wherein, as in a clear Mirror, maybe seen the Faces of the two Courts of England and France, as they then stood: with many remarkable passages of State, not at all mentioned in any History.* London: Gabriel Bedell and Thomas Collins, 1655.

Dobin, Howard. *Merlin's Disciples: Prophecy, Poetry, and Power in Renaissance England.* Stanford, CA: Stanford University Press, 1990.

Doran, Susan and Christopher Durston. *Princes, Pastors and People: The Church and Religion in England, 1529–1689.* London and New York: Routlege, 1991.

Doran, Susan. "Religion and Politics at the Court of Eizabeth I: the Habsburg Marriage Negotiations, 1559–1567." *English Historical Review* 104 (1989), 908–26.

Douglas, Mary. *Purity and Danger: An Analysis of Concepts of Pollution and Taboo.* New York: Praeger, 1966.

Dubois, John G., ed. *Chronicle of the Grey Friars of London.* Camden Soc., Old Series LIII, 1852.

Dunbar, Agnes B. C. *A Dictionary of Saintly Women.* 2 vols. London: George Bell and Sons, 1905.

Dunlop, Ian. *Palaces & Progresses of Elizabeth I.* London: Jonathan Cape, 1962.

Eccles, Audrey. *Obstetrics and Gynaecology in Tudor and Stuart England.* Kent, OH: Kent State University Press, 1982.

Eccles, Mark. *Christopher Marlowe in London.* Cambridge, MA: Harvard University Press, 1934.

Eckenstein, Lina. *Women Under Monasticism: Chapters on Saintlore and Convent Life between A.D. 500 and A. D. 1500.* Cambridge: Cambridge University Press, 1896.

Edwards, Gillian Mary. *Uncumber and Pantaloon: Some Words with Stories.* New York: E. P. Dutton, 1969.

Elias, Norbert. *The History of Manners,* Vol. I: *The Civilizing Process.* Trans. Edmund Jephcott. New York: Pantheon Books, 1978.

Ellis, Henry, ed. *Original Letters, Illustrative of English History.* 2 vols. 2nd ed. London: Harding, Triphook, and Lepard, 1825.

Emmison, F. G. *Elizabethan Life, Vol. I: Disorder.* Chelmsford: Essex County Council, 1971.

Erickson, Carolly. *Bloody Mary*. Garden City, NY: Doubleday, 1978.
———. *Great Harry*. New York: Summit Books, 1980.
Erickson, Peter. *Rewriting Shakespeare, Rewriting Ourselves*. Berkeley and Los Angeles: University of California Press, 1991.

Farmer, David Hugh. *The Oxford Dictionary of Saints*. 2nd ed. New York: Oxford University Press, 1987.
Feasey, Henry John. *Ancient Holy Week Ceremonial*. London: T. Baker, 1897.
Foxe, John. *Acts and Monuments*. 8 vols. Ed. Stephen Reed Cattley. London: R. B. Seeley and W. Burnside, 1838.
Froude, James Anthony. *History of England from the Fall of Wolsey to the death of Queen Elizabeth*. 3rd ed. 12 vols. London: Longmans, Green, and Co., 1867.
Frye, Susan. *Elizabeth I: The Competition for Representation*. New York and Oxford: Oxford University Press, 1993.
———. "The Myth of Elizabeth at Tilbury." *Sixteenth Century Journal* XXIII, 1 (1992), 95–114.
Fumerton, Patricia. "'Secret' Arts: Elizabethan Miniatures and Sonnets." In *Representing the English Renaissance*. Ed. Stephen Greenblatt. Los Angeles and Berkeley: University of California Press, 1988, 93–133.

Gairdner, James. *Henry VII*. London, New York: Macmillan, 1889.
———. *The History of the Life and Reign of Richard the Third, to Which is Added the Story of Perkin Warbeck*. revised ed. Cambridge: Cambridge University Press, 1898; rpt. New York: Kraus Reprint, 1968.
Gairdner, James and R. H. Brodie, eds. *Letters and Papers of the Reign of Henry VIII*. 21 vols. London: HMSO, 1864–1932.
Gluckman, Max. "Gossip and Scandal." *Current Anthropology* 4, 3 (1963), 307–16.
———. "Psychological, Sociological, and Anthropological Explanations of Witchcraft and Gossip: A Clarification." *Man* 3 n.s. (1968), 20–34.
Goldberg, Jonathan. *Endlesse Worke: Spenser and the Structures of Discourse*. Baltimore and London: Johns Hopkins University Press, 1981.
Goldie, Francis. *The Story of St. Frideswide, Virgin and Patroness of Oxford*. London: Burnes and Oates, 1881.
Greenblatt, Stephen. "Fiction and Friction." In Greenblatt, *Shakespearean Negotiations*. Berkeley: University of California Press, 1988.
———. "Invisible Bullets: Renaissance Authority and its Subversion, *Henry IV* and *Henry V*." In *Political Shakespeare: New Essays in Cultural Materialism*. Ed. Jonathan Dollimore and Alan Sinfield. Ithaca, NY: Cornell University Press, 1985.
———. "Psychoanalysis and Renaissance Culture." In *Literary Theory/Renaissance Texts*. Ed. Patricia Parker and David Quint. Baltimore: Johns Hopkins University Press, 1986, 210–24.
———. *Renaissance Self-Fashioning: From More to Shakespeare*. Chicago: University of Chicago Press, 1980.
———, ed. *Representing the English Renaissance*. Berkeley and Los Angeles: University of California Press, 1988.
Greene, Robert. *The Spanish Masquerado*. London: Roger Ward, 1589.

Greenhut, Deborah S. "*Persuade yourselves*: Women, Speech, and Sexual Politics in Tudor Society." *Proteus* III, 2 (1986), 42–48.

Griffiths, John, ed. *The Two Books of Homilies to be read in Churches*. Oxford: at the University Press, 1859.

Haigh, Christopher. *Elizabeth I: Profile in Power*. London and New York: Longman, 1988.

Hardy, Thomas Duffus. *Descriptive Catalogue of Material Relating to the History of Great Britain and Ireland, to the end of the Reign of Henry VII*. 1862. rpt. New York: Burt Franklin, n.d.

The Harleian Miscellany. Ed. William Oldys and Thomas Park. London: John White and John Murray, 1808.

Harington, John. *Nugae Antiquae: Being a Miscellaneous Collection of Original Papers*. Ed. Henry Harington and Thomas Park. London: Vernor and Hood, 1804.

Harrison, G. B., ed. *The Elizabethan Journals*. New York: Macmillan Co., 1939.

———, ed. *The Letters of Queen Elizabeth I*. London: Casell and Co., Ltd., 1935.

———. *Life and Death of Robert Devereux, Earl of Essex*. New York: Henry Holt 1937.

———, ed. *A Second Jacobean Journal*. Ann Arbor: the University of Michigan Press, 1958.

Hartley, T. E., ed. *Proceedings in the Parliaments of Elizabeth I, 1558–1581*. Leicester: University Press, 1981.

Harvey, John. *A Discoursive Probleme Concerning Prophesies*. London: J. Jackson, 1588.

Hardwicke, Philip Yorke, ed. *Miscellaneous State Papers, from 1501 to 1726*. 2 vols. London: W. Straham and T. Cadell, 1778.

Hasler, P. W., ed. *The History of Parliament: The House of Commons, 1558–1603*. 3 vols. London: HMSO, 1981.

Haugaard, William P. *Elizabeth and the English Reformation: the Struggle for a Stable Settlement of Religion*. Cambridge: Cambridge University Press, 1968.

Hawkyard, Alasdair. "Guardians of Claimants to the Throne: The Talbots." In *Rivals in Power: Lives and Letters of the Great Tudor Dynasties*. Ed. David Starkey. London: Macmillan, 1990, 230–49.

Hay, Denis, trans. and ed. *The Anglica Historia, A.D. 1485–1537 by Polydore Vergil*. Camden Society, 3rd series, vol 74. London: Royal Historical Society, 1950.

Hayden, Ilse. *Symbol and Privilege: The Ritual Context of British Royalty*. Tucson: University of Arizona Press, 1987.

Haynes, Alan. *Robert Cecil, Earl of Salisbury, 1563–1612: Servant of Two Sovereigns*. London: Peter Owen, 1989.

Haynes, Alan. *White Bear: Robert Dudley, the Elizabethan Earl of Leicester*. London: Peter Owen, 1987.

Hazlitt, W. Carew. *Faiths and Folklores of the British Isles, A Descriptive and Historical Dictionary*. 2 vols. 1905, rpt. New York: B. Blom, 1965.

Heinze, R. W. *The Proclamations of the Tudor Kings*. Cambridge: Cambridge University Press, 1976.

Heisch, Allison. "Elizabeth I and the Persistence of Patriarchy." *Feminist Review* 4 (1980), 45–56.

———. "Queen Elizabeth I: Parliamentary Rhetoric and the Exercise of Power." *Signs* I, 1 (Autumn, 1975), 31–55.

Hibbert, Christopher. *The Virgin Queen: The Personal History of Elizabeth I*. Reading, MA: Addison-Wesley, 1991.

Hill, Brian. *Gates of Horn and Ivory: An Anthology of Dreams*. New York: Taplinger, 1967.

Hill, Christopher. *The World Turned Upside Down: Radical Ideas During the English Revolution*. Middlesex, England: Penguin, 1972.

Hill, Thomas. *The moste pleasaunte arte of the interpretacion of dreames*. London, T. Marsh, 1576.

Historical Manuscripts Commission. *Calendar of the Manuscripts of the Marquis of Salisbury Preserved at Hatfield House*. 15 vols. London: HMSO, 1883–1976.

Hoak, Dale. "Rehabilitating the Duke of Northumberland: Politics and Political Control, 1549–53." In *The Mid-Tudor Polity, c. 1540–1560*. Ed. Robert Tittler and Jennifer Loach. Totowa, NJ: Rowman and Littlefield, 1980, 29–51.

Hole, Christina. *British Folk Customs*. London: Hutchinson, 1976.

———. *English Shrines and Sanctuaries*. London: Batsford, 1954.

Holinshed's Chronicles. Ed. Henry Ellis. 6 vols. London: J. Johnson, 1807–1808.

Holland, Thomas. *A Sermon Preached at Paul's in London to 17 of November 1599, the one and fortieth yeare of her Maiesties raigne, and augmented in those places wherein, for the shortnes of the time, it could not be then delivered*. Oxford: Joseph Barnes, 1601.

Horstmann, C., ed. from Ms. Stowe 949 (c. 1610–1615). *The Lives of Women Saints of Our Contrie of England*. London: Early English Text Society, 1886, 80–82.

Howard, Alexander. *Endless Cavalcade: A Diary of British Festivals and Customs*. London: A.Barker, 1964.

Howard, Jean E. "Crossdresssing, the Theatre, and Gender Struggle in Early Modern England." *Shakespeare Quarterly* 39 (1988), 418–40.

Hughes, Beryl. "Success in a Man's World: The Reign of Elizabeth I of England." *Women's Studies Journal* I (April, 1985), 35–44.

Hume, Martin. *The Courtships of Queen Elizabeth*. London: E. Nash and Grayson, 1926.

Hurstfield, Joel. *The Illusion of Power in Tudor Politics*. London: Athlone Press, 1979.

Hutchison, Harold. *Edward II: The Pliant King*. London: Eyre and Spotiswoode, 1971.

———. *The Hollow Crown*. London: Eyre and Spottiswoode, 1961.

Inderwick, F. A., ed. *A Calendar of the Inner Temple Records*. London: Published by order of the Masters of the Bench and Sold by Henry Sotheran and Co.; Stevens and Haynes; Stevens and Sons, Ltd., 1896.

Index of Wills Proved in the Prerogative Court of Canterbury, Vol. IV, 1584–1604, and Now Preserved in the Principal Probate Registry, Somerset House, London.

Compiled by S. A. Smith, M.D.; ed. Edward Alexander Fry. London: the British Record Society, 1902.

Inquisitions Post Mortem of the Tudor Period for the City of London, Part III, Elizabeth, 1577–1603. Ed. Edward Alexander Fry. London: The British Record Society, 1908.

Ives, Eric W. *Anne Boleyn.* London: Basil Blackwell, 1986.

James, Mervyn. *Society, Politics and Culture: Studies in Early Modern England.* Cambridge: Cambridge University Press, 1986.

Jankowski, Theodora A. "'As I am Egypt's Queen': Cleopatra, Elizabeth I, and the Female Body Politic." *Assays: Critical Approaches to Medieval and Renaissance Texts* V (1989), 91–110.

Janson, Sharon L. *Protest and Prophecy Under Henry VIII.* Woodridge, Suffolk: Boydell Press, 1991.

Jardine, David. *Criminal Trials.* 2 vols. London: M. A. Natali, 1847.

Jenkins, Elizabeth. *Elizabeth the Great.* London: Victor Gollancz, Ltd., 1958.

———. *Elizabeth and Leicester.* New York: Coward-McCann, 1962.

Jessopp, Augustus. *One Generation of a Norfolk House.* London: Burns and Oates, 1879.

Johnson, Lynn Staley. *Shepheardes Calendar: An Introduction.* University Park: Pennsylvania State University Press, 1990.

Johnson, Paul. *Elizabeth I: A Study in Power and Intellect.* London: Weidenfeld and Nicolson, 1974.

Jones, Ann Rosalind. "Nets and Bridles: Early Modern Conduct Books as Sixteenth Century Women's Lyrics." In *The Ideology of Conduct: Essays on Literature and the History of Sexuality.* Ed. Nancy Armstrong and Leonard Tennenhouse. New York and London: Methuen, 1987.

Jones, Norman. *Faith by Statute: Parliament and the Settlement of Religion, 1559.* Cambridge: Cambridge University Press, 1982.

Jonson, Ben. *Works.* Ed. C. H. Herford and Percy and Evelyn Simpson. 11 vols. Oxford: Clarendon Press, 1925–52.

Jordan, Constance. "Representing Political Androgyny: More on the Siena Portrait of Queen Elizabeth I." In *The Renaissance Englishwoman in Print: Counterbalancing the Canon.* Ed. Anne M. Haselkorn and Betty S. Travitsky. Amherst: University of Massachusetts Press, 1990, 157–76.

———. "Woman's Rule in Sixteenth-Century British Political Thought." *Renaissance Quarterly* 40, 3 (Autumn, 1987), 421–51.

Jordan, W. K. *Edward VI: The Threshold of Power.* Cambridge, MA: Harvard University Press, 1970.

Kagan, Richard. *Lucrecia's Dream: Politics and Prophecy in Sixteenth-Century Spain.* Berkeley: University of California Press, 1990.

Kantorowic, Ernst H. *The King's Two Bodies: A Study in Mediaeval Political Theory.* Princeton, NJ: Princeton University Press, 1957.

Kay, Dennis. "'She was a Queen, and Therefore Beautiful': Sidney, His Mother, and Queen Elizabeth." *Review of English Studies* n.s. XLIII, 169 (1992), 18–39.

Kendall, Alan. *Robert Dudley, Earl of Leicester*. London: Cassell, 1980.

Kendall, Paul Murray. *Richard the Third*. London: Allen and Unwin, 1955.

Kenyon, J. P. *The Stuart Constitution, 1603–1688: Documents and Commentary*. 2nd ed. New York: Cambridge University Press, 1986.

Kimbrough, Robert. "Androgyny Seen Through Shakespeare's Disguise." *Shakespeare Quarterly* 33 (Spring, 1982), 17–33.

King, John N. "The Godly Woman in Elizabethan Iconography." *Renaissance Quarterly* 38 (1985), 41–84.

———. "Queen Elizabeth I: Representations of the Virgin Queen." *Renaissance Quarterly* 43 (Spring, 1990), 30–74.

———. *Spenser's Poetry and the Reformation Tradition*. Princeton, NJ: Princeton University Press, 1990.

———. *Tudor Royal Iconography: Literature and Art in an Age of Religious Crisis*. Princeton, NJ: Princeton University Press, 1989.

Kitching, C. J. "'Prayers Fit for the Time': Fasting and Prayer in Response to National Crises in the Reign of Elizabeth I." In *Monks, Hermits and the Ascetic Tradition*. Ed. W. J. Shiels. Oxford: Published for the Ecclesiastical Historical Society by Basil Blackwell, 1985.

Kittredge, George Lyman. *Witchcraft in Old and New England*. Cambridge, MA: Harvard University Press, 1929.

Knox, John. *Works*. Ed. David Laing. 6 vols. Edinburgh: James Thin, 1895.

Lacey, Robert. *Robert Earl of Essex: An Elizabethan Icarus*. London: Weidenfeld and Nicolson, 1971.

Laing, David, ed. *Notes of Ben Jonson's Conversations with William Drummond*. London: Printed for the Shakespeare Society, 1842.

Lake, Peter and Maria Dowling, eds. *Protestantism and the National Church in Sixteenth Century England*. London: Croom Helm, 1987.

Langston, Beach. "Essex and the Art of Dying." *Huntington Library Quarterly* 13, 2 (1950), 109–29.

Larner, Christina. *Witchcraft and Religion: The Politics of Popular Belief*. Ed. Alan McFarlane. Oxford and New York: Blackwell, 1984.

Lee, Arthur Gould. *The Son of Leicester*. London: Victor Gollancz, Ltd., 1964.

Lee, Maurice, Jr., ed. *Dudley Carleton to John Chamberlain, 1603–1624: Jacobean Letters*. New Brunswick, NJ: Rutgers University Press, 1972.

———. *Great Britain's Solomon: James VI and I in His Three Kingdoms*. Urbana and Chicago: University of Illinois Press, 1990.

Lee, Patricia-Ann. "A Bodye Politique to Governe: Aylmer, Knox and the Debate on Queenship." *The Historian* LII, 2 (1990), 242–61.

Leigh, William. *Queene Elizabeth, Paraleld in Her Princely Vertues, with David, Iosua, and Hezekia*. London: Printed by T. C. for Arthur Johnson, 1612.

Leyland, A. "'Miller's Tale' [I(A) 3449]." *Notes and Queries* 219 n.s. 21 (April, 1974), 126–27.

Lilly, Joseph, ed. *A Collection of Seventy-Nine Black-Letter Ballads and Broadsides, Printed in the Reign of Queen Elizabeth Between the Year 1559 and 1597*. London: Joseph Lilly, 1867.

Limon, Jerzy. *Dangerous Matter: English Drama and Politics, 1623/24.* Cambridge: Cambridge University Press, 1986.

———. "The Masque of Stuart Culture." In *The Mental World of the Jacobean Court.* Ed. Linda Levy Peck. Cambridge: Cambridge University Press, 1991, 209–29.

Lingard, John. *The History of England from the First Invasion of the Romans to the Accession of William and Mary in 1688.* 10 vols. London: J. C. Nimmo and Bain, 1883.

Llewellyn, Nigel. "The Royal Body: Monuments to the Dead, for the Living." In *Renaissance Bodies: The Human Figure in English Culture, c. 1540–1660.* Ed. Lucy Gent and Nigel Llewellyn. London: Reaktion Books, Ltd., 1990, 218–40.

Loades, D. M. *Politics and the Nation, 1450–1660.* London: Oxford University Press, 1974.

———. *The Reign of Mary Tudor: Politics, Government, and Religion in England, 1553–1558.* New York: St. Martin's Press, 1979.

———. *The Tudor Court.* Totowa, NJ: Barnes and Noble, 1987.

———. *Two Tudor Conspiracies.* Cambridge: at the University Press, 1965.

Lodge, Edmund. *Illustrations of British History.* 2nd ed. 3 vols. London: John Chidley, 1838.

MacCaffrey, Wallace. "The Anjou Match and the making of Elizabethan foreign policy." In *The English Commonwealth, 1547–1640: Essays in Politics and Society.* Ed. Peter Clark, Alan Smith, and Nicholas Tyacke. New York: Barnes and Noble, 1979, 59–75.

———. *Queen Elizabeth and the Making of Policy, 1572–1588.* Princeton, NJ: Princeton University Press, 1981.

———. *The Shaping of the Elizabethan Regime.* Princeton, NJ: Princeton University Press, 1968.

———. *War and Politics, 1588–1603.* Princeton, NJ: Princeton University Press, 1992.

McClure, Norman Egbert, ed. *The Letters and Epigrams of Sir John Harington.* Philadelphia: University of Pennsylvania Press, 1930.

McCoy, Richard C. "'A Dangerous Image': The Earl of Essex and Elizabethan Chivalry." *Journal of Medieval and Renaissance Studies* 13, 2 (1983), 313–29.

———. *The Rites of Knighthood: the Literature and Politics of Elizabethan Chivalry.* Berkeley, Los Angeles, and London: University of California Press, 1989.

———. "'This Wonderfull Spectacle': The Civic Progress of Elizabeth I and the Troublesome Coronation." In *Coronations: Medieval and Early Modern Monarchic Ritual.* Ed. Janos Bak. Berkeley: University of California Press, 1990, 217–27.

McCracken, Grant. "The Pre-Coronation Passage of Elizabeth I: Political Theatre or the Rehearsal of Politics?" *Canadian Review of Sociology and Anthropology* 21, 1 (1984), 47–61.

MacDonald, Michael. *Mystical Bedlam: Madness, Anxiety, and Healing in Seventeenth-Century England.* Cambridge: Cambridge University Press, 1981.

McGurk, John. "William Camden: Civil Historian or Gloriana's Propagandist?" *History Today* 38 (April, 1988), 47–53.

McIlwain, Charles Howard, ed. *The Political Works of James I*. New York: Russell and Russell, 1965.

McLaren, Angus. *Reproductive Rituals: The Perception of Fertility in England from the Sixteenth to the Nineteenth Century*. London and New York: Routledge, Chapman, and Hall, Inc., 1984.

Manningham, John. *Diary*. Ed. John Bruce. Westminster: J. B. Nichols and Sons, 1868.

Marcus, Leah. "Erasing the Stigma of Daughterhood: Mary I, Elizabeth I, and Henry VIII." In *Daughters and Fathers*. Ed. Lynda E. Boose and Betty S. Flowers. Baltimore and London: Johns Hopkins University Press, 1989, 400–417.

———. "Shakespeare's Comic Heroines, Elizabeth I, and the Political Uses of Androgyny." In *Medieval and Renaissance Women: Literary and Historical Perspectives*. Ed. Mary Beth Rose. Syracuse, NY: Syracuse University Press, 1986, 135–54.

———. *Puzzling Shakespeare: Local Reading and Its Discontents*. Berkeley and Los Angeles: University of California Press, 1988.

Marshall, Rosalind K. *Elizabeth I*. Owings Mill, MD : Stemmer House, 1992.

Martin, Colin and Geoffrey Parker. *The Spanish Armada*. New York, London: W. W. Norton & Co., 1988.

Mayr-Harting, Henry. "Functions of a Twelfth-Century Shrine: The Miracles of St. Frideswide." In *Studies in Medieval History Presented to R. H. C. Davis*. Ed. Henry Mayr-Harting and R. I. Moore. London: Hambledon Press, 1985, 193–206.

Meller, Walter Clifford. "The King's Healing." In Clifford, *The Boy Bishop and Other Essays*. London: G. Bell and Sons, 1923, 81–94.

Melville, James. *Memoirs*. Ed. A. Francis Steuart. New York: E. P. Dutton, 1930.

Mendle, Michael. *Dangerous Positions: Mixed Government, the Estates of the Realm, and the Answer to the xix Propositions*. University, Alabama: University of Alabama Press, 1985.

Mercer, Eric. "Minatures." In *English Art, 1553–1625*. Ed. Eric Mercer. Oxford: Clarendon Press, 1962.

Montrose, Louis. "Shaping Fantasies: Figurations of Gender and Power in Elizabethan Culture." *Representations* I, 2 (Spring, 1983), 61–94.

———. "The Elizabethan Subject and the Spenserian Text." In *Literary Theory/Renaissance Texts*. Ed. Patricia Parker, David Quint. Baltimore: Johns Hopkins University Press, 1986, 303–40.

More, Thomas. *Complete Works*. Vol. VI. Ed. Thomas M. C. Lawler, Germain Marc'Hadour, and Richard C. Marius. New Haven, CT: Yale University Press, 1981.

Mullaney, Steven. *The Place of the Stage: License, Play, and Power in Renaissance England*. Chicago and London: University of Chicago Press, 1988.

Murdin, William and Samuel Haynes, ed., *A Collection of State Papers Relating to*

Affairs in the Reign of Queen Elizabeth from 1542 to 1596 left by William Cecil, Lord Burghley. London: William Bowyer, 1740–1759.

Nash, Thomas. *The Terrors of the Night. Or, A Discourse of Apparitions.* London: William Jones, 1594.

Naunton, Robert. *Fragmenta Regalia: Being a History of Queen Elizabeth's Favourites.* Edinburgh: A. Constable and Co., 1808.

Neale, John. *Essays in Elizabethan History.* London: Jonathan Cape, 1958.

———. *Queen Elizabeth I and Her Parliaments, 1559–1581.* London: Jonathan Cape, 1953.

———. *Queen Elizabeth I and Her Parliaments, 1584–1601.* London: Jonathan Cape, 1957.

———. *Queen Elizabeth I.* 1934; rpt. Garden City, New York: Anchor Books, 1957.

Neely, Carol Thomas. "'Documents in Madness': Reading Madness and Gender in Shakespeare's Tragedies and Early Modern Culture." *Shakespeare Quarterly* 42, 3 (Fall, 1991), 315–38.

The New Catholic Encyclopedia. New York: McGraw-Hill, 1967.

Nicholas, Nicholas Harris. *Memoirs of the Life and Times of Sir Christopher Hatton.* London: R. Bentley, 1847.

Nicholl, Charles. *The Reckoning: The Murder of Christopher Marlowe.* London: Picador, in association with Jonathan Cape, 1993.

Nichols, John Gough, ed. *The Diary of Henry Machyn.* London: Camden Society, 1848.

Nichols, John. *The Progresses and Public Processions of Queen Elizabeth.* 3 vols. London: J. Nichols and Son, 1823; rpt. New York: Burt Franklin, n.d.

Norbrook, David. *Poetry and Politics in the English Renaissance.* London and Boston: Routledge and Kegan Paul, 1984.

O'Day, Rosemary. *The Debate on the English Reformation.* London and New York: Methuen, 1986.

Orgel, Stephen. *The Illusion of Power: Political Theater in the English Renaissance.* Berkeley: University of California Press, 1975.

———. "Making Greatness Familiar." In *The Power of Forms in the English Renaissance.* Ed. Stephen Greenblatt. Norman: University of Oklahoma Press, 1982, 41–47.

———. "Nobody's Perfect: Or Why Did the English Stage Take Boys for Women?" *South Atlantic Quarterly* 88, 1 (Winter, 1989), 7–29.

Osborn, James. *The Quenes Maiesties Passage through the Citie of London to Westminster the Day before her Coronation.* Ed. J. E. Neale. New Haven, CT: Published for the Elizabethan Club by Yale University Press, 1960.

Osborne, Francis. *Historical Memoires on the Reigns of Queen Elizabeth and King James.* London: Francis Grismond, 1658.

———. *Osborne's Works.* 8th edn. London: Printed for R.D., 1682.

Oxford English Dictionary. Prepared by J. A. Simpson and E. S. C. Weiner. 2nd ed. 20 volumes. Oxford: Clarendon Press, 1989.

Paine, Robert. "What is Gossip About? An Alternative Hypothesis." *Man* II, n.s. (1976), 278–85.

Parfit, Joseph Thomas. *Saint Frideswide of Oxford and the Church of St. Frideswide.* Croydon: Roffey and Clark, 1929.

Park, Katherine and Lorraine J. Daston. "Unnatural Conceptions: The Study of Monsters in Sixteenth- and Seventeeth-Century France and England." *Past and Present* 92 (1981), 20–54.

Parker, James. *The Early History of Oxford, 727-1100.* Oxford: Clarendon Press, 1885.

Parker, Patricia and David Quint, eds. *Literary Theory/Renaissance Texts.* Baltimore: Johns Hopkins University Press, 1986.

Parman, Susan. *Dream and Culture: An Anthropological Study of the Western Intellectual Tradition.* New York: Praeger, 1991.

Parry, Graham. *The Seventeenth Century: The Intellectual and Cultural Context of English Literature, 1603–1700.* London and New York: Longman, 1989.

Patterson, Annabel. *Censorship and Interpretation: The Conditions of Writing and Reading in Early Modern England.* Madison: University of Wisconsin Press, 1984.

Pears, Steuart A., trans. *The Correspondence of Sir Philip Sidney and Hubert Languet.* London: William Pickering, 1845.

Pearson, Andrew Forest Scott. *Thomas Cartwright and Elizabethan Puritanism.* Cambridge: at the University Press, 1925.

Peck, Linda Levy, ed. *The Mental World of the Jacobean Court.* Cambridge, New York: Cambridge University Press, 1991.

Perry, Maria. *The Word of a Prince: A Life of Elizabeth I from Contemporary Documents.* Woodbridge: Boydell Press, 1990.

Petti, Anthony G., ed. *The Letters and Despatches of Richard Verstegan.* London: Catholic Record Society, 1959.

Phillips, James E., Jr. "The Background of Spenser's Attitude Toward Women Rulers." *Huntington Library Quarterly* 5 (1941), 5–32.

Phillips, Louis. "Warbeck: A Play on History." In *George Spelvin's Theatre Book* III, 2 (Summer, 1980), 95–161.

Plowden, Alison. *Marriage with My Kingdom: The Courtships of Queen Elizabeth I.* New York: Stein and Day, 1977.

Pollard, A. F. *Henry VIII.* 1902; new ed. London: Jonathan Cape, 1970.

Pollen, John Hungerford, ed. *Unpublished Documents Relating to the English Martyrs, 1584–1603.* London: Catholic Record Society, 1908.

Pomeroy, Elizabeth. *Reading the Portraits of Queen Elizabeth I.* Hampden, CT: Archon Books, 1989.

Prothero, G. W., ed. *Select Statutes and Other Constitutional Documents Illustrative of the Reigns of Elizabeth and James I.* 4th ed. Oxford: at the Clarendon Press, 1913.

Ramsay, G. D. *The Queen's Merchants and the Revolt of the Netherlands.* Manchester: Manchester University Press, 1986.

The Records of the Honourable Society of Lincoln's Inn: The Black Books. I, 1422–1586. Lincoln's Inn, 1897.

Rémond, Florimond de. *L'Histoire de la naissance, progrez et decadence de l'heresie dece siecle*. Paris: Chez Charles Chastellain, 1610.

Reynolds, John. "*Vox Coeli*, or News from Heaven." In *Somers Tracts*. Ed. Walter Scott. London: T. Cadell and W. Davies, 1809, II, 555–96.

Rice, George P., Jr., ed. *The Public Speaking of Queen Elizabeth: Selections from Her Official Addresses*. New York: Columbia University Press, 1951.

Ridley, Jasper. *Henry VIII: The Politics of Tyranny*. New York: Fromm International, 1986.

Robert Laneham's Letter: Describing a Part of the Entertainment unto Queen Elizabeth at the Castle of Kenilworth in 1575. Ed. with an introduction by F. J. Furnivall. New York: Duffield and Co., 1907.

Robinson, Brian. *The Royal Maundy*. London: Kaye and Ward, 1977.

Robinson, Hastings, ed. and trans. *The Zurich Letters*. Cambridge: University Press, 1846.

Rodriguez-Salgado, M. J. *The Changing Face of Empire: Charles VI, Philip II and Habsburg Authority, 1551–1559*. Cambridge: Cambridge University Press, 1988.

Roelker, Nancy Lyman. *Queen of Navarre: Jeanne d'Albret*. Cambridge, MA: the Belknap Press of Harvard University Press, 1968.

Rollins, Hyder E. *An Analytical Index to the Ballad-Entries in the Registers of the Company of Stationers of London*. Orig. pub. 1924 by the University of North Carolina. Hatboro, PA: Tradition Press, 1967.

Rosen, Barbara, ed. *Witchcraft*. New York: Taplinger, 1972.

Rosenberg, Eleanor. *Leicester, Patron of Letters*. New York: Columbia University Press, 1958.

Rowse, A. L. *Court and Country: Studies in Tudor Social History*. Brighton, Sussex: Harvester, 1987.

———. *Simon Forman: Sex and Society in Shakespeare's Age*. London: Weidenfeld and Nicolson, 1974.

Salter, H. H. *Medieval Oxford*. Oxford: Clarendon Press, 1936.

Samaha, Joel. "Gleanings from Local Criminal-Court Records: Sedition Amongst the 'Inarticulate' in Elizabethan Essex." *Journal of Social History* 8 (Summer, 1975), 61–79.

Sander, Nicholas. *Rise and Growth of the Anglican Schism. pub. A. D. 1585, with a continuation of the History, by the Rev. Edward Rishton*. Trans. and ed. David Lewis. London: Burns and Oates, 1877.

Scalingi, Paula Louise. "The Scepter or the Distaff: The Question of Female Sovereignty, 1516–1607." *The Historian* 41 (1978), 59–75.

Scarisbrick, J. J. *Henry VIII*. Berkeley and Los Angeles: University of California Press, 1968.

———. *The Reformation and the English People*. Oxford: Basil Blackwell, 1984.

Scheff, T. J. *Catharsis in Healing, Ritual, and Drama*. Berkeley: University of California Press, 1979.

Schliener, Winfried. *Melancholy, Genius, and Utopia in the Renaissance*. Wiesbaden: Otto Harrassowitz, 1991.

———. "*Divina virago*: Queen Elizabeth as an Amazon." *Studies in Philology* LXXV (1987), 163–80.

Schmitz, Gotz. *The Fall of Women in Early English Narrative Verse*. Cambridge: Cambridge University Press, 1990.

Schoenbaum, Sam. *Shakespeare and Others*. London: Scolar Press, 1985.

Schramm, Percy Ernst. *A History of the English Coronation*. Trans. Leopold G. Wickham Legg. Oxford: Clarendon Press, 1937.

Scot, Reginald. *The Discoverie of Witchcraft* (1584). With an introduction by Rev. Montague Summers. New York: Dover, 1972.

Scott, Thomas. "Robert Earl of Essex his Ghost." In *Somers Tracts*. Ed. Walter Scott. London: T. Cadell and W. Davies, 1809, II, 596–603.

Sermons or Homilies Appointed to be Read in Church in the Time of Queen Elizabeth. 4th ed. Oxford: at the Clarendon Press, 1816.

Shakespeare's Europe: A Survey of the Condition of Europe at the end of the 16th Century: Being the unpublished chapters of Fynes Moryson's Itinerary (1617). Ed. Charles Hughes. first published London, 1913; 2nd ed. New York: Benjamin Blom, 1967.

Shakespeare, William. *The Complete Signet Classic Shakespeare*. Ed. Sylvan Barnet. New York: Harcourt Brace Jovanovich, 1972.

Shapiro, Michael. "Lady Mary Wroth Describes a Boy Actress." *Medieval & Renaissance Drama in England* IV (1989), 187–94.

Shapiro, Susan C. "Feminists in Elizabethan England." *History Today* XXVII, 11 (November, 1977), 703–11.

Sharpe, J. A. *Defamation and Sexual Slander in Early Modern England: The Church Courts at York*. York: Borthwick Institute of Historical Research, 1980.

Sharpe, Kevin. *Politics and Ideas in Early Stuart England: Essays and Studies*. London and New York: Pinter Publishers, 1989.

Sharpe, Reginald R. *London and the Kingdom*. 3 vols. London: Longmans, Green, and Co., 1894.

Shell, Marc. *Elizabeth's Glass: With "the Glass of the Sinful Soul" (1544) by Elizabeth I, and "Epistle dedictory" and "Conclusion" (1548) by John Bale*. Lincoln: University of Nebraska Press, 1993.

Shepherd, Simon. *Amazons and Warrior Women: Varieties of Feminism in Seventeenth-Century Drama*. Brighton, Sussex: Harvester, 1981.

Sidney, Sir Philip. *Miscellaneous Prose*. Ed. Katherine Duncan-Jones and Jan Van Dorsten. Oxford: Clarendon Press, 1973.

———. *The Works of Sir Philip Sidney*. Ed. A. Feuillerat. 4 vols. Cambridge: University Press, 1912–26.

Sir Henry Whithed's Letter Book, Vol. I, *1601–1614*. Prepared by members of the staff of the Hampshire Record Office. Hampshire County Council, 1976.

Skultans, Vieda. *English Madness: Ideas of Insanity, 1580–1890*. London and Boston: Routledge and Kegan Paul, 1979.

Smith, Lacey Baldwin. *Elizabeth Tudor*. Boston: Little, Brown, 1975.

———. *Treason in Tudor England: Politics and Paranoia*. Princeton, NJ: Princeton University Press, 1986.

Smuts, R. M. "Public Ceremony and Royal Charisma: the English Royal Entry in London, 1485–1642." In *The First Modern Society: Essays in English History in Honour of Lawrence Stone*. Ed. A. L. Beier, David Cannadine, and James M. Rosenheim. Cambridge: Cambridge University Press, 1989, 65–93.

Somerset, Anne. *Elizabeth I*. New York: Alfred A. Knopf, 1991.

Sotheby Catalogue, English Literature and History: comprising Printed Books, Autograph Letters and Manuscripts, also known as the "Hotspur" catalogue (1986).

Spacks, Patricia Meyer. *Gossip*. Chicago: University of Chicago Press, 1985.

Spence, Lewis. *The Fairy Tale Tradition in Britain*. New York: Rider and Co., 1948.

Stanton, Richard. *A Menology of England and Wales*. London : Burnes and Oates, Ltd.; New York: Catholic Publication Society Co., 1887.

Starkey, David, ed. *The English Court: from the Wars of the Roses to the Civil War*. London, New York: Longman, 1987.

———. "Representation Through Intimacy: A Study in the Symbolism of Monarchy and Court Office in Early-Modern England." In *Symbols and Sentiments: Cross-cultural Studies in Symbolism*. Ed. Ioan Lewis. London, New York, and San Francisco: Academic Press, 1977, 187–224.

———, ed. *Rivals in Power: Lives and Letters of the Great Tudor Dynasties*. London: Macmillan, 1990.

Starkey, Marion L. *The Devil in Massachusetts: A Modern Inquiry into the Salem Witch Trials*. New York: Alfred A. Knopf, 1950.

Stenton, F. M. "St. Frideswide and Her Times." *Oxoniensia* 1 (1936), 103–12.

Stone, Lawrence. *Family, Sex, and Marriage*. New York: Harper and Row, 1977.

Stow, John. *Annals of England faithfully collected out of the most authenticall authors, records, and other monuments of antiquitie, from the first inhabitation until this present yeare 1592*. London: R. Newbery, 1592; London: T. Adams, 1615.

Strong, Roy. *Art and Power: Renaissance Festival, 1450–1650*. Bury St. Edmund's, Suffolk: St. Edmundsbury Press, 1984.

———. *Cult of Elizabeth: Elizabethan Portraiture and Pageantry*. Wallop, Hampshire: Thames and Hudson, 1977.

———. *Splendour at Court: Renaissance Spectacle and the Theater of Power*. London: Weidenfeld and Nicolson, 1973.

Strype, John. *Annals of the Reformation*. 4 vols. Oxford: Clarendon Press, 1824.

———. *The Life and Acts of Matthew Parker*. 3 vols. Oxford: at the Clarendon Press, 1821.

———. *Memorials of the Reverend Father in God, Thomas Cranmer*. 2 vols. Oxford: University Press, 1840.

Stubbs, John. *Gaping Gulf*. Ed. Lloyd E. Berry. Charlottesville: The Folger Shakespeare Library for the University Press of Virginia, 1968.

Stubbes, Philip. *Anatomy of Abuses* (1583). Ed. William B. D. D. Turnbull. London: W. Pickering, 1836.

Sugden, John. *Sir Francis Drake*. London: Barrie and Jenkins, 1990.

Tanner, J. R. *Tudor Constitutional Documents, A.D. 1485–1603, with an Historical Commentary*. Cambridge: at the University Press, 1948.

Taylor-Smither, Larissa J. "Elizabeth I: A Psychological Profile." *Sixteenth Century Journal* XV, 1 (1984), 47–72.

Teague, Frances. "Queen Elizabeth in Her Speeches." In *Gloriana's Face: Women, Public and Private in the English Renaissance*. Ed. S. P. Cerasano and Marion Wynne-Davies. Detroit: Wayne State University Press, 1992, 63–78.

Tenison, E. M. *Elizabethan England vol III: 1575-1580.* 10 vols. Royal Leamington Spa, Warwick: issued by the author, 1933.

Tennenhouse, Leonard. *Power on Display: The Politics of Shakespeare's Genres.* London and New York: Methuen, 1986.

Thomas, Keith. *Perception of the Past in Early Modern England: the Creighton Trust Lecture, 1983.* London: University of London, 1983.

———. *Religion and the Decline of Magic.* New York: Charles Scribner's Sons, 1971.

———. "Women and the Civil War Sects." In *Crisis in Europe, 1560-1600.* Ed. Trevor Aston. New York: Basic Books, 1965.

Tilley, Morris Palmer. *A Dictionary of the Proverbs in England in the Sixteenth and Seventeenth Centuries.* Ann Arbor: University of Michigan Press, 1950.

Tillyard, E. M. W. *Some Mythical Elements in English Literature.* London: Chatto and Windus, 1961.

Tittler, Robert and Jennifer Loach, ed. *The Mid-Tudor Polity, c. 1540-1560.* Totowa, NJ: Rowman and Littlefield, 1980.

Tucker, M. J. "The Child as Beginning and End: Fifteenth and Sixteenth Century English Childhood." In *The History of Childhood.* Ed. Lloyd DeMause. New York: Psychohistory Press, 1974.

Vansina, Jan. *Oral Tradition as History.* Madison: University of Wisconsin Press, 1985.

von Klarwill, Victor, ed. *Queen Elizabeth and Some Foreigners: Being a Series of Hitherto Unpublished Letters From the Archives of the Hapsburg Family.* Trans. T. H. Nash. London: John Lane, 1928.

Wall, Alison. "'Points of Contact': Court Favourites and County Faction in Elizabethan England." *Parergon* n. s. 6 (1988), 215-226.

Wall, J. Charles. *Shrines of British Saints.* London: Methuen and Co., 1905.

Waldman, Milton. *Elizabeth and Leicester.* London: Collins, 1944.

Warnicke, Retha. "The Eternal Triangle and Court Politics: Henry VIII, Anne Boleyn, and Sir Thomas Wyatt." *Albion* 18, 4 (1986), 565-79.

———. "The Fall of Anne Boleyn: A Reassessment." *History* 70, 228 (1985), 1-15.

———. *The Rise and Fall of Anne Boleyn.* Cambridge: Cambridge University Press, 1989.

Weber, Max. *On Charisma and Institution Building.* Ed. S. N. Eisenstadt. Chicago and London: University of Chicago Press, 1968.

Weidhorn, Manfred. *Dreams in Seventeenth-Century English Literature.* The Hague and Paris: Mouton, 1970.

Wells, Robin Headlam. *Spenser's Faerie Queen and the Cult of Elizabeth.* Totowa, NJ: Barnes and Noble, 1983.

Wentworth, Peter. *A pithie exhortation to her Maiestie for establishing her successor to the crowne.* Edinburgh: R. Waldegrave, 1598.

Weston, Corinne Comstock and Janelle Renfrow Greenberg. *Subjects and Sovereigns: The Grand Controversy over Legal Sovereignty in Stuart England.* Cambridge: Cambridge University Press, 1981.

Wilson, Derek. *Sweet Robin: A biography of Robert Dudley, Earl of Leicester.* London: Hamilton, 1981.

Wilson, Elkin Calhoun. *England's Eliza*. Cambridge, MA: Harvard University Press, 1939.

Wilson, Jean. *Entertainments for Elizabeth I*. Totowa, NJ: Rowman and Littlefield, 1980.

Wood, Anthony A. *Athenae Oxonienses*. Ed. Philip Bliss. 4 vols. London, 1813; rpt. Hildesheim: George Olms Verlagsbuchhandlung, 1969.

Woodbridge, Linda. *Women in the English Renaissance: Literature and the Nature of Womankind, 1540–1620*. Urbana and Chicago: University of Illinois Press, 1984.

Woolf, D. R. "Two Elizabeths? James I and the Late Queen's Famous Memory." *Canadian Journal of History* XX, 2 (1985), 167–91.

Wormald, Jenny. "James VI and I, *Basilikon Doron* and *The Trew Law of Free Monarchies*: the Scottish Context and the English Translation." In *The Mental World of the Jacobean Court*. Ed. Linda Levy Peck. Cambridge and New York: Cambridge University Press, 1991, 36–54.

———. *Mary Queen of Scots: A Study in Failure*. London: George Philip, 1988.

Wright, Peter A. *The Pictorial History of the Royal Maundy*. London: Pitkin Pictorials, Ltd., 1981.

Wright, Thomas, ed. *Queen Elizabeth and Her Times*. 2 vols. London: Henry Colburn, 1838.

Wriothesley, Charles. *A Chronicle of England During the Reigns of the Tudors, from 1485 to 1559*. Ed. William Douglas Hamilton. 2 vols. Westminster: Camden Society, 1875–1877.

Yates, Frances. *Astraea: The Imperial Theme in the Sixteenth Century*. London: Routledge and Kegan Paul, 1975.

Zweig, Stefan. *Mary Queen of Scots and the Isles*. New York: Viking Press, 1935.

Index

University of Pennsylvania Press
NEW CULTURAL STUDIES
Jean DeJean, Carroll Smith-Rosenberg,
and Peter Stallybrass, Editors

Jonathan Arac and Harriet Ritvo, editors. *Macropolitics of Nineteenth-Century Literature: Nationalism, Exoticism, Imperialism.* 1991

John Barrell. *The Birth of Pandora and the Division of Knowledge.* 1992

Bruce Thomas Boehrer. *Monarchy and Incest in Renaissance England: Literature, Culture, Kinship, and Kingship.* 1992

Carol Breckenridge and Peter van der Veer, editors. *Orientalism and the Postcolonial Predicament: Perspectives on South Asia.* 1993

E. Jane Burns. *Bodytalk: When Women Speak in Old French Literature.* 1993

Jones DeRitter. *The Embodiment of Characters: The Representation of Physical Experience on Stage and in Print, 1728–1749.* 1994

Julia V. Douthwaite. *Exotic Women: Literary Heroines and Cultural Strategies in Ancien Régime France.* 1992

Barbara J. Eckstein. *The Language of Fiction in a World of Pain: Reading Politics as Paradox.* 1990

Katherine Gravdal. *Ravishing Maidens: Writing Rape in Medieval French Literature and Law.* 1991

Jayne Ann Krentz, editor. *Dangerous Men and Adventurous Women: Romance Writers on the Appeal of the Romance.* 1992

Carole Levin. *"The Heart and Stomach of a King": Elizabeth I and the Politics of Sex and Gender.* 1994

Linda Lomperis and Sarah Stanbury, editors. *Feminist Approaches to the Body in Medieval Literature.* 1993

Karma Lochrie. *Margery Kempe and Translations of the Flesh.* 1991

Alex Owen. *The Darkened Room: Women, Power and Spiritualism in Late Victorian England.* 1990

Jacqueline Rose. *The Case of Peter Pan or The Impossibility of Children's Fiction.* 1992

Alan Sinfield. *Cultural Politics - Queer Reading.* 1994

This book has been set in Linotron Galliard. Galliard was designed for Mergenthaler in 1978 by Matthew Carter. Galliard retains many of the features of a sixteenth-century typeface cut by Robert Granjon but has some modifications that give it a more contemporary look.

Printed on acid-free paper.